Paul Watkins was born in 1964. He is the son of Welsh parents and was educated at the Dragon School, Eton and Yale. His first novel, *Night Over Day Over Night*, was set in Germany in 1944 and dealt with a sixteen-year-old boy's initiation into the SS and his baptism of fire in the Ardennes Battle of the Bulge. His second novel, *Calm at Sunset, Calm at Dawn*, was based on several years that he spent working on a deep-sea fishing boat off the New England coast. This book won Britain's Encore Prize for the best second novel of the year and is now being made into a film. *In the Blue Light of African Dreams*, his third novel, was set in Morocco and Paris in 1926 and was based on the true story of two men who disappeared while trying to make the first non-stop flight across the Atlantic. His fourth novel, *The Promise of Light*, was published in 1992 by Faber and Faber to critical acclaim.

Stand Before Your God

Paul Watkins

faber and faber

LONDON · BOSTON

To L.V.H.

First published in 1993
by Faber and Faber Limited
3 Queen Square London WC1N 3AU
This UK paperback edition first published in 1994

Phototypeset by Intype Ltd, London
Printed in England by Clays Ltd, St Ives plc

A CIP record for this book is
available from the British Library

ISBN 0-571-17157-5

2 4 6 8 10 9 7 5 3

CHAPTER 1

I SWEAR, I thought I was going to a party.

I had a new suit made of blue corduroy and new black shoes that came with a free pack of playing cards. I was seven years old.

My father drove me to a house that I had never seen before. Mother refused to come with us. The last I saw of her was a tear-blotchy face staring down from the window of our room at the Randolph Hotel in Oxford.

The door to the house opened and a man with a stubbly chin shook my hand. He led me into a room where dozens of other boys in blue suits and black shoes were playing board games and trading marbles.

'Goodbye,' my father said, and shook my hand. His face was hard and serious. He tasted the sherry that the stubbly man had poured for him. Then he put his glass down on a bookshelf and walked away from it.

I went around showing my cards to people. I said I knew some games. This place had a smell to it – boot polish and old bread-crumbs and spilled milk gone sour and the flannelly warmth of our blue corduroy.

'This is a neat party,' I told the man. His hair was threads of black and grey. It looked sharp like steel wool.

'Did you say something?' he asked me.

'Where's my dad?' I flipped my cards from one hand to the other, hoping he would ask about them.

'He's gone.' The man crouched down until I was no longer look-ing at the buckle of his belt but at his face. 'Your father has gone home. I am Mr Vicker and I am your housemaster. From now on, you must call me "sir".'

I reached out and touched his hair, sure that it would cut my fingers the way paper can cut you.

He swatted my hand away and stood. The hard creases of his trousers fell back into their lines.

'When can I go home?' I asked.

'You can go home in about three months.'

'Three months?' His voice reached me as if it had been shouted into a canyon. I knew then that I had been tricked and that this was no party. I ran out to the road, through the part of the house where Mr Vicker lived. This part had a different smell, of liquor and coffee and the sweetness of pipe tobacco sunk into the wooden floors.

The road was empty. The place where my father's rented car had been parked was empty, too. It was so dark, I couldn't see the tops of the trees.

I didn't know how to get back to the Randolph Hotel and imagined that my parents had already left there. They were on their way home to America. Between me and them lay a long thundering journey with only a little aeroplane window to look out of and clouds like a cauliflower jungle far below.

I tried to remember if my parents had told me I'd be coming to this place. Perhaps they did. Most likely they sat me down and gave me a long talk, but I must not have been paying attention, perhaps because the television was on in the other room and I was trying to overhear the show.

I walked back into the house and asked Mr Vicker, 'Where's the ocean?' If I could at least find the sea, I thought, there might be some ship heading home, and maybe if I scrubbed the floors and washed dishes, they would let me stow away.

Whenever I talked to grown-ups, I looked down at my feet. My mother had tried to stop me doing this, but I couldn't help it. After I'd finished talking to Mr Vicker, studying my new black shoes, I looked up. But he had walked off.

All of the parents were gone. Mr Vicker cleared away the half-full sherry glasses.

The boys in blue suits still played in their room. A couple sat in the corner crying, but the rest seemed glad to be here. A few had got into fights and had bloody noses. Others sat trying to fix their new toys which were already broken. I found myself a quiet spot between two dustbins. I squatted down and watched the crowd, trying to measure out in front of me the space of three months.

The house was huge and it went up and up. I found my name written on a piece of sticky paper in a dorm. The sticky paper was on a bed rail.

I got into the bed with my clothes on. I didn't even take my shoes off because I was afraid that someone would steal them.

There were twelve beds in the dormitory, each one black-framed and heavy. Our blankets carried a mothballed mustiness. Every boy had a locker, a brass hook for a towel, and a mug to put his tooth-brush in. The floors looked raw and splintery, the way they'd be if beds had been dragged across them.

As if he knew what I'd been thinking, a boy heaved his bed into the middle of the room. Written on the band of his underpants in heavy black marker, I read Ǝ⅃AƆИITHƆIИ. It looked like a code, the kind that you could only break with one of those code rings that come in cereal packets. Immediately, I convinced myself that I was the only boy in the school without a code name on my underpants. Just as I was about to burst into tears, I realized that this boy had his underpants on inside out and in fact his name was Nightingale, and the marker had soaked through the band. Nightingale stood on his bed and made a trumpeting noise. Two other boys pushed his bed down to the end of the room until it crashed into the wall and catapulted Nightingale into some thick red curtains.

Mr Vicker turned the lights out. He warned us not to talk. Then he told me to take off my shoes and asked me if all Americans slept with their shoes on. I dressed in my pyjamas and hid everything else from my suitcase under the mattress.

It was quiet for a while. Yellow-orange streetlamps lit up rain-drops on the windows. The lumps of my shoes and clothes and washing kit bag under the mattress made it difficult to sleep.

A rustling made me open my eyes. The other boys in the dorm were all around me. They had slithered without a sound from their beds. Stuffed into each boy's pyjama trousers was a bear. They reminded me of gunfighters, with Colt Peacemakers tucked into their belts. Nightingale leaned forward. 'Where's your animal?'

The others leaned forward as well, and I felt their breathing on my face.

I had a bear named Oscar. My father won him in a fair by throw-ing wooden balls at coconuts, which were set up on sticks. If you knocked the coconut off, you got a prize. My dad threw a ball so hard at a coconut that the nut smashed in half, but part of it stayed on the stick. You could tell it had been glued. The coconut man said no prize. When my father heard this, the veins in his neck stood out. He talked to the man in a low voice so that I couldn't hear a word. Then the coconut man stuffed a bear into my arms so quickly that it knocked the wind out of my lungs. My father asked the coconut man for his name and when the man said Oscar, that was what we named the bear. He had a bell in his ear.

When I fished Oscar out from under the mattress, Nightingale took him away. 'We got to christen him,' he said, and opened the window and threw him outside. Oscar cartwheeled into the dark, like a Superman who has suddenly forgotten how to fly.

I heard the ear bell ring as he landed in the bushes.

The crowd around me filtered away into the shadows of the dorm. Their bare feed padded on the floorboards.

'You're a Yank,' Nightingale told me, as he climbed back into bed. It seemed he was only trying to be helpful as if maybe I didn't know.

I waited a while and then whispered, 'Nightingale!'

His blankets shuddered and his head with its porcupine hair popped up.

'Nightingale, where are we?'

'You're in the Dragon School,' he said.

'For what we are about to receive, may the Lord make us truly thankful.'

Chair legs scraped across the floor and I sat down at a long table which was jammed with other boys.

Plates slid from hand to hand and on the plates were pieces of fish that smelled like a camp-fire. One time at home, a trawler dumped its catch in Narragansett bay and the fish washed ashore ankle deep. The water was rainbowed with their oil. These flat-tened-out and smokey things that found their way to each boy on the table must have washed ashore somewhere, too. Or maybe the trawler caught fire.

I stabbed it with my knife.

'Watkins.' Fingers drummed the table in front of me. They were fingers that had nails bitten down to the quick.

When I looked up, I saw a fuzz of rusty red hair and under that a face with eyes the same colour blue as on my mother's Royal Copenhagen china.

'I'm Henry Bessom.' He pulled his fingers back, as if I might stab them the same way I was stabbing the fish. 'I'm your Pater. It means you're new here and that means we can call you a new Bug.

I've been told to look after you. I been here already two terms. I can punch you if I want.'

Mr Vicker told me to eat my fish. He told me they were called kippers and I couldn't leave the table until mine was gone. He said he'd keep me there all week if he had to. Already, some boys had gone down to the linoleum-floored area where lockers lined the wall. Others were trampling the frosted grass outside.

I looked at the stab marks in my fish and saw that oil had leaked from the wounds. I remembered how oil from the dumped catch had stayed on Plum Beach, weeks after the tide had gathered the fish and swept them out to sea. You could dig down in the sand and see it still; blue and red and gold.

When Mr Vicker wasn't looking, I slid the fish off my plate and put it in my pocket. Then I went outside to fetch Oscar.

The other boys left my bear alone after that. It was only for the christening that someone could throw your stuffed animal out the window and not get into a fight. It was the worst kind of insult to have someone torture your animal and pull its head off or fill it full of toothpaste. You had to defend the animal because it could not defend itself, and it was a cowardly business to beat up someone's bear. And the first thing I learned at the Dragon School was that this was no place for cowards.

It made me laugh to see how some of the toughest bully boys had the most dog-eared, sad-faced old stuffed animals. They gave the animals dumb names like Poopie and Woo-Woo, and talked to them after the dormitory lights had been turned out. It looked as if the only reason these boys felt they had to be tough was to make up for how sappy their animals were. But that was an opinion you had to keep to yourself.

Bessom and I walked across the road to school. He had put his kipper in his pocket, too, so we both took them out and dropped them on the road. Then we waited on the pavement until a truck ran over them.

Bessom had a Swiss Army knife on a cord attached to his jacket. It had three blades, and he showed them to me. 'You have to understand,' he said. 'You are a Little Man here. Everyone who's been here longer can call you Little Man and the longer they've been here, the more times they can say it. I been here two terms already.'

'You told me that.'

Bessom fell quiet for a moment. He had forgotten what he was talking about. Then he breathed in suddenly and kept talking. 'I been here two terms longer, so I can call you Little Man-Little Man. There's another boy named Watkins in the school, and he's been here for years. He could call you Little Man so many times it would take him all day. I'm going to call you Little Man now. Just to show you.' He stared at me. 'Little Man-Little Man.'

'Little Man!' I shouted in his face.

'You can't do that.' Bessom put his hands deep in his pockets and jangled the treasures inside. 'You got to do what I say. All right?'

We walked to a hall called the Big Hall. Hundreds of boys were standing there in rows. I didn't see any girls. The teachers told us to shut up.

A man stood up on a platform at the front of the hall and everyone stopped talking. Bessom whispered to me that this was the Headmaster. The man stood there for a while, pleased with the silence he had made. From the earthy colour of his clothes and the way his feet were planted on that platform, the Headmaster looked to me like a man carved from the trunk of a giant tree. Nothing could move him, or even put a dent in the iron-wood frame of his body. Then he breathed in so deep that the sun-lit dust around his head swirled into his mouth. 'Books!'

Down the line came blue books with HYMNS AND PRAYERS FOR DRAGONS in gold on the cover.

Another teacher played the piano while we sang, and the dust that had gathered on it in the holidays now jumped from the polished wood. It swirled through sun that hung in honey-coloured beams across the hall.

I thought about the dust that would be settling now in my room at home and on my stuffed animals staring dumb-faced out of the window. It would have settled on their eyes and made them blind.

The first thing I saw when I walked into the classroom was Nightingale. Now that I had a better chance to get a look at him, I noticed he had the roundest face I had ever seen. He had so many freckles that I found myself wondering if he had more freckle on his cheeks than pink. When he wasn't looking, I tried to count the dots. He had a short, thick body that made me think it would be difficult to beat him in a fight. He was the kind of boy who could not run fast, but if he got a hold of you, then you'd have some trouble.

Nightingale was standing on a desk and the front of his jacket was plastered with fuzzy-felt animals which he had pulled from a board. Nightingale looked over my shoulder at Bessom.

Bessom pushed past me. 'You can't touch the fuzzy-felts! We'll all get extra work if you do.'

'Not on the first day, Bosom.' Nightingale jumped down from the desk. He walked over to me, until our noses were only an inch apart and I couldn't focus on him. 'Did you know that we call him Bosom?'

Bessom looked at me and then down at his shoes.

I knew then that from now on I wouldn't be doing what Bessom said and I wouldn't be letting him call me Little Man. It was an automatic historical fact that nobody named Bosom has ever ordered anyone around. It seemed to me you had to figure out people pretty quickly at the Dragon School. Who you could trust and who not. You measured them up fast and went with your instincts. And you knew that at the same time, people were measuring you up and it would take a lot to change their opinions. It brought no real respect to be good at classes, but you could change their opinion if it turned out you were good at sports, or if you were hurt in a game and did not cry. The only thing you were truly stuck with was your name. I had already seen how some names could ruin your life. With luck, news wouldn't travel across the ocean from America that I had once been called Watkins-Bare-Botkins.

There was no point having a first name at the Dragon School because nobody used it. Instead they took your last name and said it to themselves a few times, rolling it over on their tongues. They found out if it sounded like another word, or an animal or a part of your body. If nothing came up, they'd add an 'o' to the end or 'ers' and see if that worked.

You could be born with a name that you thought sounded fine until you reached the Dragon School. Then someone would spit that name back in your face in a way that would change your whole life. So if your name was Codrington, you might never have known until then that your name sounded a little like Cuddlybum. But from then on your name would be Cuddlybum, and not just until the end of the Dragon School but until the end of time. You knew suddenly that deep into the future, you would find yourself one day walking into a building in the City to ask for a job. And the man behind the desk would take one look at you, jump to his feet and yell – Cuddlybum!

I got named Watty Dog. Not because I looked like a dog or walked or smelled like one but because of the senior boy whose name was also Watkins. From then on, he was Big Watty Dog Watkins. He did walk like a dog. He didn't swing his arms when he moved and his head bobbed up and down. His paces were so long that at first the teachers thought they could make a long-jump champion out of him and for a while they had him out in the rain at the long jump pit, scrabbling down the ash runway and swan-diving into the sand. But Big Watty Dog Watkins couldn't jump like a dog. All he could do was walk like one.

It was Nightingale who named me Watty Dog, and officially changed the other boy's name to Big Watty Dog. Nightingale named most people. It was sort of his job. I wondered if in the ancient days of blue-painted Britons and armour-chested Romans crashing together in the fields of English summer wheat, whether every town didn't have someone like Nightingale to name each family and make sure the name fitted and stuck.

Nightingale said that because the other Watkins and I had the same name, we must be related, even if the link was somewhere back in the time of mud huts and Romans, when one of Nightingale's ancestors had sat on a tree stump and scraped at the crud in his beard, thinking out family names. It didn't matter that Big Watty had blond hair when mine was brown and a crooked nose when mine was straight, so you could tell he wasn't related to me.

Big Watty Dog heard about me and my new name. He took the slipper from under his bed and walked all the way across school to hit me with it at Bun Break one day. Bun Break came every morning at 10.30. Mostly there weren't any buns. Instead they gave us tea and biscuits printed with the word NICE that we used to throw at the kindergarten pupils on our way back to class. Big Watty said if I kept calling myself by his name, there'd be trouble. I tried to explain. He hit me again and I dropped my biscuits.

At least I wasn't called Cuddlybum. Or the one great name that was so cruel it didn't need to be changed. The name you didn't use if you wanted to be kind to this boy, even though it was his real name and it seemed to be everywhere – on his locker, on every item of his name-taped clothing and called out in the thunder of the Headmaster's voice across the Big Hall. Ramsbottom. You looked at him and you could tell he had been suffering since birth or even before, as if some echo of the name had found its way into his mother's stomach and the unborn Ramsbottom had heard and understood. He had grown tall but flimsily. His knee joints looked like tennis-balls under skin where the veins all showed through. Tripping him up on the soccer field, which I did most days, was like sticking a broomstick into the spokes of a fast-rolling bicycle. He'd nose-dive into the mud and yell – Just shut up! Just shut up! – even if no one was talking.

The teachers had their other names, too. Inky, Bleachy, Waa-Waa, Splash, Casc, Putty. Their beginnings all seemed lost. Nightingale and I would lie awake at night and say the names over and over to each other, waiting for the spell to break and for the meanings to come clear. But it seemed that in the old days, they had used a different method for naming. Maybe it had to do with being good at Rugby or soccer or swimming, or to do with a certain colour hair that now had fallen out. We never found out. The spells never broke and the teachers wouldn't tell.

I found a blob of modelling clay attached to my desk. It had been shaped to look like a radio. As soon as I opened the lid of my desk, people yelled, 'Bug! You've been bugged!' They cupped their hands around their ears and pretended to listen through the bugging device, as if they could hear each thought inside my head.

Then the teacher walked in, and the smiles dropped off our faces.

We didn't call our teacher Mr Winter. We called him Pa Winter and it was the same for all the teachers at the Dragon School. He wore a thick tweed suit with a matching waistcoat and had leather patches on the elbows of his coat. He also had leather buttons on his jacket which looked to me like tiny flattened soccer balls. Mostly you couldn't see his eyes, because his glasses were so thick. Once in a while, he took them off and massaged his temples. Then you could see that he had a young face and it was only the suit that made him look like an old man. His cheeks were very pink, and sometimes he held his hands gently to his face as if his skin was very sensitive and it hurt him to shave every morning.

He was angry about the fuzzy-felt board and all his fuzzy animals being crumpled. With his long-fingered hands, he smoothed out the wrinkles. Pa Winter had a temper. The first warning sign was a twitching of his lips. As soon as I saw that twitch, my bowels cramped and I wanted to crawl under my desk, as if to take cover from an air raid.

I was introduced as 'Our New Friend from the Colonies' and made to point out where I lived on a globe. It wasn't a big globe, and I almost couldn't find Rhode Island. Eventually I tracked it down. The state was painted green, like a lump of snot under the flexed arm of Cape Cod. The space was too small for Rhode Island to be spelled out, so all they put was RI.

Speaking like an American seemed far worse than having a name that could be twisted into body parts or ugly animals. I got a feeling of what was to come, and knew that the only way to stop it was to learn how to speak like the English.

At the end of the day, we all filed into our classrooms and did homework. The hardest time was after dark. Pictures of home appeared more clearly, like radio waves suddenly free of static. I picked Pa Winter's globe off his desk, found Rhode Island, and Blubbed over the spot. Crying was called Blubbing at the Dragon. With the magnifying glass attached to Bosom's Swiss Army knife, I scanned the blob of Rhode Island, looking for the contours of Narragansett Bay. But it was useless. The whole of America could hide under my outstretched hand, and the whole big blue of the Atlantic lay in the shadow of my palm.

The hallway echoed with coughing and whispering and the grumble of crank-handled pencil sharpeners. Pa Vicker walked up and down the corridor on patrol. He wore crêpe-soled desert boots that made almost no sound. I listened to how the whispering stopped as he moved from classroom to classroom. When he came close, I'd set the globe on the floor and write out my homework. Pa Winter had given us a barnyard scene and we had to name all the animals in French – La vache. Le canard. Le cheval. And then the ones I didn't know, but had to make up – Le tractère. Les cloudes. La Piglette.

Pa Winter had a system.

He'd call on you in class and you'd have to stand up from your desk. Then he'd tell you to recite your homework from the night before. If you screwed up, he'd put a black mark next to your name. If you didn't fumble, then you'd get a red mark.

Three red marks and he'd give you a chocolate bar. They were big bars, too, and he had a box with all different kinds.

But three black marks and he would beat you. You'd go to his house after school, stopping to collect your plimsoll from the gym. Before that, you'd have put on every pair of underpants that you could find as padding. He'd hit you six times with your plimsoll and then you had to shake his hand. As you were leaving he'd give you the same kind of chocolate bar you'd receive if you had three red marks, except that now your butt was on fire. Either way, you walked home with a slab of chocolate.

In the first month that I had Pa Winter as a teacher, I was beaten three times and received seven chocolate bars.

Sometimes I'd find myself at the end of a long line of boys outside Pa Winter's study. Each of us carried one plimsoll, mostly the kind made by Dunlop called Green Flash. I'd hear the fump-fump of a plimsoll connecting with a boy's butt, but couldn't see anything because Pa Winter always shut the door. As the line grew shorter, I sometimes couldn't stop from crying and even asked to go ahead of people in the line. It was the waiting that I couldn't take.

Once I stood next to Cuddlybum. He was very thin and pale, so that you could see the wandering red path of veins under his skin. Cuddly always combed his crow-black hair very neatly, which set him apart from the rest of us. He had two huge bristle brushes that he used each morning, one for each side of his parting. Cuddlybum also kept a bottle of perfume in his locker, because it was his mother's brand. He liked to smell it and be reminded of her. Like me, he almost never saw his parents in the term-time. They lived in Portugal, where his father was in the British embassy.

Cuddlybum pulled me out of line, even taking hold of my elbow the way teachers do. 'You can't let Pa Winter see you cry, Watty.'

I looked at the other boys to see if they'd been watching, and they were. From the expressions on their faces, I knew that Cuddly was right. I saw how important it was. If I cried, I let everyone down, even if these were the hardest tears to choke back.

So I never let Pa Winter see me cry again. Always I waited until I was out of his study and had gone to the end of the corridor. I touched the smoothed wooden ball at the head of the banisters and once I had touched it, I allowed the tears to come.

For the first few days, I cried after the dormitory lights were out. I pressed my face deep into Oscar Bear's foamy yellow stomach because I didn't want anyone to hear me. I didn't cry in the daytime because there was too much else going on. After a while, I also stopped crying at night. Instead, I begged to be sent home. I didn't beg to the teachers or in letters home to my parents. I lay in my bed after dark and begged the great forces of magic, good or bad – whichever would listen – to send me back across the water. I offered up toys and money, then teeth and hair and fingers.

I imagined myself appearing suddenly on the beach. I'd make my way up the steep slope of the garden and find my way inside. Wandering the corridors, I'd see the dining-room table which had been made from the timbers of a ship. I'd see the lamp with the cracked blue glass and the painting of a boy on a green bicycle.

But if the forces of magic were hard on me that night, I'd appear further from home – in Jamestown maybe – and have to cross the bridge, hundreds of feet above the water, before I could reach the house. Or out on Dutch Island in the middle of the bay, where the black and yellow spiders lived. I'd have to swim across and scrabble ashore over the barnacled rocks.

As their cruelty increased, the forces sent me further and further away. And they asked for more payment. Arms, legs, my sight. I gave them what they wanted. Some nights, if these dreams had come true, I'd have dragged myself home blind and deaf and mute and on bloody stumps from the Canadian border with nothing more than my chin to move myself.

The truth was that there were no deals to make. I would just have to wait it out. Sometimes, I felt like a bug trapped in a bell jar. I could see outside and imagine all the things I'd be doing if I was free, but the only thing to do was wait until someone set me loose.

We sat two boys in each bath, knees pulled up to our chins. A matron named Charlotte sat on a chair beside us, reading a book. Before coming in to the bathroom, she would stand in the hall and tie her long hair in a knot at the back. As the evening went on, this knot would come gradually undone, until the shiny red-brown strands fell down across her cheeks. She always had a slight squint, as if the wind was in her face.

Earlier that evening, as we scraped the last clumps of beans and toast from our plates, Pa Vicker had made an announcement that we should go to Charlotte if we had any problems we wanted to talk about.

On the way up stairs, Nightingale warned me never to discuss problems with Charlotte. 'Once a boy did that and in a week he was gone and we never saw him again.'

I looked at Charlotte through curtains of steam that rose up from the bath. I had been thinking hard of a problem I could talk to her about. It was something in her smell of worn-out perfume and the tap-tap of her shoes and her sighing that made me want to be near her.

After baths, Nightingale led me down to the Medicine Room, which was really just a bathroom.

Charlotte sat on the toilet seat and had two bottles set out by her feet. One bottle was filled with bright red syrup and the other with luminous yellow. 'Cough or a sneeze?' she asked Nightingale, when we appeared in the doorway. With one quick movement, she shook the hair out of her eyes.

'Both,' Nightingale told her. He leaned out over the bathtub and sucked down a teaspoon from each bottle. The sides of the bathtub were streaked with red and yellow dribbles of syrup. Then Nightingale pointed at me. 'He has both, too.'

Charlotte looked half asleep. Her voice didn't rise above a murmur. 'It's an epidemic,' she said.

Nightingale crawled into the bath and licked up the dribbles of syrup.

Charlotte told him he was disgusting.

The syrups both tasted the same. They burned in my throat and made my tongue go numb.

After that, we went every evening to the Medicine Room, like grown-ups having an after-dinner drink, the same as Pa Vicker with his port and cigars that kept him company at his desk as he worked late into the night.

After Nightingale and I had got back from the Medicine Room, Cuddlybum went around the dorm asking what our families did.

My dad was a scientist, I told him. A geophysicist.

Nightingale's dad was a chartered accountant.

'No, no, no!' Cuddly shouted. 'What did they do in the war and what did they do back in the time of Henry the Eighth and what is your family crest?'

So while Nightingale was railing on to Cuddly about how his grandfather had been a boxer in the Army and gave people the one-two punch, I thought about what my family had done hundreds of years before.

I didn't know. It had always surprised me that other boys could say what their great-great-grandfathers had been and where they lived and how they had become famous.

I didn't think my family had been in any wars, and they hadn't discovered any islands in the South Pacific or been in Parliament. There was a mountain range under the Atlantic Ocean named Watkins Ridge that had been named after my father and he said it was as big as the Rockies. He came home from work one day and stretched out a huge map on the dining-room table. It was a diagram of the mountain, done in blue ink and looking like a computer print-out of someone's heartbeat. But neither Cuddly or Nightingale seemed impressed since the whole thing was under water and therefore you couldn't climb it and put a flag at the top.

This threw me a little, since I had never thought an underwater mountain was any less important than one which was above water. I sat there for a moment with a grey cloud over my head, but then I had an idea. 'Of course you could climb the mountain,' I announced, 'if you had one of those special underwater climbing suits.'

All talk stopped in the room.

I didn't even wait for their questions. 'I can't believe you don't already know about them. God.' I clicked my tongue and rolled my eyes. 'Well, my dad's got one and so have I.'

'You do?' Nightingale had already begun to strangle his bear out of jealousy.

'My dad and I go walking right out into the middle of the ocean. Just like going for a walk in the park. We have special climbing boots and oxygen tanks. It's all quite dry inside.'

I didn't need to say any more. Even I became lost in the daydream of wandering with my father across the great underwater plains, through forests of kelp, and climbing the Everests of the Atlantic. I imagined all of us, Nightingale, Cuddly, my father and me, strolling along with our hands in our pockets the way we always did, as if we did this every day and were not even very impressed by it anymore.

But then the conversation turned back to what our families had done and where they came from.

My father had gone to Canada in the 1950s as a javelin thrower for Wales in the British Commonwealth Games. He came home and married my mother and they both emigrated to Alberta. After that, he worked for Shell Oil up in the Yukon, until he had enough money to move down to the States and put himself through school again.

I knew that my father's family name used to be Moore, but that one of his ancestors once got drunk in a pub with some sailors and when he woke up, he was on a ship on his way to the Crimean War. So he jumped overboard and swam to shore and changed his name to Watkins.

And I knew that people on my mum's side of the family had once come from Italy and smuggled crystal and rum into Cornwall, but got left there when their ship went down.

Cuddlybum was going on about how he could trace his family back to William the Conqueror and how his family crest had been granted by King Henry IV.

My grandfather on my mother's side designed steam engines for Babcock and Wilcox in Pembroke Dock in Wales. He was working out in Singapore when the Japanese invaded. I heard that he had stood on the veranda of his hotel and heard a strange squeaking sound coming from the hills. It was the Japanese soldiers, who were all riding on bicycles. They had come so far that the tyres had all popped or worn out, so the soldiers were riding on the metal wheel rims and that was what made the squeaking sound. He escaped just before they stormed the city, and my mother still had the compass that he used to find his way out through the jungle.

My other grandfather came from a poor family. He had been a dynamite boy in a Welsh mine at the age of fifteen. At sixteen, he ran away to London and became a policeman. He was savaged by a dog one day and married the nurse who stitched him back together. After that, they lived outside London, in a place called Sunbury-on-Thames. But years later, something happened, something that was never made clear and never talked about. The family just suddenly packed up and moved back to Wales. I heard that my grandfather had taken a bribe and later got blackmailed. So he had to run away, back to Southerndown in Glamorgan. I doubted if my father ever forgave my grandfather for allowing himself to be blackmailed.

My grandma had a maid called Hettie.

My uncle Bill was a porter at Heathrow airport.

All I knew was fragments that didn't fit together.

Then Nightingale lost his temper and gave Cuddly the one-two punch and I was glad that the subject would change now.

But it troubled me. I knew my ancestors must have done something. I knew we didn't just evolve out of a rock pool a hundred years before on Pwyllgwylod beach in Pembrokeshire.

I felt ashamed of my family for not having a coat of arms granted by Henry IV and did not know what excuse there was for not having led at least one famous cavalry charge.

I figured it would be up to me. Everything else seemed suddenly unimportant.

Just before Lights-Out, a girl walked into our dorm. She was Pa

Vicker's daughter and the same age as us. For a moment, she just smiled. Then she pulled her nightdress up around her chin and I had never seen a naked girl before.

Then we all had to show her our dicks which was the rule. Nightingale showed his first.

She ran away when Pa Vicker came up the stairs, ringing a bell and shouting, 'Pyjamas, Prayers and Potty!' He said he would read us a story.

While he read, we sat on our beds and ate toothpaste.

When the story was over and the lights had been turned out, I watched raindrops spread huge across the ceiling, projected by streetlamps outside.

As I drifted off to sleep, I dreamed that I could hear my mother calling my name from America.

The dorm lights hadn't been off more than fifteen minutes when it was decided that we would have to raid the dorm downstairs. I had been asleep, but now with a dorm raid about to start, I knew there'd be no chance of trying to doze through that. All of the dorms were named after famous astronomers. Kepler, Tycho, Galileo, Copernicus. We were Kepler, and to our minds Copernicus had already been destroyed.

An adult might not think that there'd be much in the way of weaponry in a dormitory room for seven-year-old boys. But the way we saw it, everything was a weapon. And no excuse was too small for taking your pillow and slamming it down on your next-door-neighbour's head. There were other weapons, too. Slippers. Blankets. Entire mattresses could be used against the enemy.

It was decided that Bosom would open the attack by sliding down the stairs on a mattress. Bosom was not in agreement on this, so he was tied to that mattress with several linked-together belts. And a sock was put in his mouth to discourage any lack of fighting spirit.

Unfortunately for us, and especially for Bosom, the dorm downstairs had also decided to launch a raid. They were already coming up the stairs, like a half-naked tribe of midget savages, when we pushed Bosom down on to them. He took off like a man on a bobsled and sent them flying in all directions.

My job was to stand at the top of the stairs with several toothpaste tubes lined up along the top step. When the enemy were within range, I stamped on the toothpaste tubes, one after the other, and sent jets of brightly coloured Aquafresh and Close-Up down on top of them.

Soon they had beaten us back into our dorm, and all you could hear was the thump of pillows striking bodies and grunts as the blows connected, sending boys airborne across the rows of beds. There was also a frantic squealing from the bottom of the stairs, where Bosom was trying to spit out his sock and untangle himself from the mattress.

As always seemed to happen in dorm raids, one after the other, the pillows started to rip. Nuclear mushroom clouds of feathers sprayed across the dorm, and soon we were ankle deep in what looked like a hundred exploded chickens.

We didn't know it then, but Pa Vicker was already on his way. It was his bad luck as he bounded up the stairs in the dark that he did not see Bosom and the two of them had slid half-way down another set of stairs before Pa Vicker got back on his feet.

By this time we had captured the prefect of the dorm downstairs. We made him stand on the window-sill with a pair of underpants on his head and sing the national anthem.

Pa Vicker reached our dorm and turned on the lights. Then he stood there in the mound of feathers, which lay like fresh snow on the floorboards. He was so angry, he couldn't even speak.

It was at this point that I learned the most important rule of dorm raids, which was that whenever the teacher comes in, no matter if you are standing right in front of him when the lights go on and with a pillow raised above your head, you have to run back to your bed and pretend to be asleep. That is what everybody did. I guessed it was hoped that the teacher would think he was hallucinating or maybe just having a really bad dream.

There were about four times as many boys as there were beds, so after all the commotion had died down, each bed had anywhere from two to six boys in it, all pretending to be fast asleep and not having done anything wrong. The only boy who hadn't found a bed was the dorm prefect from downstairs. He was still running around with a pair of underpants on his head, looking like someone who has lost out at musical chairs.

Since I was the first one that Pa Vicker had seen when he came into the room, he marched straight over to my bed. 'You're responsible for this!' he yelled.

I stretched and yawned and tried to look as if I'd just woken up.

I took a look around at the shredded curtains, the feathers and the empty pillow-cases. I admired the artistic squiggles of tooth-paste all over the walls. To me, it was all a thing of beauty, a cause for some genuine pride.

'This is all your fault!' he shouted.

'It is?'

'Entirely!' he bellowed at me.

'Thank you, sir,' I said.

He threatened to send me home, first back to America and then to my family in Wales, but it was almost time for the half-term break, so I'd be going there in a few days anyway. Pa Vicker threatened me with so much that even he lost track of what he was going to do and then he started to repeat himself. When he had run out of steam, he stamped out of the dorm.

But we all saw the flicker of a smile on his lips as he stepped out into the hallway. And we remembered, as he had just remembered, that he was once a seven-year-old boy, too. Perhaps, deep under layers of paint on the walls, were the toothpaste squiggles he himself had put there years and years before.

Most of my relatives still lived in Wales. My parents emigrated to Canada just after they were married, but they left their families behind.

When the half-term holiday came, I got on a National Express bus at Oxford and changed and changed and changed buses until I got to Carmarthen in West Wales. In summertime, the western English countryside would blind me with its green. I reached Carmarthen after dark, and my Uncle John was there in his duffel coat.

He and my Auntie Vivian lived in Fishguard, in a house with sharp white stones imbedded in the outside walls. The house looked out at the cliffs of Dinas Head, jutting into the Irish Sea.

Mamgu, the grandma of my cousins, lived up the road with Gerhardt Knaf, a sergeant in the Nazi Luftwaffe, who'd been sent here as a prisoner of war, but didn't bother to leave when the war ended. They stayed in the same house, and sat in blanket-covered chairs by a coal fire.

The streets were noisy with cars. Crows and seagulls marched on the chimney pots. I walked on the beach called the Parog, watching the ferry come in from Rosslare in Ireland and head out again into the foam-topped water. Mostly my cousins were away, and Uncle John was headmaster at the Dinas Lower School. Andrew was up in Scotland, senior prefect at Gordonstoun. Gail was away, too. So it was me and my Auntie Vivian and my youngest cousin Carol, careering around the little roads with the high hedges and buying ice-cream at every town we came to.

Time smashed out of its slow-puttering clocks and the neat boxes of classroom times. It ran fast and barrelled through the three days of my vacation. I was allowed to take some money for the trip, and I always spent it at a shop called Nichols' in Fishguard. There was usually a craze for some gadget back at school and I'd be sure to find it in Nichols'.

I travelled back to the Dragon on an early morning bus, just me and the driver across the Welsh countryside, with only flickering memories of what I'd done in the holiday. In Wales, I didn't have to worry about being an American. It just didn't seem to make any difference to people. But at the Dragon it mattered.

I was the only American at the school then, and at first I couldn't hide it. Everyone needed to try out their own twanging Cowboy voices and say 'Utah' the wrong way and call me 'Pardner'. Even the teachers. It was no good making fun of English accents, because then the joke suddenly stopped being funny and I saw and felt their anger.

All arguments ended with me being called a Yank and America being a place where everyone carried six shooters and where gangsters drove through the streets, squeezing off rounds from Thompson guns.

There was nothing to do but take it.

On Sundays, I'd go to the library and read the newspapers. What I read about America there seemed to make true all the things I had heard from the other boys. America did seem to be run by gangsters and Americans did always seem to be at war.

I didn't know enough to argue. I knew about the war in Vietnam, although I had no idea where Vietnam was and why it was worth fighting about. I knew we had shot up the Indians and I knew there was a Revolution and a Civil War, but I didn't know in what order.

Sometimes I missed being at school in America. I missed the hot green plastic seats of bus #2 and I missed bus driver Bill Bailey who was always kicking out the boy named PJ at the top of Champlin Road and making him walk the rest of the way home. I missed Mrs Bailey's hamburgers at the gas-station-and-restaurant called Babbie's, even though I heard a rumour that she seasoned those burgers by slapping them under her armpits.

I missed my yellow raincoat with the fireman's clasps and my Donny Osmond lunchbox.

I missed saying the pledge of allegiance every day and holding my right hand over my heart – *'I pledge allegiance to the flag of the United States of America, and to the republic for which it stands, one nation under God, indivisible, with liberty and justice for all.'*

The name of the school was Hamilton Elementary School and I used to sit next to Fred who wet his pants. And on the other side of me was Mary and as soon as she saw Fred wet his pants, she would wet her pants and I would sit with my feet up on my chair while the teacher cleared up the mess.

I guess I even missed Sam and Allen Morgan, who were always first on the school bus in the mornings. They called me and my brother the Twat Twins and called me Wat Toad to my face.

In time, I learned to hide the American accent. I could make it disappear the minute I passed through customs at Heathrow Airport on my way to school. And when I was home again, I could bring back my American voice the second I walked out of Logan in Boston. I could do it well enough that no one would question where I came from. It was a necessary thing, because it stopped the teasing on both sides of the ocean.

I did find one raw nerve among Cuddly and Nightingale. I said that Britain would never have won the World Wars without America. This got them mad. Even the teachers got mad. They said they would have won the war by themselves and they got so mad that they stopped making sense.

Sometimes war seemed to be everything at the Dragon School. We were all still fighting the Japanese and still fighting the Germans. We killed them as plastic soldiers arranged in formation across the linoleum floors of the dorms. We killed them with our plastic model kits, and sent their planes on fire down into the trampled grass of the playing fields. We killed them in the War Mags that arrived all rolled up and crispy-paged each Thursday and got handed around dog-eared on Saturday nights. They died on Sunday nights at the movies shown in the Big Hall. We killed them hand-to-hand down by the river banks, the dead ones vanishing as they hit the ground and new ones jumping to life from the bushes.

We all went down to the Army Surplus shop in Oxford and bought ammunition cans at 45p each. In these cans we carried our books and pencils and everybody had one. We also had the steel boxes of Army medical kits with the instructions still printed to the inside lid on how to administer morphine tablets under the tongue of a wounded man. In these steel boxes we kept our valuable marbles – the Vals – the Spiral Spirals and the Jumbo Emperor Trebs.

Some of us had canvas webbing belts and some had wool commando hats which we wore whenever we could.

It was war against the other teams – St Edward's, The Bedford Bulldogs, and Appleby College from Canada who came to play us in rugby and did all kinds of warm-up exercises on the field while we stood watching with our hands in our pockets and then we kicked the shit out of them.

There was war between the dorms on the nights of pillow-fighting, when toothbrush mugs came raining down and pillows burst and I would stand at the top of the stairs and stamp on tubes of toothpaste, sending jets of red, white and blue Macleans and pink Euthymol onto the people below.

The last kind of war was against a couple of the teachers. In this war we did what they told us to do, but we gave them no respect. We did not look them in the eye or show them any kindness. You could tell the ones who had been fighting hard. They were red-faced and tired and mean, always beating people. They were slowly losing the war, because there was only one of them, but there were never-ending ranks of pale-faced us, who cottoned on fast and fought back.

In the winter, the Dragon School had a Guy Fawkes celebration as soon as we arrived back from the half-term break. Then there were only three weeks to go until the Christmas holiday, and the air was filled with the spice of cold and a promise of going home soon.

Instead of Hallowe'en in America, we had Guy Fawkes Night at the Dragon School and all over England. Guy Fawkes was the one who had tried to blow up the Houses of Parliament, some time back in the days when men dressed up in clothes that made them look as if they were wearing their underpants outside their trousers. The week before Guy Fawkes Night, Bovver Boys stood on street corners all over Oxford with stuffed dummies in wheelbarrows. They'd hold out their hands and say – 'Penny for the Guy? Penny for the Guy? Oi you shit, I'm talking to you and I said penny for the fucking Guy.'

The dummy was supposed to be Guy Fawkes and on 5 November, when the real Guy Fawkes had tried to blow up Parliament, the dummy's head would be stuffed with fireworks and set on fire.

We had our own dummy at the Dragon School. He sat piled way up on a mound of old and broken desks and chairs.

After supper, Pa Vicker led us out onto the playing fields, where the bonfire had already started. Everyone in the school gathered around the flames. We ran at the flickering light and I felt the way a moth must feel when it's zooming towards a candle. I couldn't help myself, and if there hadn't been a rope strung up to keep us back from the flames, I might have run straight into the crumbling white centre of the blaze.

This wasn't like the candy-scavenging Hallowe'en of back home. Not like the time I wore a Felix the Cat costume and was running away from old man Fontaine's house with a handful of Milk Duds. The Felix mask slipped over my eyes. I ran into a tree and flattened my nose. It was different here on the Dragon field. Something more serious, as if the dummy was a real person who would scream when the flames reached his feet.

Guy Fawkes sat high above us, roped into a chair. He wore a clown mask with a huge and red-lipped smile. His stomach and his legs were bloated and I imagined sticks of dynamite packed inside him, smouldering and ready to blow.

I watched my friends in light the colour of marmalade. Their eyes were shining like glass. Teachers stood above them, serious-faced, arms folded across their chests.

The dummy's clothes caught fire. He must have been soaked in petrol because suddenly he was flames and his head exploded, sending sparks down on us like pebbles from a meteor.

We screamed and threw up our hands. The teachers grinned and showed the white of their teeth. The blaze ate up the dummy, and he fell back into the furnace-guts of the fire.

On that night, the dark and foggy places by the river were not to be feared. I wanted to walk among the gargoyle shapes that hid among the reeds, ready to chase us back home on every night but this one. The dead had one chance a year to walk beside us. And this was it.

I wondered if all the times I had begged the forces of magic to send me home, whether the ones who answered were good forces or bad. Maybe they would never collect what I offered them, or maybe they were just biding their time.

I did seem to travel. It seemed so easy sometimes, in the crackling static of my body closing down for the night. I walked towards the cliff face of my sleep, and jumped clean out of my body. Some nights it seemed so real that the next day was spent in a fog, with a numbness fizzing in my nerves and the voices of teachers reaching me as if down the length of a long cardboard pipe.

I slipped gently from the white cage of my ribs and soared up past the chestnut trees and yellow buzzing streetlamps of Oxford and the glumly tolling bell of Tom Tower. I drifted fast across the tundra of clouds, over deep-sea rollers and tankers and castaways on their life rafts a thousand miles from land. I reached the shores of Narragansett Bay and trod home by moonlight across the sand. I saw the stray red lights of cars that crossed the Jamestown bridge and heard the sail-boat cables rattling against their masts in Newport harbour.

I passed through the huge glass pane of our front window and felt the Persian carpet under my feet. I saw my parents sleeping, in separate beds because my dad thrashed about in his dreams.

Then I scurried away across the thousands of miles to my bed at the Dragon School. I came to rest again behind my ribs, before the colours of the English sunrise spread pink and blood-red across the dormitory walls.

I did this not just once, but dozens and dozens of times. I went each night for weeks, wandering with the ghosts of Conanicut Indians and the two British Redcoats who had been killed by Yankee Minutemen two hundred years before and were buried in Mr Worrel's garden.

I even begun to feel sorry for my parents, that they could not voyage like me. But then I wondered if perhaps they did the same dark travelling. Maybe our shadows crossed high over the Atlantic as they made their way back to their old homes in Wales, or perhaps they came to visit me as I lay sleeping in my iron-railed bed.

I don't know why I went home in this way. It did no good, after all. I'd be back in England by morning. I could carry nothing with me and I could leave nothing behind. I wanted to leave messages in the dust on my bedroom window, or move something – a lamp or a chair or my father's Bulova watch that he set on the bedside table before he went to sleep. Then they would know I'd been there.

I think I went back because I had found out that I could. I went back to know that I had not dreamed the Bay and rockpools and the gutted, wind-muttering buildings on Dutch Island and to see that my parents were safe.

The night we got back from the Guy Fawkes celebration, I wet the bed. I dreamed I was in the bathroom and in front of the urinal and I peed and then I woke up.

Now, I figured, they would give me one of those plastic sheets over my mattress which told everyone you were a bed-wetter. Every time you moved, the sheet would rustle. It put you lower than the littlest Little Man, lower even than Bosom.

As quietly as I could, I pulled off my sheets. Everyone else was still asleep, Nightingale swinging his legs back and forth all the time the way a dog does when it dreams.

I dragged the sheets to the bathroom and tried to wash out the pee in the toilet. I got water everywhere and started to cry because now the sheets were all wet and there was no way to dry them. It looked as if I'd stood on my pillow and peed all over the bed, not just a little in a dream.

I did wish I could die then, silently and without fuss.

Charlotte lived next to the bathroom and I woke her up with my crying. She walked in wearing a night-dress that didn't even come down to her knees. She smelled of smoke and perfume and her knees cracked when she bent down to see who I was.

I had hidden my face in the wet sheet.

She knew who I was because I had a Green Bay Packers football helmet printed on my pyjamas. I hugged her and pressed my mouth and nose into her stomach to stop the noise of my crying which now I could no longer control.

I said I would give her my pocket money to shut up about it. I'd take out the maximum amount each week until it was gone and I'd give it all to her.

She gave me a clean sheet from the linen cupboard and promised not to tell and not to give me a plastic sheet which would be the same thing as telling.

I made her swear on the Bible. She told me to hurry up and get back to sleep because I had a soccer match the next day.

I wasn't any good at soccer. Didn't have foot control. So I stood in the goal and stopped balls with my face.

There is a certain kind of noise that echoes through your head when you stop a soccer ball with your face. The ball hurts less if it is raining and plastic balls hurt more than leather ones.

If it had been raining, the explosion of mud off the ball would blind me totally. A pins-and-needles numbness scorched my nose and forehead and lips. I'd flop into the dirt that was riddled with the punch marks of soccer boot studs. But if the ball did not go in the goal, and I heard cheering that I'd saved the game, I found myself hoping that the pain would look even as bad as it felt. Some days, I'd wander back to the showers with the checker-board imprint of the ball branded on the side of my head.

The best part about being a goalie was the extras. You got to wear gloves with little rubber pebbles on them for gripping the ball. You got to wear as many clothes as you liked and you didn't have to run around, with the cold air making your lungs feel as if they had been scraped with a wire brush.

My Dad had taught me about soccer. The important thing, he said, was the Heroic Save. It was no good simply to pick up the ball. You have to dive because it looked better, and if you missed and the ball went into the net, at least you had dived to save it and that looked better than the ball running straight between your legs.

It was mostly in these Heroic Saves that I caught the ball with my face. The Dragon was divided up into four teams – Bardwell, Chad, Linton and Norham. Those were the names of streets that ran by the school. And on Saturdays, when all the teams competed, parents would come to watch the games. I'd get handshakes and pats on the back and clean handkerchiefs dabbed against my bloody nose.

I wasn't a good goalie, not first team calibre. But I was the Heroic Diving Goalie of Bardwell team number four. I wished that my parents could have seen. I couldn't tell about it properly in the letters I wrote home on Sundays.

In the first two minutes of my first game, I took a soccer ball full in the face. My lip was split. I didn't cry, and was as surprised as everyone else that the tears did not come. In that moment, I realised that I would not die of the homesickness, or the teasing or the modelling clay bugs in my desk. I would be all right, but I would have to make sure of it by myself. Even with Nightingale and Cuddly and I together as friends all the time, we judged each other separately and in that way we stood apart. As boys lifted me up and Pa Winter the referee made me open my mouth to see if any teeth were broken, I heard the other boys saying 'Well done, Watty.' I knew that this would be my name from now on, whether the other Watty Dog liked it or not. Paul and Watkins would be reserved for teachers and parents. The language of boys was different. They named you differently and judged you differently and this name was better than Bosom.

CHAPTER 2

━━━━━

EVERYTHING HAD A value at the Dragon. Each marble, each piece of toffee and each chair in the TV room. You knew how many toffees it would take to buy a Medium Triple Treb marble and how many Triple Trebs it would take to get you the best seat in the TV room. None of this was written down, but everybody knew it. And everybody knew that the most valuable thing was free time, and this could not be sold or traded away and maybe that was why its value was so great.

In our free time, Nightingale and I nearly always went down to the river. Cuddly didn't come because he hated getting his shoes muddy.

The only trouble with the river-bank was a boy named Bukovik. The only place I ever saw him was on the bank and I used to wonder if he lived there all the time. He was heavy without being fat and with short spiky hair. Even if you were trying to speak kindly about him, you'd have to admit he looked like a hedgehog. And he snuffled when he spoke with a hedgehog kind of noise.

Bukovic made booby traps in the tall grass. You'd be walking along the edge of the slow-moving water and find a rabbit dead in a snare and know it was Bukovik's work. He killed the little hedge-row animals as if to punish God for making him look like one of them. But he made traps for people as well. An open can of Coke left out, but filled with soapy water. Boards with nails in them hidden in dead grass.

Until the day I ran right into him, I had only heard about Buko-vik. Before that, I used to wonder if he was perhaps only a ghoul, like other ghouls who haunted the river bank and drifted on the foggy water and chased you back to school across the playing fields after dark.

Bukovik was making a trap when I found him. He had set up a trip-wire between two trees and laid out drawing-pins in the space where the person would fall. I walked right up to him, not knowing who he was or what he was doing. I had bought a model of a Sopwith Camel and was flying it across the fields. The model was so small that I could only hold it with two fingers. In the end I glued the model to my thumb and flew it that way.

Bukovik knelt in the dirt and set out drawing-pins one by one. When my shadow crossed his path, he raised his head. I knew it was him. Nightingale had described the pointy nose and thin, white lips. His father was a Russian professor at one of the university colleges. I wondered if his parents were as ugly, or whether there had been some kind of mistake.

I stopped making the 'brr' noise of the Sopwith Camel's engine.

Bukovik told me to fuck off. It was the first time anyone had told me to fuck off. The word was too grown-up for most of us and I had to pay Cuddly 50p to tell me what fucking was, anyway. Cuddly had found out about it in a letter from his sister. She wrote that she had done sex one time but was never going to do it again.

For the 50p, Cuddly said he would even teach me a song about sex, so I would remember more easily.

Cuddly escorted each of us in turn into an empty classroom for the lesson.

Nightingale came out from his lesson and said it was damn cheeky to be charging for crappy information like that. Then he blew apart Cuddly's money scheme by offering to tell anyone about sex for free.

A few hours after I'd been told to fuck off, Pa Vicker ran over Bukovik's trap on his bicycle and popped both his tyres. Bukovik was hiding in the bushes and not hiding very well because Pa Vicker found him. Pa Vicker went berserk. He grabbed Bukovik by the hair and bicycled back across the playing fields on his popped tyres, dragging Bukovik behind. He pedalled right past where Nightingale and I were building a fort. We had vines twisted around our heads and in and out of our buttonholes for camouflage. Nightingale was General that day and he had ordered it. We sat very still as Pa Vicker rode past. Bukovik was the only boy in the school who had never been known to cry, and even then he wasn't Blubbing. It was the harshest thing I ever saw done to a boy, but I would have done it myself if I'd been as big as Pa Vicker and if I'd had a bicycle.

If it rained, the playing fields would be out of bounds, which meant the river bank as well. Then we'd spend any free afternoons in the glue-smelling hobby hut and stick together models of Stukas or Spitfires or carve spears from tree branches with Swiss Army knives. Or we'd wander the empty corridors of the school, in and out of the silent classrooms. Our precious Saturday afternoons would trickle past while the rain stamp-danced on the playground.

The only place in the school where I never went unless I had to was the Sanitorium, which everybody called the San. The San was where you went if you were sick and Sister Mabel would feed you giant pink pills called Trigesics. The place was haunted. Even the teachers said so.

A hundred years before, a boy named Ned Morphew fell off a balcony in the Old Hall and broke his head on the floor. Nightingale said he'd heard that the boy's brain had rolled across the floor like an old pudding.

The teachers carried him to the San and he died there in a room called Little East.

Which was exactly where they put me when I got sick on my birthday.

To make things even worse, there were two beds in Little East and when I fell asleep that night, one of them was empty and I was in the other. But when I woke up at three in the morning, wind and rain doing cavalry charges up and down the street outside, there was a grey shape in the bed that had been empty.

I went out and slept in the hall. It was safe in the hall, but Ned Morphew owned Little East and you could not fight him for it.

When I heard bed-creaking and running-water noises from Sister Mabel's room across the hall, I snuck back into Little East. By then it was eight in the morning. I didn't feel like explaining to Mabel about sleeping in the hall, and I figured even Ned Morphew wouldn't grudge me that.

I'd been on the bad side of Sister Mabel ever since I broke my toe playing soccer. She wrapped my foot in a cast and told me not to go out on the playing fields.

But the first place I went was out on the fields, chasing Nightingale who had run off with my crutches. We ended up in a wrestling match. The cast got muddy and wet and started to come apart. I left a trail of wet plaster paint everywhere I went.

Sister Mabel followed my white paint trail and hauled me back to the San. This time she gave me a cast that was so heavy I could barely walk. She told me in great detail what she would do to me if I went out on the fields again.

One Saturday afternoon, I was wandering down a corridor near the TV room when I found Cuddlybum hanging from a coat peg. He hung there from the collar of his corduroy jacket and his feet didn't touch the ground. A senior boy had grabbed him and put him up there.

'Hello, Watty,' he said. 'Have you got anything to eat?'

I gave him a toffee. Then I got down on my hands and knees and let him tread on my back while he unhooked himself. Then he ran off down the hall and out into the playground. He didn't say thank you or anything else and he ran off so fast that I wasn't even up off my knees before he'd disappeared.

I didn't like walking past the long line of coat-pegs. There were hundreds of them lining a corridor in School House, bony and curvey like an old woman's finger calling you in. The pegs were meant for hanging our duffel coats, but mine had been stolen so my peg was empty.

The corridor led to the TV room, so sometimes I had to make the run, down the musty-smelling lines of coats to the huge door, skidding the last twenty feet. I imagined Bukovik hiding in one of the heavy blue coats. His arm would fly out and knock me flat and Bukovik's face would appear from the dark. Bukovik chased me even in my dreams, and in these dreams, the corridor went on for ever and the door to the TV room stayed locked when I tried to open it. The TV was on inside. I heard the munching of crisps and people laughing, but they didn't hear my shouting and Bukovik dragged me away.

We could only watch TV on Saturday afternoons and evenings. Cuddlybum watched from the moment it was turned on until the masters turned it off at 9.30. He watched through the drone of the soccer commentator's voice, listing off the scores. He watched the news. He watched commercials. By the time the Saturday movie came on, the room was crowded with people. Cuddly sat in a huge leather chair, his face only two feet from the screen. We gathered around him and watched, resting too-salty Cheese and Onion flavour crisps on our tongues until our eyes watered and the crisp dissolved. We only had crisps for dinner on Saturday night. Charlotte threw the hand-size bags into the crowd and sometimes you'd hear the pop of an exploding bag, grabbed too hard by the boy who caught it. Charlotte loved it. She'd pitch the bags high and shout 'Wheeee!,' seeing hands rise up, fingers scraping the air. Crisps were currency. For a bag, you could trade Big Treb marbles and two-year-old radiator-hardened horse-chestnuts used for playing Conkers. Crisps were power on Saturday night. They could get you a seat in front of the TV and not stuck at the back, standing on a window-sill with your butt getting cold against the window-pane. Sometimes I'd buy extra bags in town on Saturday afternoon and smuggle them in. In the frenzy of handing out, the crisps would grow in value. It was like a documentary on the Stock Market that Pa Winter once made us watch – all the hands raised and faces twisted with want. You could sit back and watch the frenzy and make it work for you. I had sacks of marbles to prove it.

Then later in bed, the last hum of the frenzy leaving my bones, I'd figure out how hungry I was. I hadn't kept any food for myself. There was nothing to do then but wait for Sunday morning and the hard-boiled eggs that always came for breakfast. We'd bludgeon off the tops and cram in butter to make the yolk seem melty. Then we'd go into chapel and fart.

The only obligation we had on Sundays was to go to chapel. The rest of the day we had free. The best meal of the week outside of eating sweets was at Sunday lunch. It was almost always roast beef and Yorkshire pudding.

I would eat most things that they served to us at school, with the absolute exception of kippers. I had seconds of a batch of steak and kidney pie that made everyone else sick and I ate the gravy-spattered gristle in the stew and I ate the salad without even scraping off the aphids, but when I smelled the oily low-tide smell of kippers heaving up from the dining-hall, I knew I'd go hungry that day.

We wore ties on Sunday, and black wool suits called B-Suits, with the school crest on our top pocket. The crest was a Dragon, whose head reached out towards the sun. Under that came the motto: *Arduus ad Solem*.

My father had taught me a song to help me do up my tie. It had the tune of 'Twinkle, Twinkle Little Star' and went – 'Over, under, over, through, pull the little end away from you.'

I didn't need to practise it much. Instead of undoing the knot when we wanted to take off our ties, we just loosened it until we could pull the tie over our heads, then hung it like a noose on our coat pegs.

I told Pa Sunderland, the music teacher, about the Tie Song my father had taught me. Pa Sunderland went over to his piano and sang the whole thing out, then added extra verses about bow-ties and Ascots. He had a bow-tie on, himself, and while he sang, his Adam's apple bounced up and down on the pink and purple knot.

He taught his classes in a little room with banana-yellow walls. He couldn't pronounce the letter R. Charlotte told us that this was because his tongue was too long.

The worst place in the world for a man to be when his tongue was too long and made him talk funny was in front of a classload of boys at the Dragon School.

We used to sing – 'Lobin Hood, Lobin Hood, liding thlough the glen, Lobin Hood, Lobin Hood, with his Melly Men.'

He bashed on the piano to make us stop but it was hopeless. 'Light!' he screamed. 'Light, you'll all in big tlouble!'

'Lound the Lagged Lock, the Lagged Lascal Lan.'

'You'll all be put on lepolt! I'm leally going to be fulious in a minute!'

I figured he must have stayed awake at nights, trying to think of songs to teach us that didn't have the letter R in them. In the end, we all sang Joseph's Technicolor Dleamcoat.

Some Sunday afternoons, the school was like a ghost town. The day before parents had clogged the school with their Bentleys and Range Rovers and Rollses and driven away their sons. The ones who remained were mostly boys who lived abroad. They weren't foreign. It was just that their parents were working in Singapore or Hong Kong or Bermuda.

We'd all be crunched together in the dining-hall, which echoed strangely to have so few people.

On one of these afternoons, I was running through the playground with Cuddly. We had a game of Tig going, our pockets stuffed with tennis-balls retrieved from the hedge by the tennis-courts. We used these as missiles. We would have been out on the playing fields, but they were muddy and a white sign by the hockey rink said they were Out of Bounds.

As my arm stretched back to launch a ball at Cuddly, I caught sight of Pa Winter at the entrance to the Old Hall. He had a stack of books tucked under his arm. There was hardly ever a trace of teachers at the weekends. Most of them drove out to the country-side or worked in their rose gardens, which were firework displays of colour at the right time of year.

I dropped the tennis-ball. You could never tell with Pa Winter. He might laugh if I beaned Cuddly on the head with the ball, or he might send me to the gym to fetch my plimsoll so he could beat me with it. I bounced the ball a few times, as if to show that I had never even considered beaning Cuddly.

Cuddly had stopped running. He stood with his hands in his pockets, chewing at his lip.

Pa Winter asked us what we were doing.

'Nothing, sir,' we told him. Our eyes grew narrow with worry.

'Playing Tig, were you?' He rocked on his heels.

'Yes, sir. Something like that.'

'Right then,' he said in a loud voice. 'Let's see if I can't catch you both!' Then he dropped his books and the next thing I knew he was running after us.

I had never seen a teacher play like this before. I had seen them roll marbles and sometimes show off by kicking back a football that got booted their way, but not Tig.

I was afraid and ran as fast as when the river-ghouls chased me.

Cuddly's eyes were open wide. He ran with his head thrown back, heavy cloggy Clark's Commando shoes slapping the playground asphalt.

We ran into a classroom and he chased us. So we dodged out the back door and into an alleyway that led out to the playing fields.

He kept chasing us, and we were frightened. By now there was sweat soaked through his shirt. He took off his glasses and ran with them gripped in his fist.

Cuddly and I got to the end of the alley and stopped. The playing fields spread out gloomy and trampled and muddy in front of us. Clots of fog hung around the Rugby goalposts.

Pa Winter still chased us. All I could see was the huge blackness of his body filling up the alleyway.

There was no other place to go but onto the fields, so Cuddly and I ran out over the boot-gouged mud. We stopped then and turned.

Pa Winter stood at the end of the alley, hands on his knees and red-faced. 'You know the playing fields are Out of Bounds. It says so very clearly on the notice-board.'

'But you chased us, sir.'

'You've broken the rules. Both of you. The rules are perfectly clear.'

'But sir . . .'

'Both of you can come to my study after tea this afternoon. And bring your plimsolls.' He stood up and walked back down the alley.

I spent the rest of the day with a fist of panic clenching and unclenching in my guts.

'I don't think he'll do it,' Cuddly said at tea time. He cut chunks of half-frozen butter from a slab on the table and set them on his toast. Then he squashed the toast up against the side of one of the big iron teapots to melt the butter. 'He's just scaring us.'

'I don't know,' I told him. 'He looked pretty serious to me.'

'Calm down, Watty. There's no use Blubbing about it.'

'I'm not Blubbing!' I yelled.

Across the dining-hall, stray heads looked up from their Marmite and toast to see what the yelling was for.

Cuddly went in first. I stood in the hall of Pa Winter's house, smelling polish and tobacco and a far-away sourness of old cider. I heard Pa Winter's muttered voice, and even though I couldn't hear the words, I knew he was telling Cuddly to bend over. I heard the Whacks coming down hard. I counted six and then breathed out, as I knew Cuddly would be breathing out.

When Cuddly appeared from Pa Winter's room, he was holding a big red bar of Cadbury's Bournville chocolate.

I remembered how we had joked sometimes about getting bad conduct marks on purpose, so we could collect these bars of dark chocolate.

Cuddly's face was red from bending over. He looked at me and breathed through his teeth. 'He's Whacking hard today.' Then he walked to the stairs, touched the greasy ball of the banisters and sat down on the top step to wait for me.

I waited for him to cry now that he had reached the stairs, but Cuddly was tougher than that. He made up for his twiggy arms and legs with sharp words that could cut you dead and by making sure the teachers almost never made him cry.

Pa Winter's study looked out into a Conker tree. The leaves were huge and emerald. The spiked balls of horse-chestnut cases hung thick on the branches.

I was losing it. I could feel my throat cramping and my eyes begin to fizz. It was the emptiness of the school and having to stay behind when everybody else went home for the weekend. It was the crappy dining-hall food when I knew other boys would be drinking ginger beer with their parents at The Bear in Woodstock. It was having to wait all afternoon, knowing that I would be beaten at the end of the day and it was not having asked Pa Winter to play Tig with us. All of this bundled up and made the tears start fizzing in my eyes. I sat down in a chair, took out my ink-splotched handker-chief and crammed it into my eyes, in case the tears tried to leak out.

'Now stop crying,' Pa Winter said. 'What do you think this is?'

'I'm not crying, sir.'

'What do you think this is?' he asked again. 'Get out of my chair and come over here.' He was still wearing his sweaty shirt from earlier in the day. He had rolled up his sleeves. 'Get out of that chair and come here!'

I could hear the floorboards creak as Cuddly tip-toed towards the door so he could listen to what was going on.

'Please not this time, sir. Please can't you let me off this time? It was just a game, sir, and we didn't go very far onto the fields.'

'If you don't get over here this instant, you'll be sitting in that chair and doing Latin homework every free afternoon for the rest of term!'

I moved foggy-eyed to his desk, bent over, and shouted in pain as he gave me the Six.

Then he was hugging me. He said it was all right. He pressed my face into his sweaty shirt and then he shook my hand and gave me a chocolate bar.

Cuddly put his hand on my shoulder as we walked back to house. I told him I hadn't cried, but I didn't think he believed me. He was trying to be nice, but it only made things worse.

Most teachers knew how much we valued our time outside of class, as they valued it, too. They would only keep us behind in the classroom for the most serious offences.

But there was one teacher who made a habit of asking boys to stay behind. To go over their work, he said. He waited until the others had left and then he shut the door. He sat down at his desk and made the boy sit, too. Then he'd go over the boy's work. But while he was doing that, he reached across and took hold of the boy's balls and squeezed. If the boy opened his mouth to say some-thing, the man would squeeze harder, so hard that it made the boy shut up and be still. Above the desk, the teacher would go on correcting the work without a pause, as if whatever else was going on had nothing to do with him. The expression on his face never changed. The pitch of his voice never rose or fell.

Cuddly told me about it, and from his face, I knew it was the truth. He was in the teacher's class and had seen one boy after another stay behind. He had heard from the others. He figured his turn would come soon. Nightingale and I agreed that Cuddly would have to give the teacher the one-two punch. Nightingale said his grandfather had laid out people all over the world and listed off the battles in which his grandad had fought. I listened and was impressed. Afterwards, I checked out the dates of the battles and figured that the grandfather would have to be over three hundred years old to have fought in all those wars.

We practised in the dorm against a pillow. I held up the pillow and Cuddly punched it, shouting out 'One-Two' as each fist struck the sack of feathers.

Teachers did different things when they got mad. Some only shouted and gave you Latin hexameters to write out. Others sent you to the Headmaster, who scared you, but didn't whack very hard. Some pulled hair and gave you the knuckles. Others grabbed your sideburns.

This teacher grabbed your sideburns. So one time after practice, we snuck into Charlotte's private bathroom and borrowed her leg razor. It was pink with flowers printed on the plastic. I shaved off Cuddly's sideburns and then put Savlon on the shaved place, because I had cut him up pretty badly. He looked like one of the aliens who show up one time only on a Star Trek episode and then get killed.

I wondered to myself if Cuddly really would get picked to stay behind. I had seen the boys that the teacher picked, and they were Pretty Boys. These were boys who could have dressed up as girls and look more dainty than half the girls I'd ever seen. But Cuddly wasn't pretty. His eyes were too close together and his skin pasty like the flesh of the halibut stored in a jar of alcohol in the bio labs. It seemed to me that Cuddly almost wanted to be picked. If the news ever got out about him giving the one-two punch, the school would echo with his name. But I would rather have turned and faced one of the river-ghouls that chased me home across the playing fields, than I would have dared to rabbit-punch that teacher's bony chin.

Nothing happened. We got tired of practising the one-two and had moved on to stamp collecting.

Then Cuddly came up to me one day in Bun Break and he pulled me out of line. He said the teacher had kept him after class and grabbed his balls, just like the others had said.

'So did you punch him?' I asked, eyes flicking back to the bun tray and knowing they'd all be gone before I could get back in the line.

'No, Watty.' He started taking things out of his pockets and inspecting them – a Conker, barley sugars, his dirt-crusted Opinel knife.

'But why not? Why didn't you give him the one-two punch?'

'Because he had hold of my balls, you damn Yankee.'

From the way Cuddly said it, I knew there was no more to be said. We had known about what would happen, but we had not known how it would be. The one-two punch would go unnumbered and undone.

My father came to visit, on his way to a scientific conference in Brussels. I woke up one morning and looked out of the window and there he was standing in the garden. He wore a dark suit and an old sports tie and his size 13 shoes that I once tried to sail out into a pond as boats. At first I thought he was a ghost, and then I asked myself if perhaps my father had perfected the technique of voyaging in his dreams, just as I was trying to do, and now there he was, having travelled like a spirit across the vast waves of the Atlantic.

He said we were going to the best restaurant in the world and told me to bring some friends. So Nightingale and Cuddly came, too, because by now I knew that even with us teasing and thumping each other sometimes and arguing about who would have won the war with whose help, we three were the best of friends.

'That,' Cuddly told me, 'is the tallest chap I have ever seen.'

'My uncle was taller,' Nightingale said. Then he remembered that he had to have good manners, so he added, 'Well, maybe an inch or two shorter.'

We drove in a rented car to The Bear in Woodstock. It had clay pipes hanging on the walls and we drank Schweppes Ginger Beer from dark brown bottles with orange labels. By the end of the meal, my dad was laying down 10-pence pieces in front of us and saying we could have them if we'd finish such and such a potato or such and such a piece of meat.

Then we drove, but he wouldn't say where. The car he had rented was too small for him and every time we went over a bump, his head would bang against the roof. He would shout 'Ouch!' and then say sorry to apologize. There were lots of bumps on the road, and for a while all the three of us could hear coming from the front seat was – 'Ow! Shit! Sorry . . . Ouch! Christ! I beg your pardon . . . Ah! God damn it! You didn't hear that.'

Nightingale and Cuddly were all polite and not calling me Watty Dog. We called each other by our first names, the words sounding awkward and foreign. After a while, my dad turned around and squinted at us in the back seat. He said, 'Don't you chaps have nicknames? All anyone ever called me at school was Stretch.'

They called him Stretch because he was so tall. I had seen an old newspaper picture of him standing in a doorway and the caption said he was the tallest schoolboy in Britain.

When he heard that my name was Watty Dog, he laughed so much, he almost drove through the front door of a big thatched-roof house.

We came to an airfield and my dad said this was the place. A little orange plane was waiting and a little man to fly it. My dad called Nightingale's parents and asked them if it was all right to send their son up in a plane. Mr Nightingale said he wished he could come, too. But from the look on my dad's face, we could tell Cuddly's parents didn't like the idea. When he hung up, he turned to Cuddly and told him – 'Well, Cuddly, I'm afraid your mother would rather I drop you head first down a well than send you up in that machine.'

The little man wore a leather hat and goggles, but we weren't even in the plane yet before I'd begged them off him for the ride. The engine shook through our feet and backs and arms. When we'd cleared the ground, I looked down at the green pom-poms of trees and towns with their brick-red roofs, each one like an octopus, with the arms of roads spreading out into the green and pale green and yellow and gold. For the first time, I saw the sense in the pattern on my dad's Harris Tweed jacket. All of the colours were there, even the neatness of fields blocked out by hedges.

The little man let me take hold of the controls and I dropped us 300 feet before he could steady the plane again.

On the ride back to school, I had the same ugly heaviness in my guts as when I first arrived at the school and found out I was staying.

My dad said goodbye and drove away. I chased the car, but he drove fast and didn't stop.

There was an awkwardness when you had taken friends out or they had taken you out and then you got back to school. It was awkward because you felt as if you had to be nice and you didn't know whether or not to keep calling each other by your real names or by your school names.

Soon enough it all got back to normal, with teasing and one-two punches and all of us beaten for talking about the day, after Pa Vicker had turned out the lights.

The word spread through school. A teacher named Pa Dimbleby came up and asked if these rumours were true about me and Nightingale and Cuddly dive-bombing Blenheim Castle in a Piper Club with a little old man trying to grab the controls out of my hands. I knew my dad would have wanted it this way. I hoped that one day I'd be able to take him up in a plane and I hoped I'd be flying it myself.

The only other contact I had from home was in letters. Some days it seemed that I was living from one delivery of mail to the next.

At the end of breakfast, Pa Vicker would walk in with the stack of letters and everyone stopped talking. I scanned the stack for the pale blue of an aerogramme. Those letters would be from my mother, and I could never figure out how to open them. Sometimes, in the hurry to read my mother's big-looped handwriting, I just tore the aerogramme into pieces and stuck the parts together like a puzzle. I kept all the letters, but I never read them twice. It became a superstitious thing, which I picked up from Nightingale, who only read his letters once and then always dumped them in the same dustbin on the way over to school. It was the same bin where I stuffed my breakfast kippers whenever we had them, hating how my pockets and my hands would stink all day of low-tide.

I could never predict where my father's letters would come from. He travelled all over the place on his scientific missions and his passport was stamped with a grid of foreign names. In most pictures I had seen of him, he stood on the deck of a ship in the middle of the ocean or was drilling holes in the rock face of some desert island.

Once he sent me a tiny letter in a huge envelope, plastered with stamps from French Antarctica. He wrote that he had been to the building which Captain Scott used as a base camp when he set out to reach the South Pole. Everything was the same as Scott had left it, even with yellow tins of Colman's mustard powder still standing on the shelves. He wrote that whole whaling villages had been abandoned, with whale bones all up and down the beach and pianos left in the houses. He found a warehouse filled with exploding harpoon heads for shooting into the whales.

Cuddly begged for the stamps and Nightingale begged me to ask my father to send him an exploding harpoon head. He went on about it for weeks. Then as a last resort and because he had become obsessed, he went over to the woodwork shop, which we called Barsonry, and tried to make his own harpoon. Pa Barson helped him at first, but then realised what Nightingale was making and pulled his hair as a punishment.

My father sent me an arrowhead that he had pulled out of a mudbank in the Mississippi river. It was a real arrowhead, and maybe hundreds of years old. Boys came from all over the school to see it. And each one in turn would take the sharp end and press the arrowhead against his palm to see how sharp it was. It made me famous for a while. Sometimes I would let Nightingale borrow it for the day. He wanted to make an arrow shaft and tie the arrow on the end, but he couldn't find any feathers for the flights. He wanted to make a bow as well, and fire the arrow at Bukovik.

In the end, I gave him the arrowhead. I don't know how he persuaded me. I think I made up my mind after Nightingale asked me if he could have the arrowhead in the event of me dying unexpectedly.

A letter arrived from Borneo, where my father had gone on another expedition. He said the people were smaller than me and had put out little wooden carvings of aeroplanes beside the jungle runway. They did this for the same reason that hunters in America stuck out wooden decoys of geese in the fields, hoping to lure the birds in. I imagined my father, climbing from the plane and towering above the Borneo people. He was six foot seven and towered above everybody. I pictured him sitting by a camp-fire with one Borneo person on each knee, telling them about the Dragon School and letting them listen to the high-pitched whine of his Bulova Accutron watch.

Cuddly frowned when he heard about the little stick aircraft set out beside the runway. 'I did that once,' he said, 'in a field behind my house.'

'They're cannibals in Borneo,' Nightingale told me. 'They've probably stuck your dad with a poison dart and eaten his brains.' Nightingale didn't say it to be mean. He had just read about cannibals in *Look and Learn* magazine and figured my father must be leftovers by now.

For a while after that, junior boys would walk up to me in the playground, tug on the back of my jacket and ask – 'Was your dad really eaten by cannibals?'

Nightingale cornered me one day at Bun Break. He had a shifty look on his face, so I knew something was up. I figured he must want to borrow something of mine, but I couldn't think of anything that he didn't already have. But then he said, 'I'm taking you out with my parents this weekend.'

'Gosh, thanks, Nightingale. That's very kind of you.' I felt bad to have misjudged him, and figured he must be paying me back for my having taken him out when my father came to town.

'My sister's having her tenth birthday party.' He added this in a quiet voice, looking over his shoulder at the bun line, as if it was only an unimportant detail.

Now I saw that I hadn't misjudged him at all. I stayed quiet for a minute, scrambling my brains for an excuse not to go.

In the silence, Nightingale's face went from shifty to desperate. 'Oh, look, Watty. You've got to *come*! I can't go to this bloody thing by myself. Oh, look, please! I'll pay you. I'll do whatever you want, but you must come to my wretched sister's wretched birthday party!'

'No chance.'

'But you have to.'

'Never.'

He followed me back to the playground, pleading and offering me money. Then suddenly he stopped and grabbed hold of my arm. 'I'll kill you if you don't come.'

'You will not.' I shook off his grip.

'I will. I'll kill you when you're not looking.'

'Then you'd go to prison.'

'It would be better than going to this damn party by myself.' Then he got down on his knees and clawed at my legs. 'Oh, please, Watty. I won't ask for another favour as long as I live.'

I gave in eventually. Mostly it was out of embarrassment at seeing Nightingale grovel on the asphalt. That afternoon, we both went into town. Nightingale's father had given him five pounds to buy a present for his sister, whose name was Fiona.

First we agreed to spend four of the pounds on Fiona and keep one for ourselves. But we ended up spending one pound on Fiona and pocketing the rest. We bought her a necklace from a shop where they sold incense and little Indian carvings and foreign cigarettes. Then we each bought a woolly commando hat and a giant bar of Bournville chocolate.

As soon as I walked into Fiona's party, I saw what Nightingale had been afraid of. If I'd been him, I would also have got down on my knees to persuade someone to come with me.

Fiona was bigger than Nightingale and she slapped him around. She had five girl friends with her and they slapped him around, too. They dressed him up in a stupid hat and told him to bark like a dog.

When the time came for opening presents, I had never seen anyone rip off the wrapping paper as viciously as Fiona. She yanked the necklace out of its box and put it on. It seemed as if everyone was giving Fiona necklaces this year, and she wore them all at the same time, like the princess of an African tribe.

Our necklace was in the shape of a bird and had a little spoon dangling from its claws. It was the cheapest one they had in the shop.

'What is it?' Fiona asked. She held it up and let it drop again onto her chest. 'Well, what is it?' she asked again.

Nightingale's parents edged forward, squinting to see what it was. Then Mr Nightingale's eyes opened very wide, as if he had just been slapped in the face. He grabbed the necklace, grabbed Nightingale and walked him out of the room.

I followed, not wanting to be left alone with Fiona.

'This is outrageous!' Mr Nightingale waved the necklace in our faces. 'What is the meaning of this?'

'It *did* cost five pounds.' Nightingale had on his Honest-and-Desperate face. 'It cost . . . it cost.'

'Four pounds ninety-five.' I said.

'Yes!' Nightingale jumped up in the air and raised his hands over his head as if he had just scored a goal in soccer. 'Four pounds ninety-five!'

'I don't care how much it cost. Do you have any idea what this is?'

I stepped forward and took hold of the necklace. Obviously the entire Nightingale family were Wallies and now I would have to explain everything. 'Well, you see, sir. This is a bird. It's a special type of bird called an *eagle*. An eagle is a very *big* bird. And this thing is a *spoon*. It's just like a regular spoon only smaller.'

Mr Nightingale stared at me with his mouth hanging open. Then he turned to his son, whose mouth was also hanging open. 'Where did you get this, boy?'

'And the eagle is carrying the spoon in its *claws*, as if maybe it found the spoon on the road someplace and picked it up . . .'

Mr Nightingale snatched it out of my hands. 'It's for snorting cocaine, you idiots! It's a drug spoon. What the hell do you think you are doing, giving this to your sister for her birthday?'

They were all Wallies. I was sure of it now. 'You see, sir, it's only a *pretend* spoon. Not a *real* spoon.'

Mr Nightingale didn't let me finish. He ordered us both out to his car and drove us back to school.

Nightingale and I stood outside our dorm in a cloud of exhaust smoke as Mr Nightingale zoomed away up the street. For a while, neither of us said anything. Then we heard the clink of knives and forks on plates in the dining-hall.

'We didn't miss lunch,' Nightingale said.

So we ran to the dining-hall and ate. Then for the rest of the day, we lay in the grass by the river and made rude noise whistles by putting blades of grass between our thumbs and blowing through them.

Being at Fiona's party was the closest I'd been to a girl my age in a long time. A girl was called a Haggis at the Dragon School. You had to call them that, even if you didn't want to. There weren't many girls at the Dragon, only a couple who were the daughters of teachers. Sometimes we saw them in the distance. To us, girls were things that belonged outside the school, to the streets of Oxford and to home and to the holidays. Even if there had been many around, we wouldn't have known where to put them.

Apart from Fiona's party, the last time I'd had anything to do with a girl my age was back in America before I arrived at the Dragon. I met her at a gumball machine and she was crying. I always used to wait by the machine while my mother was shopping, in hopes that people might give me a penny to spend on a gumball. That day I had found a penny and was chewing on some bubble-gum. This girl couldn't get her penny into the gumball slot, so I helped her. I set the coin in, cranked the handle and heard the gumball rattle into the pick-up slot. It was a Big Red, the kind that tasted of cinnamon. I held it for a second in my palm, the colour already painting my skin. The girl stood next to me, hand held out for the gumball. Then I had an idea. I took the chewed piece of gum out of my mouth, dropped it in her hand, then stuffed the Big Red in my mouth and ran away. She screamed and tried to hunt me down in the grocery aisles, but I was out in the parking lot.

A whole squadron of Haggises lived at a school up the road from the Dragon. It was called Wychwood and had high brick walls and barbed-wire around it. Once a year, the Wychwood Hags came to our dance.

We had been practising for weeks. A lady came to teach us. Pa Sunderland the music teacher bashed out tunes on the piano until the lady clapped her hands and told us all to stop and do it again right this time. Nightingale and I swung each other around for weeks and when the Hags came we were ready.

They walked into the Dance Hall and we were all over them. I saw girls danced with in a way that reminded me of sumo wrestlers grappling in the ring. Some girls were kissed without mercy. After five minutes, most of them had run away into the dark, so I danced with Nightingale instead.

I wanted to dance with Charlotte. On bath nights, Cuddly and Nightingale and I always waited until the end so we could sit in the lukewarm water gone grey with other people's grime. Then we would all talk with Charlotte, who sat on a chair in the corner. She was pretty all right and I didn't have nearly enough courage to dance with her and nor did Nightingale and Cuddly. Bosom tried. He went up and bowed to her and asked if he Might Have This Dance. Charlotte snorted with laughter and had to go and sit down. After that, the teachers danced with her instead. They held her hand high and stared straight into her eyes, which we were too short to do.

Charlotte didn't stay long at the Dragon School. She got tired of mending socks and handing out clean underpants and sitting in the corner of the bathroom. I didn't blame her. With all the jets flying everywhere in the world and the cars to drive and boys who had more than 10p a week to spend on her, it made no sense for her to stay.

But for Ma Blek it made sense. A long time ago, her name had been Blake, but now not even the teachers called her that. She was ugly in a way that you could not even joke about. She looked as if she used to be a cartoon. Her legs didn't bend when she walked. The only time I ever saw any expression on her face at all was when I jammed a cream puff up the exhaust pipe of her car and she tried to start the ignition. At first nothing happened and then there was an explosion and the cream puff shot across the car-park and exploded against the Headmaster's greenhouse.

The way she got back at us for being rude and setting booby-traps was to put our names down for haircuts.

The haircut men came by once a month. One of them carried a huge suitcase and the only things inside the case were two Buzz-Hackers for shaving heads. They never used scissors. What I saw them do to boys' heads would have been funny if they had not done it to me as well. I saw ladders of fluff up the back of Cuddly's skull and a fringe on Nightingale that made him look as if he was wearing a German helmet. And for me, it was as if they had heard about my other name being Watty Dog and did their best to make me look the part.

The haircut room was in School House. The shelves were lined with copies of a single book, which must have been made up as a kind of commemorative thing. The book contained pictures of boys who had gone to be soldiers in the First World War and died. The pictures were milky coffee brown and had tissue-paper in front of them. A page told how they died. It gave me goose-pimples one time, when I realized how many people had gone to the war from the Dragon and stayed there. I wondered if they all went together and all charged at the same time, bayonets fixed, at the German trenches. I imagined there was a field some place in France where they all lay and their ghosts talked the same Dragon slang as us and knew the same jokes and had the same values for Yo-Yos and balsa-wood gliders and Jumbo Triple Treb marbles.

Apart from with our parents and on holidays, the only other chance we had to leave the school was on field trips.

The first trip I went on was with Pa Dimbleby, who taught us about the Romans. He was kind to us, and often when we didn't deserve it. We paid back his soft voice and easy homework assignments with whispering in class and Spit-Ball barrages whenever he turned his broad back. I always thought Pa Dimbleby never belonged here, and I was not surprised to see him leave the school before I did. I heard he went to be a sheep-farmer in Wales. He looked the way I had always imagined a shepherd would look, with his face cut deep with grooves like rock that's been shaped by the wind and rain, and he had a scrubby beard that sprouted from his face like a bramble bush. His hands were strong and knuckles tufted with the same almond brown hair.

He was always telling us to go out and make something of our lives.

'Go out *where*, sir?' Cuddly asked him.

There were posters on the walls of Pa Dimbleby's classroom that showed Roman legionaries and how they marched and what they wore.

The way Pa Dimbleby explained it, the ancient Britons never stood a chance. The best they could do was paint themselves blue and throw rocks. I thought of my ancestors, up to their necks in some Welsh swamp and watching the Romans clank past in their armour.

We went in a bus on a field trip to Chedworth Villa, which was a dug-up Roman house. I had no idea where it was. I knew the Dragon School and I knew a piece of Rhode Island, but I knew nothing in between.

A guide led us around a pile of stones set out at knee-height. He said this was where the main room was and this was where the storeroom was and here were the stables and here was the kitchen.

You needed a lot of imagination to see any of these things among the knee-high stones. Besides, none of us were paying attention. A Mister Softee ice-cream van had appeared in the car-park. Vaguely in the distance, I could see the list of different coloured lollies stuck up on a poster in the ice-cream van's window. A plastic cow stood on the roof of the van. A couple of times, the ice-cream man blew his horn. *Moo-moo-mooooo-moo.*

When the horn sounded, our heads snapped up and we stared with narrowed eyes and gritted teeth towards the van. As soon as the guide let us go, there would be a stampede towards the car-park. It would be every boy for himself. We were all afraid that he might leave before the lecture was over.

As soon as the guide paused for breath, Pa Dimbleby threw up his hands and said – 'All right! Go and get your bloody ice-creams, then, and see if I care!'

I ran out ahead of the rest. I could hear them all trampling the ground behind me and I was afraid of tripping and getting crushed. As I ran, I saw the face of Mister Softee. He stood with his arms braced against the counter. From the look in his eyes, I knew he was afraid we might tip over his van.

We left ten-foot skid-marks in the grass in front of Mister Softee's window.

As I walked away through the crowd, all with hands raised and

10p pieces shining in their fingers, I saw a few of the boys who had fallen and lay Blubbing. They knew there would be nothing left but Cider Lollies by the time they made it through the queue. No Strawberry Mivvies or 99s or SunMaid Oranges. Pa Dimbleby walked from one Blubbing boy to the other, telling them to get up and stop being Weedy.

Nightingale and I ransacked the hedge that ran along the edge of the villa's grounds. He said there might be stuff there that hadn't been dug up. He said a few years before, some farmer had ploughed up a big plate made of solid gold.

We hacked at the bushes with our Swiss Army knives and scraped away snail-shells and old leaves to reach the soil.

I tried to imagine how it must have been for the Romans in the villa. I thought of them, used to the sun and heat of Italy, trying to live in the rain and fog of England and trying to sleep at night when they knew the woods were filled with blue-faced ancestors of Watty Dog and Nightingale, ready with sharp rocks to throw.

Pa Dimbleby dragged us out of the hedge by our feet. He started to yell at us, saying that the more we understood about our ancestors, the more we would understand about ourselves. But the Moo-moo noise of Mister Softee's truck interrupted. By the time Pa Dimbleby remembered what he was saying, we had disappeared.

We would all gladly have eaten Mister Softee's ice-cream until we puked. For us, the only things worth eating were sweets. Sweets were as good as money at the Dragon School. In a way, they were better than money, and the way you showed that you were friends with someone was to share your chocolate with them.

You could buy chocolate at the tuck shop. It was a brown hut with a tar-paper roof in the middle of the playground.

I always bought white chocolate mice for a penny each, then cut them into pieces and traded the bits for Cuddly's Liquorice Allsorts or Nightingale's Chewyfruits. If they didn't have anything to trade, I gave them pieces anyway.

Along with the tuck shop, there was a padlocked tuck cupboard back at the dormitory. Boys arrived at school each term with boxes of chocolate which were stored in the tuck cupboard. The cupboard was opened each day after lunch and you could take out your box and have a piece of chocolate, but first you had to show Charlotte how much you were taking. This was a dumb rule, because Charlotte could be easily distracted by walking slowly up to her and saying with a very calm voice, 'Please Charlotte, Bosom is in the Hobby Hut and he's just poked his eye out with a pencil. But don't worry because Nightingale has some glue and we're sticking it back in.' Then when she screamed and went tearing out to the Hobby Hut, you could fill your pockets if you wanted to.

I didn't know about the chocolate and I didn't arrive with any. So in the beginning, before I had Cuddly and Nightingale as friends, I used to sit with an empty box by the cupboard every day at lunch break. I sat there like a leper and collected bits of chocolate and liquorice. I got good at being a leper, and learned never to let the can become too full.

One day I was caught robbing the cupboard. It was a Sunday afternoon and most of the boys had gone out with their parents for the day and I was bored. I unscrewed the latch of the padlock with my Swiss Army knife and was just about to take out a can, when I was caught by Bosom.

This was bad luck, being caught by Bosom. He had a lot of chocolate in the cupboard. He cried too much and always told on people for teasing him. Then he had tantrums when the teachers told him to stop being Weedy. Nobody liked a Sneak, teachers included.

Bosom said he was going to tell on me. He told me I was being Reported. Then he changed his mind and said he wouldn't Report me but I had to let him hit me twice.

I said – Any place but in the balls.

He hit me once in the eye and once in the gut. The eye puffed up big and black. It didn't hurt, but it looked bad and I had to say I'd fallen out of a tree down by the river-bank. It was the stomach punch that hurt, turning purple yellow and thumping with pain for days.

Two weeks later, I was out on the fields being goalkeeper. I had caught a save and was going to kick it back down the field.

Bosom was there. He tried to block my kick, jumping up and down with his too-big feet and his springy red hair flapping on top of his head.

I looked at Bosom long enough for him to realize what I was going to do, but not long enough for him to do anything about it. I punted the ball square into his face and watched him slap down spread-eagled into the mud.

He couldn't even cry, it hurt so bad. He just made wheezing sounds as they carried him off the field.

I kept my eye out for Bosom, since you could never tell with people who threw tantrums the way he did.

Bosom challenged me to a duel on Sunday morning out on the playing fields. He said to be there half an hour before chapel. His nose had puffed up like a mango.

Nightingale said that since we were friends, he supposed he would have to go out with me and defend me. He made himself sound very weary as he told me this, as if it was a favour that he didn't want to do. But I knew him better than that. I knew he would have paid me for the chance to fight a duel. Still, it was the greatest sign of friendship that he would offer to stand beside me when I was in trouble. So the next morning, we both showed up to face Bosom.

We had made spears out of sharpened branches. Nightingale carried a towel and I carried the lid off a dustbin. We got the idea from Cuddly's book on Roman Gladiators.

Cuddly offered to be the one who said when to stop the duel. He said there was always someone who did that in real duels.

'No!' Nightingale shouted. He knew that Cuddly would try to stop the duel if anyone got hurt and hurting Bosom was what he wanted to do more than anything else in the world.

Bosom was waiting for us on the field, where morning fog weaved in and out of the soccer goalposts. Bosom had rolled up his sleeves.

Nightingale and I clattered onto the grass in our Gladiator outfits. 'We're going to kill you,' said Nightingale cheerfully.

For a moment, it looked as if Bosom was going to hold his ground. But then he turned and ran screaming down towards the river-bank.

We chased him all the way down to the river and then made him walk the plank on the old diving board. When he came up from the water, his hair was speckled with pondweeds.

After Bosom had run away back to house to find dry clothes and Report us, Nightingale and I still had energy to spare. So we fought a duel, careful not to hurt each other. Because we were like blood brothers now, and that meant friendship forever.

In the last few days of term, I made myself sick with the waiting.

Charlotte brought down our suitcases from the attic and we all started packing to leave.

On the night before we left, we all crowded into the Old Hall for the Sing Song. The teachers dressed up in their old Army clothes or jammed their butts into a pair of boy's corduroy trousers and made fun of themselves on the stage. They threw sweets out into the audience. Pa Sunderland bashed on the piano until it looked as if he was going to pass out.

We all sang the song about the Dragons coming in One-by-One-Mostly-With-Their-Buttons-Undone and Two-by-Two and up to Ten-by-Ten-and-Then-They-All-Went-Back-Again. We sang this to the chorus of Inky-pinky parley-vous. It was a tune from the First World War called 'Mademoiselle from Armenteers'. The soldiers used to sing it as they marched up to the line.

People leaving for the airport had to get up early the next morning. I couldn't sleep anyway.

I put on my B-suit and went around the dorm, shaking everybody's hand. Now suddenly from having been jealous all term of the ones who lived nearby and who could get home in twenty minutes by bicycle, they were all jealous of me. I didn't have to walk past the empty school during the holidays, or even set foot in the same country.

A coach took us up to Heathrow. In the yellow-lit tunnel that led from the motorway to the terminal buildings, we all tried to hold our breath to the end, but never could.

The ones who were flying far away were dropped off with the British Airways Nannies at Terminal 3. That was where I got out. I was handed over to the British Airways Nannies and kept in a corral until my flight was called. I got a red and silver badge that said Young Passenger Travelling Alone. Then the Nannies walked me to the front of the passport line and took me to my plane.

All through the flight, I kept my face pressed to the little fishbowl window, seeing veins of ice form on the glass outside. I studied the clouds below and tried to imagine where I would build a house among the powdery white valleys if the clouds could hold my weight.

I got to see the cockpit. I sat with the pilot and co-pilot, feeling as if I was balanced on the edge of a cliff, with all the clouds spread out and seeing icebergs off the coast of Labrador or the brick-red Nova Scotia sand.

I was a member of the Junior Jet Club. I had a set of plastic Captain's wings. On each flight, I handed in my blue Junior Jet Club book and had the captain log the distance. Each flight across the Atlantic was 2435 miles.

I couldn't sleep. I'd read *Mad* magazine and try to get the jokes. I wanted to watch the film but I'd already spent my last few coins on chocolate and you had to pay extra for the head-sets. I swivelled the arm rest up to my ear and tried to listen through the two tiny holes where the earphone cord plugged in, but then I couldn't see the screen. So I alternated from watching to listening and tried not to lose track of what was happening in the film.

A German man sat next to me. He explained that he had seen America but had never been there. When I asked him how, he raised his fists up to his ears and I knew he was pretending to look through the periscope of a submarine. He had been a Nazi U-Boat man.

The flight went on forever and my stomach burned with the waiting.

In the last few seconds before the plane touched down, my heart beat so fast I could barely breathe. The plane came in low over Boston harbour, looking as if we were going to land in the ocean instead of on the runway. Then came the roar of the engines switching into reverse and I felt the bars of muscles release from around my guts.

As my parents drove me out of the chaos of Boston, I looked around at the buildings and highway that I'd been visiting in my half-sleep all this time I'd been away, and I wondered if I wasn't just having a slightly more vivid than usual dream voyage to my home. I waited for the yellow streetlamp light of Bardwell Road to bleed into my thoughts and land me back in bed.

We ducked into the Callaghan tunnel with its bronze angel lounging on a plaque at the entrance, and for a while its yellow lights seemed to be the threat that I was only in my dreams. But the clear blue winter sky returned as we cruised south on Route 95.

England dissolved and I never talked about it and none of my friends ever asked. The place stayed frozen in my head, and it wouldn't thaw until I was on my way up to Boston airport again.

I didn't go to Boston in the holidays. The place belonged to school.

This was home, although I still didn't believe it completely.

Small things had changed. My parents didn't tell me off any more and I no longer walked around naked in front of them. I could stay up as late as I wanted. Now instead of being sent to the back room with the fuzzy orange carpet to watch TV whenever guests came by, I had to sit in the living room and try to follow the talk. I could see that some of the neighbours didn't like the idea of me being sent away to school in England, and telling them about Nightingale and Big Watty Dog Watkins and Haggises and the Heroic Diving Goalie of Bardwell team #4 only made things worse.

At school, I listened to the noises. I learned to track the crêpe-soled plod of Pa Vicker in his desert boots, as he moved from dorm to dorm after lights-out, prowling for people who talked. Or there was the school bell. Or a distant three cheers being given for a team out on the playing fields.

Here, I heard the silence. Winter sunset spread sad pinks and violets across the bay. The sea grew strangely calm and clear. I walked along the beach, where frozen waves gripped the sand. My windows spider-webbed with frost until I could see nothing out of them but the colours of these sad sunsets.

The snow fell deep and made the silence stronger. I pulled my toboggan down Wilbur Hazard road, following the tracks of other toboggans and the distant laughter of Chuck Hesketh and the Palmer boys sledding, until I came to Hesketh's Hill.

It was the biggest hill in the neighbourhood and Chuck Hesketh knew it. He was tall and older than the rest of us, with rosy cheeks that always looked as if they'd just been pinched. Chuck made you grovel for the chance to slide down the slope, which was so steep it would take you across the road and into some crab-clawed bushes on the other side. He invented little plays and made you act in them. The plays had you being hurt and pretending you had a broken leg. Then he would come down in his toboggan and rescue you. If you laughed in his face or flipped his toboggan as he pretended to take you to the hospital at the bottom of the hill, he would start crying and get his mother to come out. She was the only mother in the neighbourhood who would actually send all the friends home if her child asked her to.

When I once went bawling to my mother, telling her to send everyone away because I hated them now, she sent me to my room and let all my new enemies watch the TV.

But when I reached the top of Hesketh's Hill, ankles hurting from having to take side-steps all the way up, I'd do anything for the chance to slide down. I'd lie flat on my toboggan and start to slide. The speed would pick up so much that often I tipped over deliberately, rather than go any faster. Then snow exploded around me and packed itself into every crevice of my clothing.

It was the only time of the year Chuck Hesketh could bully anyone, so he made the most of it. There were times I even went home before dark because of his mouthing off. But his mother was so kind to us. She'd take out mugs of hot cider and bring us all in to get warm, not caring about the snow that melted all over her kitchen.

The other problem was that Chuck Hesketh also had the biggest toboggan. We all had to grovel some more for the chance to sit on it, all of us hugging each other to stay on.

We'd set off and lose someone at the first bump, then a few more as we slid over a tree stump. By half way down the hill, there would only be a couple left. We'd hit the road and we would hear the grind of toboggan wood scraping the road. After that came the whoosh of Chuck's toboggan disappearing into the hedge.

Then there was the time when everybody fell off except Chuck. The rest of us were balled in snow at different stages down the hill. Chuck stayed on, sitting cross-legged like an Indian, heading for the bump that we knew would make him airborne.

And he did go airborne. His toboggan hit the bump and split into five different pieces. Chuck flew off, sitting like an Indian but upside down now and screaming, hit another bump and rolled away under the bushes.

He was still screaming when we dragged him out, but he was always screaming, so we didn't take much notice. He said he had broken his leg.

We told him to stop being feeble and my brother Clive, who was two years younger than me, even booted him in the leg a few times.

Chuck's mother drove around the hill and down in her black Mercedes. We stuffed Chuck in the back seat and watched them drive away.

It turned out he had spiral-fractured his femur. There were attempts to make us feel guilty and my father's huge hands raised in disbelief that my brother had actually booted Chuck a few times. We went to visit him in hospital.

Chuck said he had a pin in his leg and if we pulled it out his leg would swivel around and face the other way. He stayed in the hospital for months and then in a body cast.

It ruined the sledding for ever. Now parents watched and called us in if we went too fast. Or they stopped us from going altogether.

Snow covered the tracks on Hesketh's Hill and the slope stayed smooth and untouched.

I remember looking up Hesketh's Hill one time as I crawled out of a snow bank. I was laughing, I recall. Then I saw all the parents lined up along the veranda of Hesketh's house. They had drinks in their hands and were looking down. But they were far enough away that I couldn't see their faces. There was something bad-dream about those faceless people watching down on us. I felt the trouble coming, the way I could feel the approach of thunder as a pinch at the back of my neck.

The neighbourhood changed. Maybe it was changing anyway, and the toboggan accident only came at a time when things were already in motion.

One day not long after that, Mrs Hesketh came home and found her husband snogging Mrs Palmer on their living-room couch. The Heskeths divorced. Mrs Hesketh went to live in Newport. The Palmers divorced, too. The last I heard, Mrs Palmer was working for a radio station up in Warwick and Mr Palmer had married a woman with half a dozen kids.

It was a damn strange thing meeting up for the few times we did after that. Damn strange seeing Chuck Hesketh and the Palmer boys looking at each other a little helplessly and knowing that their mom had snogged his dad and everything was on its way to hell. The Palmer boys stood in their matching snow suits and boots and yellow, black and white Boston Bruins snow hats and looked like echoes of each other. And Chuck Hesketh stood there on his crutches, the blood flushed in his face. And beside them my brother and me. And we just stood there. Nothing to say. Not understanding the terrible thing that had happened, but knowing it was terrible all the same.

Soon the Palmer boys moved away. I never saw Chuck Hesketh again.

Often I wished it could have stayed the same, or at least not have fallen apart as quickly as it did. Only the echoes remained of our flashlight Tig games that ranged across the neighbourhood or the times of sledding or the drift of costumed ghosts at Hallowe'en.

Still, years later, my brother and I would laugh when we walked past Hesketh's Hill. My brother would jerk one foot forward, as if punting a football, and I'd know he was remembering the time he booted Chuck Hesketh and his spiral-fractured femur. Chuck Hesketh would laugh, too, if he ever came by any more.

*

One winter evening, when the sky was streaked with rose, my father was out chopping wood. His axe glanced off a frozen log and wood chips flew up in his face. One of the chips dug itself into his eye.

I was building an igloo, not far away.

He walked over to me, squatted down and said, 'Pull this wood chip out of my eye, will you?'

I saw the piece sticking out and the blood that had welled up around it. 'Nasty,' I told him. 'I can't do it.' I didn't want to stick my finger in his eye. I asked him how he could speak with such a calm voice while he must have been in so much pain.

Then he took hold of my wrists so hard I thought they would break. 'Don't think about the pain. Just do it.'

I pulled the splinter out and looked at it, all bloody and pinched between my fingers. I wanted to ask him how he could stand the pain, but he had already gone back to chopping wood.

My parents held a party. People filled up our house and then spilled out over the lawn. A truckload of belly-dancers pulled up. They danced all over the house and had jewels stuck in their belly buttons. I didn't think they'd been invited. When I asked my father about it, he looked baffled and said he had no idea where they had come from, but then he burst out laughing and gave the game away.

I ran by to see Eric, who used to pretend he was on a motorcycle everywhere he went, changing gears in a high-pitched whine as he ran up and down Champlin Road. He was a cousin of the Morgan boys, Sam and Allen. They were the ones who used to call me and my brother the Twat Twins on the school bus. It would always get to the point where I couldn't take it any more and was about to start a fight; then they'd say something kind and I'd forgive them for another couple of weeks. Eric had curly brown hair and a laugh that made you laugh with him, even if you didn't get the joke. As I zoomed into his driveway, I made the same gear-changing noises. But I soon discovered that this was a mistake. The motorcycle noise was a thing of the distant past and so, for a while, was I.

The new thing was Estes rockets. They were expensive balsa-wood kits that needed launching-pads and hand-held remote control launchers and booster charges for rocket fuel and more patience than I owned to go and find them again after they had been launched.

But Sam and Allen Morgan and Eric had got it all down to a science. The rockets were launched in old man Fontaine's field. Each person had the parts they always carried to the launch site. Eric set up the rocket because it was his and he made it, yelling at anyone who offered advice about launching.

Sam would keep hawking and spitting because he had a permanently blocked-up nose. Allen watched everything with a calm and steady gaze, which made you think he was clever until he opened his mouth and then Sam would roll his eyes in embarrassment at what was said and give him the mandatory smack on the head. Allen had been smacked so many times, I wondered if he might have brain damage. We all had to stand back five paces from Eric's rocket and there was much argument about the distance of five paces until Eric measured out five paces for each person.

If this was England, I was thinking, Nightingale would have grabbed that little remote control unit by now and set off the rocket whether it was on the launching-pad or not.

When the rocket took off, it made a sound like a bottle of seltzer exploding. It blasted way above the power-lines and a second explosion opened the parachute.

Then we all grabbed our bikes and cycled after the drifting Estes rocket, and sometimes spent the rest of the day untangling it from a tree or fishing it out of a pond.

Eric had a German shepherd named Fang, who had been driven out of its mind by all the tricks people played on it. Whenever it barked too much at night, Eric came out to its kennel with a big gob of peanut butter, which he stuck on the roof of Fang's mouth. Then all you'd hear would be tongue-smacking noises.

The other thing they did to the dog was to start the count-down for the Estes rockets. Ten! Nine! Eight! Fang hated these rockets, and when the count-down began, it would bark and run around in circles. Fang seemed to spend half its life running around in circles with peanut butter breath and woofing like something insane.

The American school ran at different times than the English, and in the weekdays I found myself alone in the house watching TV, or kicking through washed-up seaweed at the high-tide line, looking for fish-hooks and messages in bottles. I fished off my father's dock for the orange-spotted winter flounder. I used clamworms, dodging their black pincers and making them eat the flounder-hooks.

A couple of times I got stopped by the police, who thought I was skipping school. I'd tell them about England and it would all go fine until they heard that my school was named the Dragon School. Then they would take me home and make my mother explain, if she was in.

I checked out FBI wanted posters in the post office, then wandered across the beach and stood on the Jamestown bridge, hoping to catch sight of a criminal as he sped past over the water.

During the day, my father was teaching at the Oceanographic Institute and my mother studied at the University of Rhode Island, getting a degree as a librarian. My little brother was still at Hamilton Elementary School and I was jealous of him for inheriting my yellow raincoat with the fireman clips and my Donny Osmond lunchbox.

Sometimes my father took me with him to work. He was a pro-fessor, but his study, instead of being lined with shelves of books, was lined with rock samples. That was what my father did. He travelled all over the world and collected rocks. It seemed so strange to everyone my age that we were convinced that this was just a front. We thought he was a spy, and that the rocks weren't really rocks but gems, or pieces of explosives designed to look like rocks. My father would take one particular lump off a shelf and hand it to me so carefully that you'd have thought it was a living animal like a baby bird or something. 'This,' he would say, 'is forty million years old.'

He had an entire room full of rocks that were strange purple colours with streaks of yellow in them. They were kept in a glass case as if they might try to escape. He would shut the door to this room and turn off the light. Then he would turn on another, bluish light and all the rocks would glow. I sat for hours in the room of glowing rocks, realizing that the secret of their trapped and ghostly light was so far beyond my understanding that I might never know.

My father had a stack of books that he had published. In all of them, the only things I could understand were the introductions, which would usually begin with something like – 'It is common knowledge that . . .' The rest looked like hieroglyphics to me. It was all about his undersea mountains and their shape and magnetic fields. If he'd told me this was proof he had climbed these moun-tains from the bottom of the sea, I would have believed him.

My mother had my dad on a diet. She said he couldn't eat red meat. He didn't complain about this, so my mother grew suspicious. My father also didn't lose any weight, and he had a pretty good gut, so my mother knew something was up.

I knew my father's plan, but had been sworn to silence. My father's secret was that he kept a pile of steaks frozen in a refrigerator for scientific specimens at his lab. Sometimes he and I would cook one over a bunsen-burner. He even had some Worcestershire sauce tucked away amongst those rocks from the beginning of time.

I liked being his accomplice in steak frying. I liked that he trusted me with the secret, because I got the feeling he did not trust a lot of people. Mostly I think he just trusted himself.

On the days when I was not with my father in his office, I listened for the wheeze of bus #2 coming down the hill and the creak of the doors letting my brother out in our driveway.

Patiently, I waited for the weekends. Then less patiently. Time had come unhinged again and was speeding out of control towards the point when I would leave for England.

None of the people my own age cared about school in England. It didn't matter to them and when I was home, it didn't matter to me either. I realized after a while that I would never fit back into the neighbourhood. With a nickname like Wat Toad, I wasn't sure if I had ever fitted anyway. New words had crept into my talk. The English jokes and sports and ways of settling things were different and they did not travel well.

It was already clear that I would never fit into England. The English were too good at spotting intruders and had special ways of dealing with each kind. Even if you came from Wales, you were intruding and the stand-by battery of jokes would be unleashed as if from the multi-barrelled cannon of a Stalin Organ.

From now on I would be intruding in both places. I saw no way out and there was none. I began to feel like the governor of a mid-Atlantic colony with a population of one.

Sometimes I wrote stories, as if somehow to increase the number of people on my mid-Atlantic island. It was in the stories that the same sense of voyaging returned. Here, I could travel freely, without the momentary fear of stepping out into the darkness as I left my body behind.

We kept losing Eric's rockets. The ones he bought as replacements kept getting bigger and more expensive. I had seen the Estes catalogue, and I knew it was only a matter of time before he bought the V2. It was the largest rocket Estes sold, almost three foot tall with Double 'D' Explosive charges and a ceiling of a thousand feet.

Sure enough. A couple of weeks later, we were standing in Fontaine's field with the launching-pad all wobbly from the weight of the V2.

This time we stood back ten paces and Eric didn't need to count.

I bet my brother 25 cents that the whole rig would blow up on the launching-pad.

The noise it made when it went up left a shriek in my ears. It charred the launching-pad black and melted the orange launching-pad legs.

The V2 hissed up into the sun and I heard the pop of the chute opening, but not one of us ever saw the rocket again.

We cycled all over the neighbourhood, and from a long way off I could hear Eric shouting orders at us to go this way and that way and maybe it was over here and he was going to write to Estes and get his money back.

Not a trace. I imagined it drifting out miles over the sea.

Eric did build a few more rockets out of kits he had already bought. He fitted them with charges way too big for the rocket and we watched them shoot up above Fontaine's house and blow apart into matchwood when the parachute charge ignited.

But then that was the end of the Estes rocket days.

There was an old button factory beside the highway that led into Boston. It looked as if the factory had closed down and only the name of the place had stayed painted on one wall of the building.

When we drove past that building, always at sunset and about fifteen seconds before the Callaghan tunnel swallowed us again, the holiday was over and I considered myself already back at school.

I hated seeing my parents in tears as they said goodbye and the night flight and the strange colours of sunrise at thirty thousand feet. I hated the way my eyes dried out and the acid-burning orange juice that the stewardesses handed to us in tubs when it was time to wake up.

At Heathrow, a teacher was there to meet me and anyone else coming back to the Dragon.

The school was empty when I got there. The beds had been made and names on stickers taped to the end of each bed rail. Each year, they moved you to a different dorm and then on to School House.

I walked across the playing fields with the outlines of pitches new and white on the ground. I knew it would only take a day of trampling for the lines to disappear. Then we would judge the boundaries by patches of white that had somehow gone untrampled. Everything else would stay machine-gunned with boot stud holes until the half-term holiday.

At night, the others arrived with new toys and comic books. It was quiet in the dorms when the lights had been turned out. It was always quiet on the first night, and sometimes you could hear boys crying in their beds.

CHAPTER 3

PA WINTER WAS gone by the time we got back to school. I heard from Charlotte that he had been fired.

One night in dorm, Cuddly and I told Pa Vicker about how Pa Winter had chased us onto the fields and then beaten us. We thought that Pa Vicker might laugh, but instead he got furious and yelled at us that we should have told someone at the time. Then he stomped away down the corridor.

I thought we were going to be beaten again for not having told sooner.

It was bad to be on the wrong side of a teacher, but even worse to be on the wrong side of a friend. Sometimes you had to make your choice, because you could find yourself in a situation where it would be one or the other.

This happened to me on the day we took a field trip to the Imperial War Museum.

We spent the day being chased out of the cockpits of old planes by men in blue uniforms with hats like railway conductors. They chased Cuddlybum out of an Italian midget submarine and I got caught trying to shove a dummy out of his pilot's seat in a Lancaster bomber, so I could sit there myself for a while. We climbed on the tanks and tugged at the welded-shut hatches. We saw a film on Hitler and then goose-stepped into the cafeteria.

The teachers handed out packed lunches on the grass in front of the museum, where two huge cannons from a ship pointed across the road. There was no point them giving us packed lunches with the chewy pork pies and throw-at-Cuddlybum-tomatoes. No point because Mister Softee in his ice-cream van had stopped in front of the museum and was blowing his horn. *Moo-moo-mooooo-moo!*

We charged Mister Softee and he gave out a little cry as the first blue-suited body skidded into his truck. There was combat for

Strawberry Mivvies and the left-over people who had been trampled in the charge were left with Cider Lollies.

As I sat with Cuddly at the base of the huge cannons, he told me his plan. He said he was running away.

'But where to?', I asked him. I didn't know where we were.

'Home! I live just down the road. I know this place as well as I know school.'

I looked around. I wondered what it must be like to live so near a museum like this and I wondered if they let you spend the night here and I wondered how old you had to be to be one of the guards who stayed there all day. 'You can't run away, Cuddly. The teachers would kill you.'

'I don't care. I'm never coming back to school.'

'They'll whack you. They'll send Pa Winter out here specially to Whack you, even if you aren't in the school.' It was making my guts flutter to hear about Cuddly running away. He couldn't survive. He didn't have any food or any money. 'You really live just down the road?'

'It's no more than twenty minutes by Underground.'

Now he had gone too far. It was all very well walking twenty minutes, but I knew he couldn't go in the Underground by himself. 'You can't do it, Cuddly. Just go home on the weekend, instead.'

'I'm doing it, Watty. And you got to make sure you don't tell. They'll ask you, because you've been sticking with me all day, but you got to say you don't know.' He made me shake hands and promise. Then he dodged away behind the building and a minute later, I saw him crossing the road and disappearing down a staircase that led to the Underground.

I felt sick when Pa Sunderland called out Cuddly's name as we all piled onto the bus. The seat next to mine was empty. It was Cuddly's seat. Pa Sunderland asked me – 'Have you seen Codrington?' – and I said 'No.' Then he asked everyone on the bus. I could see Pa Sunderland all red in the face and chewing at his thumbnail. All the way home I felt sick.

Back at the house, Pa Vicker called me into his study and asked me where Cuddly was.

I said I didn't know.

He took me by the arm and shook me and yelled at me. He said that Cuddly could be dead by now and I was lying and he knew it. He said I'd be Whacked if I didn't tell and I was pretty sure I'd get Whacked if I did, but I had shaken hands and sworn to Cuddly.

Pa Vicker shook me some more and his yelling was making me deaf. I thought of Cuddly lost in the maze of the Underground. I thought he might be dead or maybe calling out for help in some black tunnel where no one could hear him. The picture of his pale and frightened face glimmered in front of me as if he was already dead and a ghost. I knew then that I would have to tell and break the promise and take whatever punishment came with it. So I told, and I was crying when I said the words.

Cuddly's parents called five minutes later to say he was safely at home.

Pa Vicker pulled my sideburns and brought his face very close to mine, so that I had to breathe his milky breath. He said if I ever lied to him again, he would thrash me within an inch of my life. Then he threw me out of his study and I ran and hid in the Hobby Hut.

Cuddly found out that I had told. Sneaked is the word we all used. Pa Vicker let him know. That was Pa Vicker's real punishment to me, because the word got around and I found out that the worst thing to be is a Sneak. The news wasn't that Cuddly had run away. The news was that I had Sneaked. It took a week before Cuddly spoke to me again, and I thought for a while that we would never be friends again.

No one could Sneak, Nightingale told me, no one who was any good in this world. If you Sneaked, bad things would happen to you. You'd end up like Kissack, Nightingale said, as if you had been cursed by God himself.

Kissack was a boy at the Dragon who had haemophilia. Sometimes he'd be in a wheelchair and sometimes just on crutches. Nightingale explained that if you had haemophilia you could cut yourself, even just a little, like with the small blade of your Swiss Army knife, and you would bleed to death because your blood wouldn't clot. He was always going to the Sanitorium.

I couldn't understand how Kissak had lived as long as he did. The rest of us were bleeding all the time. Just that day, Cuddly had stapled the web of his thumb to his desk and then for no good reason stapled Nightingale's head. And I had a cut in my neck from Nightingale's pen. He had been trying to flick ink on my homework, but let go of the pen by mistake and the pen's nib stuck in me. It seemed as if everything we did got us wounded at one time or another.

Whenever I saw Kissak, I would stare at him and feel sorry. He would die soon, I felt sure, and there was nothing to do but feel bad about it.

After Pa Vicker had threatened to thrash me within an inch of my life if I ever lied, I swore that I would tell the truth for the rest of my life, no matter what had happened.

Then I got on the wrong side of Pa Pushcart, the gym teacher.

He was always yelling at me because I was slow changing for gym class.

On one of those slow days, I looked in my locker space and saw that my plimsolls had been stolen. I was late, so I grabbed the plimsolls from the locker belonging to Big Watty Dog Watkins and put them on. We all had the same Green Flash Dunlops and I knew no one would notice.

As soon as we were all in the gym, Pa Pushcart lined us up against the wall. We knew there was some trouble, and out of instinct, our hands crept down to shield our balls.

Pa Pushcart's shoulder hunched the way a grizzly bear's shoulders hunch when it stands up on two feet. 'There are thieves among us,' he said.

God damn it, I thought. God damn it to hell, I am busted.

Then Pa Pushcart locked his hands behind his back and began to pace in front of us. 'There have been some instances,' he said, 'of people stealing other people's gym things. Shorts, T-shirts, shoes. And this thieving will stop, gentlemen. We will nip it in the bud and strangle it in the cradle. I want you to know right now that if anyone today is wearing clothing that belongs to someone else, I am going to beat them.'

I had the cramp of knowing-about-going-to-be-beaten in the small of my back and my bowels. Well God damn it, I thought again, at least I don't have to run and fetch my plimsolls the way Pa Winter made us do.

'You can make things a lot easier on yourselves,' Pa Pushcart told us, 'if you own up and admit you are wearing stolen clothing. Those of you who are, take one step forward.'

I stepped forward. The rest of the class seemed to have disappeared into the wall behind me. Suddenly I stood way out in front. I felt as if I was standing at the edge of a cliff.

'Watkins!' Pa Pushcart howled in my face. 'I might have known it was you. What did you take?'

'Plimsolls, sir.'

He took hold of the back of my neck and moved me over into the storeroom, where he kept the medicine balls and hemp mats and rope. He made me take off one of the stolen shoes and he started to give me the Six, keeping his hand on my neck.

But on the fourth, he stopped. 'Your name is *Paul* Watkins isn't it?' he asked.

'Yes, sir.' My butt was on fire. He was the hardest Whacker in the school.

'Well, you bloody idiot! I am beating you with your own shoe!'

Big Watty Dog Watkins had used his own plimsolls to make a Guy Fawkes dummy. Then he stole my shoes and put them in his locker. I stole them back but did not know they were mine.

I did some more thinking about my promise never to lie no matter what happened. I figured that from now on I would take it on a case-by-case basis.

Later on I learned that if you are going to get whacked whether you lie or tell the truth, well, Hell, you may as well enjoy yourself a little and the least you can do is be rude to the person who's whacking you.

I had made a tape recording during the holidays. On the tape were opening jingles to all the TV shows I watched while I was home.

The only thing I had to play them on was a clunky Panasonic.

I lay in my bed at night, covers pulled over my head, and listened to the jingles. I got to know them so well that they turned into one song. I sang them through without a pause.

One night as I listened, the sheets disappeared off my bed and Pa Vicker stood trembling angry in front of me. He had ripped back the sheets and now he let them drop to the floor.

He picked me up and led me by the arm all through the house, upstairs and down, stamping along the corridor and me hugging the Panasonic to my chest.

When we had gone past all the dorms, he turned to me and did what he usually did which was bring his face close to mine and breathe milk and tobacco breath in my face. 'Well now, Watkins. What did you hear?'

'What do you mean, sir?'

'What did you hear as we were walking around the house just then?'

'Nothing, sir.'

'And why do you suppose that was, Watkins?'

I knew what he wanted me to say. He wanted me to say that everyone was asleep. Then he would say I should be asleep too and he'd confiscate my Panasonic and maybe Whack me as well. I saw it all coming from miles away. But I didn't say what he wanted. Instead I told him – 'I guess it was quiet, sir, because you made so much noise walking up and down the halls. Not like you usually do, sir. You know, in your crêpe-soled desert boots. So they had time to shut up before you heard them. Sir.'

I was surprised he let me talk it all the way through.

He took the Panasonic. I just handed it to him. And he beat me, right there in the hallway. It was the first time he had beat me that I did not cry, and the last time a beating ever hurt.

I got beatings after that, for dumb things like talking in homework, but something in me took the pain away and kept my eyes dry and my teeth clamped shut so that the only sound I made was a quiet grunt as each blow came down.

There was a life that we lived separately from the teachers and that was the life of the crazes. It was separate because each carried its own language and its own sets of values for objects. A bag of marbles that would not get you a cricket ball in trade one week would get you a whole set of cricket equipment, bat and pads and ball, two weeks later. There was no telling what the next craze might be or how long it would last. The only sure thing was that the new craze would come, and whatever it brought with it, you would kill to have.

At the Dragon there seemed to be about one craze every week. Sometimes you would have to have a Rotring. They were drafting pens which used black ink that never washed out. Your fingers got tattooed with the stuff and it was cool to have black smudged fingers. Sometimes one Rotring was not enough and you had to have all different sizes and a plastic case to hold them in. Then over the space of a few weeks, the Rotrings went out of fashion. The black smudges would disappear and be replaced by the same old blue stains of the Dragon school fountain pen ink that came in gallon tubs and washed off. Parents who had heard about Rotrings all holiday gave their son a Rotring set for Christmas and never saw it used. Instead all they heard about were Yo-Yos, especially the glow-in-the-dark kind, because it had become the latest craze.

Stamp collecting took hold one spring when the playing fields were more mud than grass and mostly out of bounds. Some boys living in exotic countries like Singapore or Hong Kong would become instantly popular and have the stamps from their parents' letters begged off them. Penny Blacks and Reds and even rarer stamps would appear from fathers' collections at home, taken with permission or without.

One year, we all wrote away to the Corona soft drink company to get free stickers. Within two months, there wasn't a desk in the school or an ammunition can or a window that didn't have some smiling bubble-faced troll on it, advertising Corona. The company received so many letters, they wrote one of their own to the Headmaster, who announced that the sticker supply line had been cut.

Skateboards gave us permanently bloody knees and elbows. They were crappy boards, too, with roller-skate wheels that were quickly replaced by wider boards and fat rubber wheels. But by then the interest had gone and we moved on to gliders.

I made a mini-cricket bat in woodwork. It had become the thing to do.

All these went together with the ancient playground games. In the spring time we brought our collections of marbles – Triple Trebs and Spirals and Big Reds and Big Blues and Big Greens. We kept them in military medicine boxes lined with cotton wool to prevent chipping. When class was over, we ran like hell to claim our spots in the playground and set up our Shows. We set the marbles down on a shallow bed of sand gathered from the sand-pit and drew a ring around them. With a piece of chalk stolen from class, we marked out the distance that the rollers had to stand. Then we yelled across the asphalt – 'Roll up, roll up, two Spirals and a Jumbo Treb out!' When the boys came, and they always did come, they either knocked the marble out of the ring and kept it, or they didn't and they lost what they bet. The more valuable the marble, the more chances they had to roll.

Or we dragged out one of the dustbins and flipped over the lid. We set a marble in the middle and let people roll their own marbles around the edge, to see if they could knock our marble out of place. If they did, they kept it.

You could lose your whole damn collection in one Bun Break. I did it a couple of times.

In winter, you brought out your radiator-hardened, two-year-old Conkers. You drilled holes in horse-chestnuts and hung them from pieces of string. You found yourself some Little Man with a big fat, new and shiny conker and challenged him. He'd hold up the string and let you take a swing. You watched his face as your shrivelled rock-hard Conker blew his prize into white chips across the playground. When he cried, you'd tell him – 'Don't Blub, Little Man.' But then you'd meet a senior whose Conker looked strange and transparent. He had hollowed out the middle and filled it full of glue which hardened into something stronger than rock, but you didn't know that yet. Your Conker disintegrated when he swung at it. And he told you not to Blub even though you weren't Blubbing – you were tougher than to Blub – at least in the middle of the playground.

It was possible not to take part. Some boys stayed locked in the Hobby Hut building Fokker Triplanes and sniffing the little white tubs of Airfix glue. Others fixed their brains on playing Risk and were never able to stop – just quietly conquering the globe over and over again. Some played with Action Man down by the river-banks. A few turned Patsy and played with stuffed animals and talked in squeaky voices.

One boy named Sheldon set up a whole radio network connected by wires and started broadcasting from a room at the top of the Big Hall. He called it *Dragon Radio* and spent weeks soldering all the wires together and buying up old radios to use as receivers. Sheldon gathered records from all over and got his parents to cough up for a record player. Then he tried it out and it ran brilliantly for a day or two. But then on the third day, Sheldon was looking out of the window of his little broadcasting station and he could see Nightingale, who had been trying to get a song called 'The Sun has Got his Hat On' played all week. But Sheldon didn't have it and besides, Nightingale had not been asking. He had been threatening. Sheldon saw Nightingale pick up the big old radio receiver set up on the window sill of his third-storey classroom and then had to sit there helplessly while Nightingale threw it out of the window. It sailed out into space trailing wires, and blew apart on the playground below. But not just that radio. The wires were all connected, so one radio after another flew across the classrooms and exploded against a wall or sailed out of the window. Sheldon watched Nightingale smash the whole rig in less than ten seconds. He could have put it all back together, but by then his nerves were shot. *Dragon Radio* disappeared forever and Sheldon was heard to be contemplating joining Pa Dimbleby out on his sheep farm in Wales.

A newspaper started up. *The Dragon News*. It was sold for 2p a shot. This was more money than Nightingale or Cuddlybum or I would ever have paid, but we strongarmed free copies off some of the playground sellers, who gladly handed them over to avoid having their Teddy Bears injected with toothpaste.

You could chase after a Haggis, if you could find one. Snog her in the squash court gallery and feel the barely feelable bumps of her tits. See the way people look at you now. Wait for the girl to get offended about something you did or about something you didn't do. She'll dump you in private and then dump you in public by telling the other Hags. The Hags will move through the school like the BBC World Service until everyone knows what a shit you are. Then you'll become such a hero that your fame might even spread to America and Nightingale would gladly become your Slave for Life.

The craze when I arrived at school was to have an Action Man.

I wished I could meet the real Action Man. I wondered how it felt to have your face shrunk down small and remade millions of times, with the life-like fuzzy hair and sometimes a beard and sometimes not and saying Brave Things when the cord was pulled from your chest.

I had an Action Man who talked. He used to have five different sayings, but after five minutes with Nightingale, the only words that ever came out of him again were – 'Mission Accomplished. Good Work Men.' In the games I invented, imaginary people were always doing things right, so Action Man could pat them on the shoulder with his Kung Fu gripper hands and say, 'Mission Accomplished. Good Work Men.' My dad had bought a kit that made Action Man into a member of the French Resistance. He had jeans and a black turtle-neck and a black plastic beret. I asked my dad if he didn't think Action Man looked a little Patsy in a beret. My dad said the French Resistance were tough, so it was all right to wear a beret.

I worried that he didn't speak French when I pulled the cord. I was always worrying about the little things.

I used to carry Action Man in my ammunition can. I'd check on him in the breaks between class. Sometimes I'd hide him in a tree outside the classroom where only I could see him. All through class, I'd catch his eye.

While I was in art class, Action Man would be foxholed away in the shrubs.

He was foxholed on Saturday morning when a huge machine suddenly rumbled past the window, with one of the school's caretakers riding on top. It all happened very quickly. At first it looked as if the caretaker was riding a mechanical bull that had broken loose from its hinges and was stampeding across town and he couldn't get off.

When I got to the window, I saw that he had been riding a power mower. Chopped grass lay pale green and damp in a mat along the ground. Action Man was in the grass. I counted maybe fifteen pieces of arm and leg and sliced-up rubber beret.

I put all the pieces in my ammunition can and ran down to the river-bank and didn't come back until the night-ghouls chased me home.

I asked Pa Vicker to mail home the remains. I wanted to bury him in the yard at home, the same way I'd buried gerbils and fish and Timmy the Hamster who got clawed out of his cage by the cat and mother wouldn't even let me see what was left.

Pa Vicker said I was being absurd and for a while he acted as if he hadn't mailed the pieces, but two weeks later I received a package from America at Mail Call. It was an Action Man in the package, with the same clear eyes and fuzzy beard and Kung Fu gripping hands.

Then the new craze was to have a handwarmer. Handwarmers were small steel boxes, which came with fuel sticks and a velvet bag. You'd light a stick and set it in the box and then put the box in the bag. It didn't matter how hot it was outside. Suddenly you weren't anybody unless you had a pocketwarmer burning a hole in your thigh.

Then of course the thing became to have the hottest pocketwarmer and of course that had to be Nightingale. He crammed his little box with all the fuel sticks he could find and lit them and stuffed the whole bloated thing in his pocket. His trousers caught fire and he had to pull them off in the middle of the playing fields.

Ma Blek sewed a patch over the burn hole. The corduroy line of Nightingale's trousers was going in a different direction to the corduroy of the patch, but Nightingale was not the sort to get worried about a thing like that.

'What I don't understand,' Ma Blek said, 'is why you bother to have handwarmers when it is warm outside. It's already cricket season, for Heaven's sake!'

We didn't have an answer. Handwarmers were the craze and the fact that they had come along at the wrong time of year didn't make any difference to us.

Only two things ever happened to me in cricket. Either I would hit the ball so hard that it would fly off the pitch and the umpire would raise both his arms straight up in the air, showing I had six runs. Or the ball would shoot past me and mash into the three stumps of the wicket and the wicket-keeper would shout – Owzat? Then the umpire would raise one finger, to show I was out.

Mostly I sat on the bench with Nightingale, who could not bat or bowl or catch a ball, but who had more cricket equipment than anyone else in the school. He had a Grey-Nichols bat with the red handle and pads and a smart sweater and a hat.

He also had a game called Owzat, which was made up of two things like dice that you could roll and pretend to be the score-keeper in a cricket game. Nightingale kept score in an Official Scorekeeper's Book and I was the Official Roller of the Dice.

There was always a big fuss choosing the teams. Churchill and Hitler and Mussolini and Caesar were always in the game. It went without saying. Then George Best the soccer player and Barry John the Rugby player and sometimes the Queen and Prince Philip.

Nightingale made sure that he starred in these games. He would bowl out Hitler and then get six runs off Mussolini.

I cheated with the dice when he brought himself up to bat, in order to keep the game going. He often finished the games early if he got bowled out or had too many runs hit off him. He'd tear the page neatly out of his Official Scorekeeper's Book and stuff it in his mouth and eat it. Then there'd be nothing to do.

Cuddlybum had a radio and listened with a little white plug in his ear to the cricket at Lord's.

Nightingale and I couldn't care less about cricket in the real world. In our minds, fat-bellied Churchill hit a ball thrown in by Prince Philip with his chest of medals and Hitler made a Hitler salute and caught the ball somewhere out in the field.

Whether you played cricket or not at the Dragon School, you had, every now and then, to stop what you were doing and pretend to bowl a cricket ball. You took the last three paces of your run-up and your right arm swung up and down. Then you raised your fists and whispered – Owzat? – as you imagined a grump-faced batsman wandering back to the bench after being bowled out.

You also had to own a cricket ball and not the rubber pudding type but a real one that would leave a stain on your shirt where you rubbed it before you bowled. We all had red stains on our grey shirts.

I don't think my dad knew too much about cricket. He never said so, of course, but sometimes in the holidays, when we'd be out in the garden and practising, he would pause and open his mouth to give advice but then stop. I think for a moment, he had convinced himself it was the soccer season again, when he had more advice than he knew what to do with.

We also did athletics in the summer and here was where my dad knew more than anyone. I had seen the sack of medals and the pictures of him throwing the javelin. He was a star of the Thames Valley Harriers and of Birmingham and Leicester Universities. He had a track suit with Wales in big letters on the back and he had thrown and won in the Commonwealth Games.

He bought a javelin and took me down to the beach. Then he set out rocks at different distances along the sand. On each rock he set some money, more as the rocks got further away. If could I could throw the javelin past the coins, I'd get to keep them.

He taught me the run-up and the throw but I believe I was a disappointment.

One time when I was whining, he swore and grabbed the spear from my hand. 'Don't quit on me,' he said. 'Don't quit on anything. If there's one thing I want you to do with your life, it is not to quit.' Then he moved faster than I had ever seen him move before. He took two huge paces forward and his arm snapped back. I heard the grunt as the javelin left his hand. It sailed out, rising and rising as if carried by angels, over the water until I had lost sight of it. It slipped under the waves. He never taught me the javelin again.

A couple of months later, I figured it out on my own. I was running down the ash-covered path in an athletics meeting at a place called Eagle House, javelin raised high above my head and ready to throw. Suddenly I knew what I was doing. All my muscles worked in the right way and I was not gangly and stumbling any more. When I let go of the spear, I saw it rise and rise, carried by the angels, and I blew out the Eagle House record by three and a half metres.

I wish my dad could have seen the way it flew and the way the angels carried it. It only sounded like bragging when I wrote home about it on one of those pale blue toilet-paper aerogrammes.

I was never the same after that. I didn't tell my parents or anybody else, because I had no idea how to say it. It was as if, for a couple of seconds, a huge reservoir of strength had been shown to me. If I had done it once, I knew I could do it again. It did not have to do with simple strength. It had to do with knowing how to use the strength. There was some code. Some straight path of thinking that would open up these things for me. I thought about it on the bus as we went back to school. It haunted me, the way it had haunted me when Nightingale had showed me a magazine article that said we only use one fifth of our brains and the rest is all there ready to be used but we don't know how. The first thing I thought when I read was – maybe I can voyage after all, with that untapped part of my brain.

People said congratulations on breaking the Eagle House and the Dragon School record, but I barely heard them. I was working on the code, before this whole thing stopped making sense to me, like a dream does sometimes, after you wake up.

CHAPTER 4

I NEVER THOUGHT much about the passage of time. There was only the black and white of school time and holiday time, class time and free time, and the gradual shift from one dorm to another as I moved up the school.

Nightingale and Cuddly and I all stayed the same. Or we grew at the same rate and never noticed it. We each had the things we were better at, Nightingale at sports, Cuddly at school-work and me at telling stories to keep us happy through the rainy afternoons and in the dark of our dormitory after the lights had been turned out.

I knew that one day we would have to take the Common Entrance exam and leave this place for another school. If I passed Common Entrance my parents had told me I would go to a school called Eton, but I had never seen Eton and I didn't know where it was. For a while, I thought it was back in America. I came to understand that Eton was a different place from many of the other schools that boys would go to from the Dragon. Nightingale had been signed up for Eton, too. His parents put his name down for the place even before he was born. I knew that my parents had signed me up at the age of six months. You had to do that, I heard. Otherwise you'd never even have a chance of getting in. None of the boys seemed to care one way or the other where they went. They had been signed up for Harrow, like Cuddly, or Sherborne or Winchester or Westminster and that was where they were going if they passed the Common Entrance exam, so there was nothing more to say about it. I heard about Eton from the teachers. Some said it was a snotty kind of place that was hopelessly out of date. Others would give me a knowing nod when I told them I was bound for Eton, as if they knew a secret that I was about to find out. I was not impatient to know. Time could not be rushed. I had learned that from my years of begging to be transported home in the middle of the night. Besides, I didn't give myself better than a fifty-fifty chance of getting through the Common Entrance exam.

By the time I could call people Little Men, I didn't know who they were and didn't want to call them anything. That was the thing. You hardly ever got to see people above you or below. If you hung about with older boys, people would say you were being their Servus. And if you hung about with lower boys, you were being a Patsy and mostly those were the ones who talked in squeaky voices, pretending to be their Teddy Bears, or who couldn't be tough in their own year of boys, so went down a few years to be tough.

Being a Servus meant thinking an older boy was so cool that you would do anything he wanted you to do. It was embarrassing to watch lower boys running around after seniors and prefects, carrying their ammunition cans and waiting for them after class.

There were the ranks that had names, like Prefect and Head Boy and Captain of the Rugby Team. I knew almost from the beginning that I wouldn't have a rank like that. Neither would Nightingale or Cuddly. But then there were the ranks without names that spread out through the school like veins through a person's body. They told us where we belonged in the school, and made us feel a part of it.

My brother Clive had started at the Dragon School, but I hardly ever saw him. Sometimes I caught sight of his coal-black hair in the assembly hall and sometimes we walked across the fields on Sundays, but the school had its natural ways of keeping the years separate.

There was one time on a winter day when some boys had thrown gallons of water down the slope of our playground and it had frozen into an ice slide. Of course what happened was that 500 boys were trying to slide down it all at the same time and most of them fell over before they reached the bottom. There was a wall of bodies at the end, a pig-pile of blue corduroy and Clark's Commando shoes. After a while, senior boys were just grabbing younger boys and using them as buffers as they slid down the ice, making sure to fall backwards if they slipped so as not to get anyone too badly hurt. I grabbed one little boy and began to slide down with him and it was only after a couple of seconds that I realized the boy was Clive. We made a joke of it, but I felt terrible, and it was the first time I could ever remember apologizing for something to my brother.

Apart from that, the only time we caught up on what the other was doing, was on the plane home at the end of term.

The rest of the time, it was always Nightingale and Cuddlybum and me, with Bosom throwing tantrums in the background and Kissack in his wheelchair and Bukovik setting traps and blowing up river rats with home-made explosives. The cycle of who was popular and who was not passed through each one of us and started back at the beginning. There didn't seem to be room for anyone else. We went everywhere together and were always in the same dorm and took baths together and beat each other up and all ran screaming down the hallways in the middle of the night, armed with toothpaste and pillows. And we never Sneaked on each other except for the one time when Cuddly ran away and I would never forgive myself for that.

I was lying on my bed one Sunday afternoon and waiting for Nightingale to come back to school from visiting his parents. Suddenly Nightingale ran into the dorm. He had already ditched his parents, who were downstairs trying to choke back some of Pa Vicker's sherry. Nightingale said he had something to show.

We sneaked out the back way, just in time to see a confused-looking Mr and Mrs Nightingale get into their car and drive away. They kept looking around, as if to see their son swinging from a tree branch or popping up like a rat from a hole in the ground. Pa Vicker stood in his doorway and waved goodbye. He was grinning like a skull. When the Nightingales were out of sight, Pa Vicker sheared the smile off his face and wandered back inside.

Nightingale and I ran down to the river-bank. Then he showed me a whole cigarette that he had swiped off his mother. He told me it was a Sobranie Black Russian. It had a gold-coloured filter and the cigarette was dark like a cigar.

We lit it with the burning end of a twig which we shoved into the musty-smelling smoulder of a compost heap.

I ballooned my cheeks with the smoke and spat it out again.

Nightingale did the same, the cigarette wedged between two extended fingers.

When the cigarette was done, I wondered out loud if he could get any more.

Nightingale said this was a bad sign. He told me I was probably hooked on cigarettes now and the fact that I was looking for more could only mean I was addicted.

I thought about being an addict and about this being a fine way to start off the term. It made me so angry that Nightingale was the one who started me off on my life of addiction that I punched him in the head.

He had on a brand new pair of National Health glasses, which broke very neatly in half right on the bridge of his nose. He held up the two pieces, like long-stemmed monocles now, and began to Blub loudly. He wailed that he would be blind from now on.

I imagined us wandering across the country, me an addict and looking in all the gutters for cigarettes and Nightingale stumbling after me, holding onto my belt because he was blind.

Pa Vicker took the two long-stemmed monocles that Nightingale held out to him. Then he roared with laughter. He put them back together and pulled them apart and bowed over breathless as he was laughing so hard.

I'd been expecting the worst.

Nightingale had been playing up his blindness all afternoon and tripping over things and telling me how expensive glasses were and how they weren't just regular glasses.

But now with Pa Vicker laughing and the danger gone, I took a look at Nightingale. He had even gone a little hunchbacked that afternoon, as if all blind people were hunchbacked. I wanted to hit him again and as soon as Pa Vicker was out of sight, his laughter still booming across the playground, I gave Nightingale another smack in the chops.

He didn't get new glasses. Instead, he just taped them together. This made him look as if he had a sloping forehead like a gorilla, which he did a bit anyway.

One afternoon, coming back from Rugby, Cuddly told me I smelled bad.

I said the same about him.

Cuddly rested his hand on my shoulder. 'No really, Watty. You do.'

I felt like telling him that he was sometimes a little too honest for his own good. But I could tell he didn't mean any harm. So I kept my mouth shut.

That afternoon, we went into town to buy deodorant.

But when we got to the chemist, Cuddly suddenly grew shy about buying deodorant, and decided to buy aftershave instead. I asked him what was any less embarrassing about buying deodorant. He gave me some long lecture, right outside the chemist's, about how deodorant was for getting rid of a bad smell, whereas aftershave was only for getting your face to smell nice after a shave.

'But anyone can see that we don't need to shave.'

After half an hour of discussion, we eventually agreed to say it was a present if anybody asked us.

We bought a kind called Hi-Karate because there was a commercial on TV where a man kicks and chops his way across town like Bruce Lee and then someone slaps him in the face with some of the Hi-Karate aftershave. The man looks relieved and says – 'Thanks, I needed that.' We had no idea what the commercial was about, but we bought the stuff anyway and it was damned expensive.

'It's for my uncle,' we said in unison to the cashier woman.

'Oh yes, I'm sure it is.' She turned the bottle around in her hand, looking for the price tag.

'It is! It's for both of our uncles!' Cuddly looked as if he was going to take a swing at the lady.

'Are they going to share it?' She punched the numbers into the cash register.

I wondered if it was going to be this hard every time I bought deodorant or aftershave. I wondered if I could just buy one giant size deodorant bar the size of a Volkswagen and have it last my entire life.

'Are they going to share it?' Cuddly imitated her shrill voice as we walked through the park on our way home.

I laughed and then did my own imitation, as if we had come out on top of that little conversation, but we both knew that the cashier lady had wiped the floor with us back in the shop.

We stopped near the cricket pavilion and splashed the Hi-Karate all over each other. Cuddly got it in his eyes and staggered around blind with pain for five minutes. I splashed it under my arms and for the first time in my life I knew the meaning of excruciating. There was almost none left by the time we made it back to school.

Pa Vicker threw us out of the dining-hall because he said we were giving off noxious fumes. Then he called us back in and introduced us to his nephew who had come over from Canada and was going to study at the Dragon for a term. The nephew's name was Marcus. He was a loud-mouth and bragged and I felt glad at least that he wasn't an American. This didn't make much difference to Cuddly, who called him a Yank anyway.

When I thought about it, I realized that he couldn't have been a part of our group anyway. He was too much of a stranger and we were so close that we practically had our own private language.

Two weeks into the term, Pa Vicker's nephew broke into the tuck shop and robbed a bunch of sweets. He was caught within twenty-four hours.

And the way I heard it, Pa Vicker pulled up in his car right outside the Headmaster's study, where the nephew was getting told off. Pa Vicker told his nephew to get in the car and drove him straight to Terminal 3 of Heathrow Airport. He put the boy on the next plane back to Canada. We all avoided Pa Vicker for a few days after that.

Pa Vicker could be a frightening man. Even the thought of him being so angry gave me chills at night and cramps in my bowels and the small of my back.

Cuddly was always getting kicked out of Pa Vicker's Latin class for not knowing anything. Sometimes it seemed to me as if he got himself kicked out on purpose. I felt almost sure he deliberately messed up his work.

Pa Vicker would pick on him to translate something.

Then Cuddly would begin to speak very slowly and carefully and sometimes he would stop speaking altogether.

That was when Nightingale, who sat behind him, would whisper a Latin word in Cuddly's ear. But Nightingale never said the right word. He just made one up.

So Cuddly would fall silent and then a second later he would yell out – 'Eggibus!'

Then Pa Vicker would take his blue-covered Whitbread's Shorter Latin Primer and slam it down on the desk. Chalk dust coughed up in his face. 'Why is it, Codrington . . .' he would start to ask, 'that every time I call on you . . . Why is it?'

I never once heard him finish his sentence.

He would take Cuddly by the collar and lead him from the class to go and stand in the hall. Cuddly would grin at us as he was led out.

On one of these days Pa Vicker turned to us and said – 'It seems none of you will ever amount to much in Latin.'

Then Cuddly shook himself loose of Pa Vicker's grip and yelled – 'And whose fault's that?'

Pa Vicker threw him out into the hall and stood there trembling while he thought of a terrible punishment. After a moment, he shouted that all of Cuddly's comic books would be confiscated for two weeks. 'Even your *Look and Learns*!' Then he slammed the door so hard he blew it off its hinges.

I knew that as soon as my bowels uncramped, I would be jealous of Cuddly for saying what he'd said. Perhaps even Pa Vicker would be jealous.

But there was something not quite right about Cuddly getting himself in trouble. I had a feeling he did know the right answers but got them wrong on purpose. He seemed to like being shouted at and shoved and having his hair pulled. Nightingale noticed it, too. We mentioned it to each other, but then had nothing else to say. And so the conversation died.

It was a harsh punishment for Pa Vicker to confiscate all of Cuddly's comics, even if just for two weeks. Nightingale and I had come to rely on Cuddly for magazines and hardly ever bought them for ourselves. Cuddly didn't have to buy them. His parents had them delivered every week.

Thursday was comic book day. *Beano, Topper* and *Eagle* and *Look and Learn* arrived rolled up into pipes.

In every comic was a page where jokes sent in by readers were printed. A cartoon was drawn above them, which had some clown with sticking-out ears who said the funny thing.

Cuddly once had a cartoon printed in the *Beano*. Nightingale and I could not hide our jealousy. The joke had a man driving his truck off the edge of a cliff. The man was leaning out the window and shouting – 'I just wanted to test my air brakes.' He had got the joke from his father.

Nightingale began to send off cartoons every day. He stole them from me, stole them from Cuddlybum, stole them from Cuddlybum's grandma when she came to visit. He sent off the same joke that Cuddly had got published. Nothing ever happened. The reason it never did was because Nightingale's handwriting looked as if he was writing with a pen jammed between his toes instead of his fingers.

My grandma sent me a bunch of pre-addressed and stamped cards to write on and send back to her. I put white stick-tape over her name and address and wrote down the *Beano's* instead. Then I sent some jokes of my own, and even drew cartoons to go with them.

We spent money on joke books in town.

Eventually we each had little notebooks for writing down jokes, and we brought our notebooks to the Sunday films in the New Hall in case there might be a joke from the movie that was worth writing down.

We also asked our parents for jokes.

My dad wrote back – What has sixteen legs and two boobs? Snow White and the Seven Dwarfs.

I sent it in. I figured what the hell, and it was only when they did not publish it, that I realized how much I had wanted them to.

Cuddly woke up screaming for the fifth night in a row. He said it was the Tango Ladies. They were after him again. The Tango Ladies were old women with handbags and umbrellas who chased him across the playing fields in his dreams.

I lost count of the number of times I sat with Cuddly on the wide dormitory window-sills and watched the sun come up through the Conker trees down by the river, because Cuddly couldn't get back to sleep.

Cuddly was doing some strange things. Even stranger than usual. He got Nightingale and me to play strip poker with him in a classroom one Saturday afternoon. It was freezing cold in the classroom and I said I'd only play if I could sit by the radiator.

As we watched the sunrise one day, and the sweat of Tango Lady nightmares was still on his face, he told me that if you went and stood by the Cricket pavilion in the park, people would come along who would pay you money if you let them touch you. He said they would pay you five pounds.

That changed the way I thought about Cuddly. There had only been little things before now, but they were starting to add up. And now with this story about the Cricket pavilion, I could see the balance tipping against him, and our friendship starting to fade.

Hearing about the people who would pay you five pounds if you let them touch you changed the way I thought about a lot of things. It made me see for the first time that there were many rules outside the Dragon School rules and that the adults who made the rules and enforced them had rules of their own that they were supposed to obey but sometimes didn't.

It shook me up pretty badly. I ducked some rules, but I didn't duck many. Mostly I did what I was told and was obedient to the point of stupidity. I did what I was told. That was the absolute rule above all other rules. And I often took pride in the speed that I obeyed and in doing the job well, whatever it was.

This was hard to explain to my friends in America, where it seemed that every rule came with explanations of that rule and discussions and statistic charts shoved in your face.

In the weeks that followed, Cuddly didn't hang around with Nightingale and me as much as he used to. Some afternoons, he disappeared and when he came back, he wouldn't say where he had been. He rarely talked any more.

A while later, I was walking back from the river-bank one Sunday night and Cuddly appeared suddenly out of the shadows of an empty classroom. Nightingale had galloped on ahead to the dining-hall, terrified as he always was of missing his dinner. Cuddly asked me to come inside the classroom, so I did. We stood there in the dark in silence.

'So what do you want, Cuddly?' I asked him.

He asked if he could touch my willy.

I took out my Swiss Army knife and pressed him against the wall and held the blade against the hollow of his throat. I didn't say anything. He couldn't say anything. If he'd even breathed in, the knife would have cut him. Then I ran away across the road to the dining-hall.

It was only later in the dormitory, sitting next to Nightingale and watching him stuff Fruit Chewys into his face, that I thought of the things I should have told Cuddly. It was too late by then. He had gone too far and he knew it. Things would be different from now on between him and me.

I went to Sister Mabel, thinking maybe I could talk to her about Cuddly, maybe not mention his name but still ask for advice, and it might not count as Sneaking. Even if he had become strange, I knew he was still my friend, and I still cared enough to try and help him.

'Oh, it's you, Watkins! What do you want this time?' Sister Mabel was nailing an eye chart up on the wall. She talked with a hammer in her hand and two nails held between her teeth.

Right there, I changed my mind on telling her about Cuddly. But then I was stuck, because I had to invent some reason for being there.

After a minute of coming up with excuses, saying I felt a bit tired and a bit itchy and a bit something else, Sister Mabel announced that she thought I had worms. I had to take tablets every day for a week at breakfast. For a while, she was saying that the whole house might have to take tablets. I begged her not to do that. I knew I would never be able to live it down and I lay awake at night, thinking of the new nicknames I would be called from now on.

Pa Vicker found out about it. He walked up to me in breakfast one day and said – 'I hear you've got worms!'

I pretended he wasn't talking to me.

'Watkins, I hear you've got worms. How did you get them? Because I can tell you, you didn't get them here. You must have got them in America. Perhaps you got them on the plane on the way over. But let me tell you, young man, you did not get them from here.'

For a while I took the hits about everyone having worms in America. I told them it wasn't that I had worms inside me. It was just that I kept a box of worms in my locker. I even went out and dug up some earthworms and put them in a box and showed them around for a while. For a while, it became a craze. Everybody had a box of worms. I even made a calendar to count the days until the craze faded away. When it finally died, I felt but didn't show the relief when people called me Watty Dog again. Besides, the Common Entrance exams were coming up soon, and there'd be no time for crazes or anything else.

Nightingale and I sat side by side on Sunday evenings for the film that was shown every week in the New Hall. The chairs were brown with metal frames and canvas seats that gave you Wedgies. Cuddly used to sit with us, but more and more lately, we saw him sitting up at the front by himself, the film light shining off his neatly combed hair. We didn't chase him away, but there was a coldness and an awkwardness that had grown between us which there was no denying.

The films were mostly war films – 633 *Squadron*, *Cockleshell Heroes*, *The Guns of Navarone*.

After 633 *Squadron*, the tuck shop would sell out of model aeroplane kits and after *Cockleshell Heroes*, the Army & Navy store in the town sold all its woolly Commando hats.

We watched Errol Flynn in *Captain Blood*. For weeks afterwards you could hear booming across the playground – 'Haaaaayaaaaah! Up the Jolly Roger!'

Then we saw *Zulu*, and something happened to me after seeing that film. It changed the way I thought, as if God had picked me up off the smooth train tracks of my life, set me down on a new set of tracks and given me a push to get going.

The film was set in a time that I knew nothing about. I did not know where the Transvaal was. I didn't know why the South Wales Borderers were there and why they were fighting the Zulus. Maybe they explained it in the film, but I didn't get it.

What I got was afraid. There was a point in the film when the Welsh soldiers in their blood-red coats were barricaded in a little farmhouse. Thousands of Zulus with short spears and horsehide-covered shields were getting ready to rush the barricade. The Zulus stamped and chanted and beat the spears against the shields. It sounded like a giant heartbeat racing out of control and even to us in the New Hall, the noise was deafening. I was as scared for the Welshmen as I would have been for myself.

And of course in the end some of them survive and others get killed, the Zulus go away and the Welshmen get a lot of medals, which was why they bothered to make the film and why anybody remembers Rorke's Drift, which was the name of the farm.

But that didn't matter to me. I could not get out of my head the noise of the chanting and the drumbeat of the shields.

'It would have been damned hard,' Nightingale said, 'to hold your ground against that.'

Nightingale and I agreed. We talked about it in low voices, without jokes or Nightingale saying his uncle was there giving one-two punches or Cuddly in the background making some announcement about his family crest.

That night I dreamed I was at Rorke's Drift. I was at the barricade in a blood-red tunic and I heard the Zulus chanting ten times louder than I'd heard them in the film. It was hot and I was sweating. There were other people around me and I heard the singsong of Welsh in their voices. I hoped the Zulus would charge soon because I didn't know how much longer I could stand the drumbeat of their shields.

This was no grainy-edged half-nonsense dream like all the others I'd had. This dream had the same sharp smell and touch as the times I had voyaged back home.

It didn't last long. It was as if I slipped for a minute behind the eyes of one of those Welshmen who had lived and died before I was born. And maybe he slipped behind my eyes, finding himself in the chalk-dusty air of a classroom in a faded blue corduroy suit with his pockets full of Conkers and a Swiss Army knife.

When daylight came and I told the others about it, they said they had had the same dream. At first I didn't know if they were just saying that, but then I began to wonder whether perhaps we had voyaged together. Together and alone at the same time. All of us, flickering across time for a moment and into the bodies of the South Wales Borderers and feeling the fear they felt.

Nightingale wondered if the great-grandchildren of the Zulus ever dreamed of being there but on the other side.

I couldn't get over it. I felt as if my life had been jolted off course. Time itself, the whole order of terms and holidays and classes and breaks and sports in the afternoon and supper time and dorm time and sleep time had somehow all run off the rails that night.

I tried to write down what I'd seen and what I'd felt. I spent all afternoon on it and then another and another and went to Sister Mabel, saying I was sick so she would put me Off Games. Because games were suddenly not important. I had to write this stuff down and it had to make sense.

The words wouldn't come. I could put words down, but I could not read them and make the fear jump in me again.

From then on, all I seemed to be doing in my free time was writing. I was no longer just the one who told stories and let them slip away like helium balloons into the sky, never returning. Now I set them on paper and kept them, stored like the specimens of luminous butterflies in the school museum. I should have been studying for my Common Entrance exams, but I couldn't help myself. I sat down at my desk with stacks of blank paper and slipped away into another world, time hurtling past, as if my mind had found itself suddenly set loose of the bone box of my skull, and was free to travel across the centuries, in and out of people's hearts and souls.

But it seemed that even to mention this other world was somehow to devalue it. So I didn't talk of this to Nightingale. It was one of the only secrets that I ever kept from him.

The teachers said you couldn't prepare for Common Entrance. All you could do was take it and hope you passed. So I didn't worry. Boys were talking more now about how they hoped their new schools would be. The idea of leaving the Dragon seemed so strange to me that I couldn't imagine any other place. All I thought about was the summer, and the shimmering blaze of sun off Narragansett bay. I thought of diving off our dock and disappearing into the cool water in a shower of silver droplets. The holidays had already begun in America and I could barely stay calm, knowing that there were fish to be caught, clams to be dug from the low-tide mud, and forts to be built in the shadowy green woods.

But lying between me and that was the grey of all these exams. It stopped my day-dreams dead in their tracks. I knew if I failed, I'd have to stay on an extra term and try to pass the exam again. If I failed after that, I'd get sent home to America for good. I thought about failing on purpose, about writing Nightingale's made-up Latin words for the whole Latin exam. There was something evil and sweet about the idea.

I don't know what happened. I went into the exams and tried as hard as I could. I couldn't help myself.

A few weeks later, the Headmaster called all senior boys into the drawing-room and read out the names of the people who had passed.

When I found out that I had, I ran down to the river-banks with a crowd of other boys and we all jumped into the river. We threw mud at each other and swam to the other side and blew water through our noses. I caught sight of Cuddly, and waved to him and smiled. He waved back, with a crooked grin on his face. When I saw that crookedness, I knew that it was over between us. It was just as well that we were leaving for other schools. I dived under the water and swam away through the reeds.

Then I remembered Nightingale. I hadn't heard his name. I was so excited about passing, that I hadn't stopped to wait for him.

He had failed. He got nine points out of a possible sixty-five and you needed at least twelve to get into Eton.

I found him Blubbing in the sand-pit at the entrance to the fields.

It was strange, as if he had suddenly faded far into the distance and no one could touch him. I was going on and he would stay where he was no longer supposed to be. He knew the names we called boys who stayed behind to try a second time. He had invented half of them.

I felt something strange one day in my last term at Dragon, when all of the classes competed in athletics against each other. I was the last runner in the 4 x 100 metre relay and had just started to gather some speed, arm held out behind me to take the baton from the runner coming up behind. We were out in front. The ground seemed to be shaking with spiked shoes thumping the ground.

Then the baton slipped into my palm and I gripped it and ran. In the first huge leap of my sprint, I felt a strength in me that had not been there before. It was the strength of not being a child any more. Perhaps it had been growing in me for a while, but I had never felt it until now.

I had to try not to laugh as I moved down the track. I knew I would come in first. The boys behind me were still flip-flopping along with child's muscles and I had got new ones.

I was never the same after this, as when the javelin left my hand at Eagle House and the angels had carried it up. I knew, as I knew then, that if I could figure out exactly how to use the new strength and the technique, I would be able to go a long way. It was a simple combination, if only I could find out what it was.

We all knew about the Official Sex Talk. It was legendary. The way we had heard it from the older boys, on the last biology class of the last day at school, Ma Ponsonby the science teacher would show a sex film of people doing it and then she would take off her own clothes and show us all the parts.

There was even a rumour that she would select one boy from the class to do it with her while we all watched.

I couldn't believe it, but couldn't get it out of my head either.

On the day of the last class, I sat back by the window, next to a huge jar of formaldehyde containing a halibut which was used for animal anatomy classes.

My heart was beating fast enough that I thought it would shatter my ribs.

But it turned out that Cuddlybum had told me a lot more for my 50p than Ma Ponsonby ever let on in that class. She drew a floppy willy on the blackboard and then a picture of a pair of legs without a willy in between them and that was supposed to be the girl. She mumbled something about the sperm and the egg and that was the end of the class.

I saw then how the legend worked and would continue. The Sex Talk was so bad, it was humiliating. So to hide the shame, we would fuel the rumour and lie about it, knowing that by the time the next class of boys found out, they would already be leaving the school and would have humiliation of their own.

The school was having its hundredth anniversary that term. There was going to be something called a *son et lumière* which meant that School House would be emptied. The performance would be in the evening. Lights were to be set up in the rooms and when the lights came on, voices would be heard.

I got to be a voice because of my American accent. All I said was – 'We'll be late for supper.' My mother wrote – How appropriate.

It gave me a chill to watch the *son et lumière*. It was as if we had already gone and our voices were now only echoes. It happened so quickly that new boys came to take our places in the beds and classrooms and sports teams. I and all of my friends had become like the shadows of the river-ghouls and like the Dragons who went away to the war and never came back.

I knew that I would probably never return.

The places we had owned and called secret would now be secret for somebody else. We had grown too big in our bodies, even if our minds were not quite ready to leave. Soon the smells of boys in this place, and the smells of everything that kept us warm and fed and clothed would be bitter and strange in our nostrils the same way they were for the parents.

Until then I had not thought much about leaving. I rarely thought about the future. But now for the first time I wondered if I would ever see those boys again. I knew we could write letters to each other, but it would hardly be the same. I realized too, that I would miss grumpy Pa Vicker, and the boggy-smelling river-bank and the peg-legged shuffle of Ma Blek coming to wake us up in the mornings.

In the farewell ceremony, as I collected my Leaver's Book from the Headmaster, I still couldn't believe it was ending.

Something caught in my throat in a way that had never happened before, the morning that I woke early to be on the bus that went up to Heathrow Airport. I said goodbye to Nightingale with his hair all like a hedgehog from sleeping face down in his pillow. We agreed we would meet up at Eton.

Then I shook Cuddly's pale, outstretched hand for the first and final time.

I should have said things then that I never did say. But perhaps in truth there were no words to sum up our time together. No words, at least, that we didn't already know some place inside us.

By the time it truly dawned on me that all of this was over, I was going down the huge main staircase with my duffel bag. I could hear the engine of the airport bus, and Ma Blek's voice calling out names on her checklist.

I walked out into the foggy summer morning, smelling honey-suckle and the fresh-cut playing fields. I only returned once, a couple of years later. It seemed to me that in the time between, the Dragon School had faded to a mass of echoes in my head. But when I got there, I realized it was not the Dragon which had become an echo in me. It was I who was now nothing more than an echo in the school.

CHAPTER 5

BY THE TIME I arrived home for the summer holidays, the American schools had already been out for a month.

As I stepped off the British Airways 747 and onto the ramp that led to US Customs, I caught a sliver of the blazing summer heat that blew in off the runway.

At home, Sam and Allen and Eric already had their hair sun-bleached blond and their skin was dark from living all day on the beach.

But things were different this summer. My father was dying. He had cancer in his guts. They cut him open and took out what cancer they could find. Then they started shooting him with radiation every day in case they had left some of the disease behind.

On my second day back, my mother and father walked into the TV room and shut off the TV. That was when they told my brother and me about the cancer. My father lifted up his shirt and showed us the operation scar, which made him look as if he had been bayoneted, and the strange blue and red and yellow lines drawn on his stomach for aiming the radiation gun when they zapped him.

My mother drove him up to Boston every day for the treatment. Sometimes neighbours drove him instead, to give my mother a break.

My brother and I stayed behind, with five dollars given to us each day, which we spent on fried clamcakes bought from a shack down by the beach.

I rode my stuck-in-third-gear bike miles from home and was happier when my parents were away. They both looked sick, and didn't laugh the way they used to. The summer heat drilled into us. Elvis died.

For the first time, I looked forward to going back to England. Besides, it was Eton now.

You had to be careful going over to Sam and Allen's house. If you went at the wrong time, you could find out that today was chore day and before you knew it, you'd be raking leaves or digging a Mystery Hole that was later to be Mystery filled-in and nothing more said about it.

Considering that their father sold garden supplies, I couldn't believe how we ended up with such badly broken rakes, half the forks missing, or trowels with the handles snapped off, or lawn-mowers with the blades so blunt that they just slapped the grass around and didn't cut it.

It rained one night after he had just scattered grass seed on his lawn. Over the next few days, little stubs of grass began to appear in his stone-chip path that led down to the sea.

My brother and I showed up that day, since we wanted to walk out to the cliffs with Sam and Allen.

Instead, we spent our day sifting through each stone on the whole damn walkway, using children's beach sieves with little plastic flowers for the handles.

'When I get old,' Sam said, 'I'm going to have fifteen kids and they can all spend their lives working in my back yard.'

Their father would get mad if you didn't do the work right.

It was true that when he did a job, he did it well. They were old Yankees, my mum said, and they did the job until they got it right. You could tell it in the things they made from wood, all neatly joined and polished. And you could see it in their gardens and the way they cut timber for the winter fires.

This did not help me at all. There were a couple of years when it seemed as if I broke everything I touched. Pocket calculators blew up in my face. Glasses filled with sticky orange juice or permanently-staining grape juice would fly out of my hand every time I came near a valuable carpet or piece of furniture.

So there wasn't much help I could be to Mr Morgan.

He gave me a can of creosote and told me to paint his dock. He didn't tell me I had to stir the creosote, so when the job was over and the paint was dried, his dock looked like a brown rainbow, all dark at one end and smudging its way to light brown as I got to the bottom of the can.

He gave me the keys to his tractor mower and told me to mow the lawn. I rode it out of the garage and straight over his portable Hibachi barbecue grill.

After that, I just got off the tractor and ran into the woods and kept running.

People started to go crazy in the neighbourhood. It was the mad-dog summer heat.

A boy named Jason Miller stole his father's car, spun the wheels on the lawn of his father's best friend, grabbed his girlfriend and left town. He stole some credit cards, too. By the time they found the car, Jason had gone all the way to the Florida Everglades. I heard the car was filled with pots and pans.

Jason's brother went nuts, too. He took the one credit card that his younger brother hadn't stolen, and went and bought a Porsche.

A lady drove her car up to the top of the Jamestown bridge, 200 feet above the water, got out and jumped. I remember standing on the beach and seeing the blinker lights flashing red on her car. I saw speed-boats racing out to the huge thick centre pillars of the bridge. I heard that the body drifted all the way to Wickford before they found it.

You'd look out on the bay some days and see the water frothing with a kind of fish called Menhaden. The stubby-toothed Bluefish were chasing them.

My brother and I rowed out until we were in the middle of the frothing fish. The water churned and flickered, as if filled with sheets of tin foil. We cast in treble hooks and gaffed a Menhaden. Then we rehooked it and let it swim back into the school. When a Blue struck, it would almost tear the rod out of our hands. We killed the Bluefish with a baseball bat before we pulled it on board. I'd heard stories of people having their toes bitten off by Bluefish. It was true, their teeth were vicious.

The Blue Angels airplane acrobats came to Quonset and flew. One year a father and son team touched wings at 400 miles an hour. They blew up and painted the sky. A week after that, an older boy in the neighbourhood told me he had gone over to the place on Jamestown Island where some of the wreckage came down. He said you couldn't recognize anything. There were wires and melted bits of plastic all clumped together. He said he picked up one piece of junk and was pulling at the wires, when suddenly it began to bleed. He realized it was a piece of the pilot. It was a true story. I knew it from the face of the boy who told it to me, with that haunted gaze that I heard people talk of as The Thousand Yard Stare.

It was the mad-dog heat, all right. Each day I slipped away under the water with my fins and diving mask and swam in the cool and the quiet. Sometimes I'd swim at night and see green sparks of phosphorescence in the blind man's total black.

I could feel the craziness brought by the heat. I could feel it in the dust of the flea-markets – the sense of everything coming unhinged with sweat and brightness and noise. I felt it up by the road when I went to fetch the mail from the post-box; it was there in the tarry smell of the sun-melted pavement, in the huge froth of honeysuckle bushes and in bubbles of wild grapes that grew tangled in the hedge.

I didn't go crazy in the summers. Under the water, I made it go away.

But I saw other people go nuts and figured that with me breaking almost everything in Mr Morgan's house, I might have pushed him a little down that road.

At least once we had to get to Dutch Island. It sat in the middle of the bay and no one lived there. The place used to belong to the Navy and old buildings still stood on the island, their guts burned out by vandal fires and windows broken with rocks. Giant gun-pits lay in the middle of the island, the guns taken away, but the concrete bunkers still there. I didn't know when the buildings had been built. I guessed in the First World War.

My father took a day off from his trips up to Boston and sailed us out in his boat. Mr Morgan sailed in his. We anchored in a cove, near a lighthouse.

While the parents stayed on the boat, or barbecued hot dogs at a grill on the beach, I ran with my brother and Sam and Allen to find a window that had not been broken or a door still left on its hinges.

Black and yellow spiders lived on the island and I never saw them anywhere else. I stared at them in their huge webs and poked with sticks at their bodies swollen with poison.

There was an underground place, where barrels were stacked in a corner. You could climb down a ladder and see the light as almost solid bars beaming down through other ladder shafts. You could scream and no one would mind. So we howled until our lungs ached.

We rode home on the bow of my father's sailboat, the water all sunset colours until the sun was gone. Then the water turned black and we pulled our trailing feet from the waves. By the time we reached home it was dark. Newport glowed pink on the horizon. The Newport bridge was a necklace of lights, nudging the sky.

Dutch Island had a feeling of no rules, and we all turned into animals there. It was something in the empty, roofless buildings that whispered in our ears to smash and burn and scream. The whispers promised we'd never get caught and their word was good and they kept it.

I lied about my age and got a job. I was paid minimum wage: $3.10 an hour before taxes. I worked at the Windy Acres Restaurant. The first day I was there, the Health Department tried to close the place down for sanitary violations. I got sent into a room called the Potato Room where potatoes had long ago turned into mush and now were growing up the walls and creeping along the floor, looking for the light. The staff bathroom was so bad, I took a spray can of disinfectant, taped down the nozzle so that it would spray and keep spraying, threw it in and shut the door.

I washed dishes from one in the afternoon to midnight. The cooks would yell 'Hot pan!' and throw the thing over my shoulder into the washing water. I had tracks of grease up and down my back from the flying pans.

They wouldn't give me any food. The head chef said if I worked in a shoe store, I wouldn't get free shoes, so I shouldn't expect free food in the restaurant.

I didn't try to argue with him that if I worked in a shoe store I might at least get a discount on the shoes. Instead, a couple of times a night, I'd lock myself in the walk-in refrigerator and stagger around in the dark, eating whatever my hands met – chocolate mousse, shrimp cocktail, potato salad.

They put me to work making cakes. The head chef gave me a bottle of cheap brandy and said to drizzle some on the sponge part before I put on the frosting.

I made cakes for two days. I soaked the sponge in brandy and while it was soaking, I poured two gallons of cream into the giant whipper, which was like a small bathtub with a paddle that flippered everything around until it was cream. I turned the thing on without looking to see the speed setting. Two gallons of cream exploded all over me and the paddle flippered out of control at top speed and for a while there was so much cream everywhere, on the ceiling, walls, over in the Potato Room, that I couldn't find the switch to turn it off.

The head chef walked up to me with one of my cakes. 'What in God's name do you think you are doing?'

'Making the cakes like you told me.'

He set it down on the sink, took out a lighter and lit the side of the cake. It blew up handsomely and scorched the ceiling and what was left of the cream up there.

'I shouldn't be able to do this with a cake,' he yelled at me. 'It shouldn't go up like a god damn . . . god damn . . .'

'V2,' I said, thinking of Eric's old rocket.

They took me off making cakes and set me to work peeling potatoes. They had an automatic potato-peeler, which was like a washing machine with a hard sandy inside for taking off the peel.

I packed it full of spuds and turned it on.

Then I locked myself in the refrigerator and ate two handfuls of mousse and a handful of chicken tarragon.

When I got back to the machine, it was still running. I opened the door and couldn't find any potatoes. It was all peel. Eventually at the bottom of the slippery pile, I found the spuds ground down and looking like peeled grapes.

I carried a smell with me from the kitchens. It wasn't the smell of any one thing. Instead it was the smell of a bit of everything, mixed together and fried in grease and allowed to go bad in the sun.

Even with all the talk about cancer and the dozens of people who came to supper after they had driven my father up to Boston, I did not truly believe anything was wrong. It was just the summer. Everyone went mad-dog in the summer. This time, their madness just seemed to be more organized.

The first time I truly understood that we had a problem, was when my father and brother and I and all the Morgans went over to Jamestown Island to cut brush.

My father had bought waterfront land over there and then sold a chunk of it to Mr Morgan. We were going over to scout out the path for a driveway and then build houses overlooking the bay.

It was jungle. Grapevines and pricker bushes and the glowing green heads of skunk cabbage popping up from the black earth. This was where the Conanicut Indians had lived, before the settlers chased them into the Great Swamp and massacred them in what the locals called King Philip's War. I knew they had trodden without sound across the marshy soil, tree to tree in the half light where only the thinnest threads of sunlight came down through gaps in the trees. If I had been a settler, I would never have come here. Too afraid. I would have let the Indians keep their dark woods and their silence.

We all had machetes. They belonged to Mr Morgan, which meant that they were falling apart. The handle on mine had come loose. When I whacked a tree-trunk or a heavy vine, the vibrations shook back so hard through the steel that they split the skin of my palm.

The vines gave off a heavy damp heat that made it hard to breathe. My brother, Sam and Allen and I stood shoulder to shoulder, hacking through the jungle.

Mr Morgan and my father were hacking in a different direction.

Us boys took a break and walked back to the road. On my way, I caught sight of my father and Mr Morgan. Mr Morgan was still cutting, but my father had stopped. He sat on the ground with a handkerchief pressed to his face. The machete lay across his leg and I could see his palms were bloody like mine.

This was when I knew he might be dying. There was no other way he would have quit and let Mr Morgan go on cutting by himself. At worst, he might have persuaded Mr Morgan to take a break as well, but he would never have stopped by himself, like the time he went on chopping logs with his eye filled with blood.

It had not mattered what they told me about him being sick. Not mattered about the tattoo scars which framed his stomach like a TV screen. Not mattered this constant river of grim-faced people eating dinner at our house. But seeing him quit. If he had seen my brother or me quit, he would have been ashamed and it would have been a while before forgiving. And I knew from that time when he got a wood chip stuck in his eye while chopping wood, that he did not like to admit it when he was in pain.

So now I knew that the pain in him was killing-pain. Or maybe it was worse. Maybe it was the kind of pain that drained all his strength bit by bit. I knew right then, before there was ever any talk of death, that I would rather stand the full force of killing-pain, than the slow drag, like age catching up with you long before it should.

I had never thought about that kind of death. I had thought of shark attacks and car crashes and plane crashes and the last ditch stand against the Zulus. But that was about all.

I would have rather blown my brains out than see myself wither away and have others see me and feel sorry for me and have to fuss about me the way you'd fuss about some slobber-chopped old relative who wets his pants and doesn't know he's done it. I knew that cancer could move through a family in the blood, lying like an unexploded mine in my guts and waiting to be trodden on. So I made my choice then, and it was final.

It gave me a strange feeling when I realized this. I was still gripping the machete, passing a canteen filled with warm water from Sam to Allen to me and on to my brother, all of us too tired to wipe the spit off the top.

It made me grow up a bit to know this so suddenly and have it staring me in the face, not blurred by a dream or day-dream world.

That's how I grew up; not gradually with the shifts from dorm to dorm and teachers cautiously passing on of fragments of power as I moved through the school. I didn't grow up with religious confirmations.

I grew up in jolts, from one suddenly realized thing to another. I couldn't ever tell when they were coming. I didn't know what they were before they appeared. It seemed as if some years I would stay the same and at other times, I would be jolted four times in a week.

It was a jolt being sent away to the Dragon School. Perhaps an even bigger jolt to come back home again for my first holiday. It jolted me when the angels carried my javelin up into the sky at the Eagle House athletics meeting and when I found out about Cuddly going to the park. It jolted me the first time Pa Winter handed over a piece of his Whacking chocolate. I felt it when I walked past the war memorial at the bottom of the playing fields.

As I walked back into the grapevine hot-breath jungle and swung the machete some more, I knew that if my dad died, it would be more than a jolt. It would be my own personal Nagasaki mushroom cloud and would shove my whole world off course.

My brother and I didn't talk about it. To speak of it would only mean to bring it closer. We were superstitious.

Late in the summer, the jellyfish came. All through July, you'd see a couple now and then, looking like unpeeled grapes slopped from wave to wave across the Bay until the tide spat them up on the sand and seagulls pecked them apart.

Sometimes there'd be a Portuguese man-of-war, trailing long and ugly veins of poison and carrying a blue bubble on top that looked like someone's brain exposed. They could kill you, I heard. Paralyse you with their poison. If it had been my job to make up animals for hell, I would have sent down a sea of men-of-war to waft through the current and sting with their vast acid tentacles.

I was as afraid of men-of-war as I was of sharks, which also came in August. Once a small fishing boat was off Block Island, reeling in Blues, when suddenly a shark stuck its head out of the water and bit off their transom, which is a rail at the back for stepping onto the boat. They said the shark was twenty-two feet long. They even had a picture of it, which the newspaper printed.

Others appeared, too big to catch with a rod and reel. So men went out and harpooned them. I heard there was a man down on Montauk Long Island, who spent his whole life warring against sharks.

I screamed like everybody else when that dead man fell out of the bottom of the boat in the movie of *Jaws*. Like everyone else, I threw my popcorn in the air and for a while it was coming down like rain.

But that shark was made of rubber.

The grey monsters I saw heaved off the decks of trawlers in Newport and Galilee were big enough to swallow me whole. I never did see a shark when I was swimming in the bay, but the water was never quite clear, so it always made you think you could see something huge slipping in and out of the murkiness at the edge of your vision.

We found a speargun at the dump, broken so that the spear stood as much chance of firing backwards as forwards, but a speargun all the same. It made us feel safer, and we took it in turns to swim out looking for a shark. Mostly we shot jellyfish and things that couldn't move, like clams. Then one day I shot at a fish under the dock and the damn spear stuck into a piling. It wouldn't come out and that was the end of the speargun.

The jellyfish seemed to appear overnight. The few we'd been seeing all summer were just scouts, clear and camouflaged, rippling rainbows on their sides. The jellyfish which clogged the beaches and made swimming impossible were the same shape and size, but rosy pink.

The summer was pretty much over when they came. They washed in like a warning, as if to tell us that the great icepacks of the Arctic were drifting down towards us now, and soon the water would be killing cold, snuffing out the lives of the trawlermen who fell overboard or whose boats sank from under them in the sea off Martha's Vineyard.

My father took my brother and me out sailing one breezeless day and the jellyfish were so thick that they jammed his little outboard engine. They changed the colour of the bay and dulled the edges of the waves. So we turned around and went home. By then my dad was really too sick to have taken the boat out. He looked the same jade colour as the waves.

I knew the jellyfish would be gone when I returned from school on my next holiday. Instead, the Greenland glacier water would lie calm and clear on Narragansett bay.

The summer fizzled out, but the mad-dog heat still crabbed at me inside.

The storms were coming, too, as they did every year at this time. On the news, we'd see weathermen pointing at satellite photos of white swirls off Bermuda. These were the hurricanes, and while the parents put masking tape on windows and stowed away the deck furniture and took their boats out of the water if they could, my brother and I prayed that the storm would reach us without weakening into a tropical storm, or dying away altogether.

In 1938 and again in 1956, hurricanes had raged down Narragansett Bay, flooding Providence and smashing down every tree and building and breakwater that got in the way. I had seen pictures. The boardwalk at Narragansett beach looked like a spilled box of breadcrumbs. Boats were washed across the road and into the Narragansett pond.

The sky turned brassy as the storm moved up the coast. Policemen closed the Jamestown and Newport bridges. The bay turned ruffled and grey.

I woke up one night in a storm, sure that I could hear the Dragon School's class bell, but it was the cannon blast of thunder, over and over in the sky. The lightning flashed so close one bolt after another, that it looked like daylight at three in the morning and I could see right across the bay to where the cows were huddled in the field on Jamestown. The lightning rods on Old Man Fontaine's barn were glowing green. The bay looked as if it was boiling.

I never did see a hurricane. I felt the house groan with the wind and watched Old Man Fontaine row out to bail his motor-boat just in time to see it sink under the waves. But it was only a tropical storm by then.

Branches down, leaves down, power lines down. Still, I felt cheated by the weathermen. These were the same damned liars who said on Christmas Eve that they had charted Santa Claus's course down from the North Pole. For years I believed them.

The storms usually broke the summer's heat and the craziness as well. It was the last rage of the season and people always seemed calmer afterwards.

The summer people began to pack up and leave, and the year-round people didn't mind watching them go.

Sam and Allen and Eric all disappeared to school and usually we didn't say goodbye, as if it had taken us all by surprise.

I spent a week more wandering the empty beaches and watching the beach clubs close down. I watched the Jerry Lewis Labor Day Telethon, seeing him get more and more tired as the hours went on, until he began to look as if he had been stuck in a time-machine and turned into an old man.

The fall was coming. Poison ivy leaves turned red like spots of blood and I knew that soon all the leaves would start to change. I didn't belong here in that season, and when the time came to leave for Boston, I had been ready for a while. My brother still had a few days left in his holiday. But mine was over now. I packed my bag and we all drove up to Boston. The button factory zoomed up on the horizon and I sat in the back seat, gloomy and going to school.

The last time I saw my father, he was wearing his sheepskin jacket and a big cowboy hat. I turned once as I walked down the long rampway that led to the plane. He had his hand up, waving to me. I waved back and turned and stepped into the plane.

For me, he was already dead and he knew it, but he never said a word. At least he was still on his feet when the time came for saying goodbye. That kind of thing meant a lot to my father, and looking back, it meant a lot to me too.

CHAPTER 6

'WELCOME TO OUR King's College of our Lady of Eton beside Windsor, founded by King Henry the Sixth in the year 1460.' The senior boy who was giving us the tour spat all this out in one breath, and so quickly that I barely understood him.

All of the new boys in Mr Rosser's house had been told to show up for this guided tour of Eton. We shuffled through courtyards, classrooms and out on to the playing fields. All the time, we gave each other shifty looks and sized each other up.

I saw a boy who looked like a girl, a fat boy, an ugly boy and a snot. They already knew I came from America, even if my voice no longer gave me away. I saw from their expressions that they had slotted me into a file that said – Foreigner. It was a file big enough to fit any Oriental, African, Continental or even Irish person that they came across. In fact, that file held everyone who didn't come from England, and preferably the southern counties.

In the opening meeting Mr Rosser, the Master of Carter House, had introduced me as 'one of our Colonial friends'. Then he went – 'Bwah Ha Ha.' I thought – Jesus, it's going to happen all over again.

'If you have any questions,' the senior boy told us, 'you can ask them at the end.' Then he gave us a look that said we wouldn't be asking any questions if we knew what was good for us.

We walked into the huge school courtyard, with its bronze statue of King Henry the Sixth, the Founder, and the chapel so huge it cut out sunlight from the yard by three in the afternoon. I saw the school crest on the clock tower and a war memorial that went on for ever.

Some boys had already been put on punishment detail and were picking moss from the flint courtyard stones.

I thought how, when this place was built, the Conanicut Indians still ruled on Narragansett Bay. They owned the grapevine jungles on Jamestown. The young Indian boys trying to grow up probably jumped from the cliffs at Fort Wetherill, just as we did, before there was a fort or even a Wetherill to name it. In 1460 they hadn't even seen a white man, and it would be another 250 years before the settlers loaded their muskets and kicked the shit out of the Conanicuts once and for all.

I had already begun to understand that what made Eton strong was not its age, but how little its age had changed it. I'd walk past walls graffitied with names and dates that were more than 300 years old. I had walked the chapel steps, worn down into U-shapes by centuries of use. I'd been led through the oldest classroom still in use in the world. I saw the vast sombre-metal war memorial plaque with its lists of names so long that the plaque stretched the entire length of the main school yard.

That evening, in a long hall over the main entrance to the school courtyard, Headmaster McCrum gave us a welcoming speech. The only part I remembered from it was that he said if we were late for an appointment, we should run. The reason I remembered so little was that I kept staring at the marble busts that were lined up along the hall. At first, I thought that they were Roman emperors. They had the same half-angry faces as the ones in the British Museum. They were all done in white marble and their eyes, although open, had the wide blank blindness of dead people whose eyes had rolled around into their heads. But these weren't emperors. These were people who had gone to the school – Prime Ministers, Statesmen, Rulers of the Empire when people still used that word with respect. Over the words of the Headmaster, it seemed to me that I could hear a different voice. It told us to look at these statues and to see what these people had made of their lives. It made us remember how far we still had to go. But it said that if we worked hard and made friends and had luck, that one day we might find ourselves in the ranks of these Rulers of the Empire. I thought back to the hundreds of names that I had seen on the war memorial earlier that afternoon, and it seemed to me for a moment that all of those people had not died in the wars, but had died trying to become one of these rulers.

This voice passed through a veil of silence and boomed inside my head. It told me what was at stake, where the winners stood and where the losers lay.

The great steamroller of time stalled when it reached Eton. In places you could see where progress had gained some ground, at the Music School or the School of Mechanics, but mostly you just noticed the old stone and stained-glass windows that stood like barricades against the years.

And I knew that now I had arrived, I could never leave this school behind. One look around me and I knew that you did not stop being an Etonian. Some people would use it as an insult and others as the highest praise they could find. Besides, it was one thing to wear a blue corduroy uniform like at the Dragon, but you couldn't come to Eton and dress up as a goddamned opera conductor for four years and not have that do something to you.

This was, it seemed to me, the all-time brotherhood, with its black-and-turquoise old school tie, so sacred it was hardly ever worn.

I had myself in tears the first morning of classes, trying to get dressed in the Eton uniform. The gold studs that attached the starch-stiff collar to my shirt kept popping loose. My sleeves hung down almost to the tips of my fingers. My trousers were too big, so I had to buy big clown-type suspenders for keeping them up.

The Lower Master, who we called the Lower Man, kept coming up to me and saying that my shoes weren't clean. The Lower Man was in charge of the junior boys in the school the same way that the Headmaster was in charge of the senior boys. The Lower Man had a nose like a hawk and eyes that stared straight through you. He'd come up from behind, so it was always a surprise when his arms slithered around your shoulder. He asked my name and my house and my tutor.

I didn't like polishing my shoes. I'd been in trouble for it at the Dragon School as well. So I went down the High Street, bought some floor polish and painted my shoes with the stuff. After that, the shoes would wink and blind me on a sunny day.

I learned about not doing up the bottom button on my waistcoat, and I learned that the tail-coats looked strange but were actually very comfortable.

We wore the uniform all day and every day. It wasn't like at the Dragon, where we had our Sunday best suits and then the blue corduroy for the rest of the week. When the weather got cold we had to buy old Army or Air Force greatcoats because it was a rule that our winter jackets had to cover the tails. The only coat that I could find came from a flea-market up in Slough. It was a grey Russian thing with red lining and a place for a sword to be worn.

On Saturday afternoons we could wear Standard Change. This

meant jacket and tie. But even here, there was kind of a uniform, because everyone wore Harris Tweed jackets, baggy corduroys and army sweaters. You had to wear Standard Change when you went down the High Street and crossed the bridge into Windsor, because there were people who would chase you and beat you up or throw you in the river if they knew you went to Eton. They were called Oiks or Camden Town Bootboys or sometimes the Great Unwashed. With them, there was no fooling around. If you didn't run, they'd kill you, and if you stayed to fight, they always had something to cut you with, like razors or Stanley knives or bits of broken bottle.

I was not a Pretty Boy. If I'd been pretty, I wouldn't have been last choice on the list of servants to the senior boys.

It was a tradition at Eton. All first year boys had to be servants to the senior boys.

In the end, the house captain took me on, to set some kind of example. His name was Sacker and, even though he was only eighteen, he looked so old to me that I kept calling him Mr Sacker. When he told me to call him George, I called him Mr George.

At 7.15 every morning, I made him a cup of coffee and then knocked on his bedroom door. I opened the window while he still lay in bed, sipping the coffee. Then while he was in the shower, I set out his clothes for the day.

After lunch, I had to stand outside the prefect room, which was called the Library although there were no books anywhere near it. If Sacker had a message that he wanted to send to someone in another house, he'd call me and I'd have to do the job. He gave me strangely-folded pieces of paper that were impossible to unwrap without tearing, in case I felt like reading what he wrote. All of the new boys had to wait outside the Library.

Then at tea-time, I made toast and coffee and tea for the senior boys. I spread marmalade or Bovril or lumpfish caviar on the toast and handed it over. Sometimes the senior boys got bored, made me spread peanut butter on bread slices, then had a competition to see who could throw the most slices at the wall and have them stick.

Another time, when it had snowed outside, I was given a dustbin and told to bring it back filled with snow. Once I'd done that, the senior boys had a snowball fight inside the Library.

If I was rude to them, they made me sit in the corner and eat tea bags.

There were fifty boys in Carter House and we each had our own room. The rooms were so small that our beds had to be folded up into the wall. But it was still better than being in a dorm.

I had been in my new room five minutes when a boy named Markby came in with a poster of Farah Fawcett. He said he'd sell it to me for two pounds. I didn't have any posters, so I bought the thing and then heard him laughing in the corridor that I had bought The Farah Fawcett Poster.

It turned out that the poster had been sold every year for the past five years to some new boy and it was believed to be the ugliest poster in creation.

Now that I looked at it, there was definitely something wrong with the picture. The lady had just finished some kind of a running race and she was standing at the finish line, covered in sweat. At first glance she maybe looked a little sexy, with her eyes screwed up and mouth hanging open. But when you studied it some more, you saw that she looked a little sick, as if any second she might drop to her knees and puke.

I spent my whole first year looking at Farah Fawcett on the verge of throwing up. Her expression seemed to change if I stared for long enough. Sometimes she was laughing at a bad joke, sarcastic, with her head tipped back and rolling her eyes. Other times I saw the glimmer of some passion in her face, then quickly she would be back to almost throwing up. I couldn't afford a new poster and it was better than looking at the blank wall, but not by much.

The boy who had been in the room before me came from India. He had painted the place Army green and lived off cans of Indian food he brought with him from home. I could still smell the food. It reminded me of the mixed-together and gone-rotten stench of the back alley behind Windy Acres Restaurant.

My window looked out at a brick wall. The wall was six feet away. Carter House was much older than the building opposite, so maybe there had once been a view from my room, perhaps quite a nice view. But now there was only the wall.

If I leaned out the window at about three in the afternoon, I could get sunlight on my face and sometimes shit on by a pigeon. The window was made up of diamond-shaped panes framed in lead. The frames were loose and on stormy nights the window-panes rattled like a wind chime made of bones.

It was the room right next to the prefects' Library, and that combined with the fact that I had bought The Farah Fawcett Poster did not help me at all.

Senior boys could stay up late in the Library and make all the noise that they wanted and no one could tell them to shut up. They had a record player but only one record, which was an old song by Manfred Mann's Earth Band about two people getting together over a glass of champagne. They played it maybe ten times a day and then a couple of times after dark.

I heard it when I was awake and in my sleep. I'd lie on my bed and rock my head back and forth like a mental patient, singing along with the music for the fifteenth time that day.

When the senior boys had wandered off to bed, I'd tiptoe in across spilled sugar and smashed light bulbs, past slices of bread still welded to the walls with peanut butter and the toaster smouldering in the corner like a clump of molten lava. I'd stuff my face with whatever food I could find. It was my revenge for them keeping me up half the night. I ate their marmalade and their lumpfish caviar with its taste like a mouthful of low-tide and I poured sugar on bread and ate that. I made cups of tea and stretched out on their beat-to-hell couches and listened to the train clatter on the tracks out by the river.

Sometimes I listened all the way through the night, until the electric-motored milk-floats puttered by, milk bottles jangling in their crates.

One of the first things you had to do was try out for the choir. It was compulsory. I waited in a line of boys, who walked one after the other into a soundproofed room at the Music School. When my turn came, the teacher banged one finger on a key and asked me to sing that note. He raised his eyes and looked at me, then hit the note again. Bong Bong Bong Bong.

'Bong Bong Bong Bong,' I sang.

'Don't say Bong, you idiot. Say La.'

'La la la la.'

His eyes narrowed for a moment. 'Are you putting any effort into this, at all?'

'Yes, sir. Lots.'

He told me to send in the next boy on my way out and that was it for me and the choir.

All the new boys in Carter House came from schools that I had never heard of. In the beginning, we followed each other around, to chapel and the dining-hall, and we huddled in each other's rooms for company. We flinched at the roar of men shouting in angry voices. At the Dragon, only the teachers had broken voices, but here the pupils did too, and they were roaring all the time.

After a few days, things began to split up. We saw each other's faults and pointed them out. I was a Yank and mostly in the lowest classes. Moriarty was overweight with a little Buddha-belly that made him walk funny. Wittingham looked like a girl, and what were all these fiddly little gadgets he kept in his room? Manson was ugly in a big-nosed spotty-faced way that even he could not deny.

Then there was Rupert Holiday, who didn't talk much and always carried a look on his face as if he had just woken up and didn't know where he was. He combed his hair with a harsh parting that let you see the whiteness of his scalp. If he'd been able to grow a moustache, he could have made money impersonating Adolf Hitler. When he wasn't wearing school uniform, he wore the kind of clothes that you see on old photographs of people out hunting or fishing in the country. Most of these clothes were so old and so ratty that you had to wonder if they weren't the same clothes that had been worn to pose for those photographs a century ago. As ratty as these clothes were, senior boys would often stop him in the street and ask him if his jacket wasn't a Gieves and Hawkes or if his umbrella wasn't a Swaine, Adeney and Brigg, or his shoes an old pair of Lobb's. I would stand there next to him while he gave the senior boy a lecture about how his grandfather had owned the jacket and his uncle the shoes, and I would look down at my own clothes and realize I was not the least bit surprised that no one asked me about them.

The rest of the time, Rupert Holiday strolled around with his hands in his pockets and hummed at the sky. The only thing that seemed to wake him from his walking coma was if someone started talking about the Labour Party. If you said a bad thing about it, he would look up and stare at you with sharp and focused eyes and say 'Damn right, too.' But if you said a good thing, his neck would get very red and he would call you a Bolshevik. He'd go on about people sponging off the state and not doing a day's work for a day's wages.

He knew a lot of names and had a lot of phrases which he punched out in the same monotone way that we said the Lord's Prayer all the time in chapel.

I didn't understand half of what he talked about, and had no wish to read the political magazines that he had mailed to him each week. I never talked politics with my friends in America. It would have been considered almost rude, the way it seemed rude to talk about money in England but which never bothered people back in America.

In the first few days I grew to like him, although he gave no sign of liking me or anyone else. He seemed entirely unimpressed by everything around him, as if he had always worn a tail-suit and as if his family at home was governed by as many rules and punishments as this school. I imagined him wandering the empty corridors of his mansion at home, scowling at the portraits of his ancestors and saying rude things to the servants. In spite of all this, I liked him because he seemed to be the only one of us who knew what he was doing here. It was as if he had been briefed in some quiet room away from the rest of the new boys, and he was taught what made this place work.

Wittingham's room looked like a hardware store. He had clamps and rolls of wire and nails and broken radios. He also had a TV, which he had told Mr Rosser didn't work. Mr Rosser fiddled with all the knobs and dials and convinced himself that this was true. Then as soon as he was out of the room, Wittingham flipped a switch somewhere in the tangle of wires, and the TV was working again. This didn't last long. Wittingham was discovered and the TV wheeled out of his room on a trolley, down the corridor and into Mr Rosser's part of the house. Wittingham followed the wobbly-wheeled trolley with gloom on his face, as if he was following a funeral procession.

I sat in Wittingham's room some afternoons while he took apart a radio and soldered it back together. He had rigged up an alarm system, which triggered if there was any loud noise in his room. So I sat very still, eyes closed but not sleeping.

Wittingham had friends from his old school. They would come by the room and speak in code and then laugh so much I got worried they were making jokes about me.

Wittingham was spindly-looking, with black and curly hair. He had the complexion of a girl, his cheeks all rosy and sparkle in his eyes. It looked to me as if he had once been a water-bird, like a heron, standing still at the edge of a lake on long and beanpole legs for hours at a time, then jabbing at fish that swam past.

He was popular with the older boys, because he was the prettiest. The members of the Library would often stop by his room. They stood in his doorway with their hands in their pockets and asked how he was getting on. Sometimes they would let him into the Library to boil water for the ugly-smelling health drink his mother sent with him to school. I wondered if perhaps he was like Kissack at the Dragon School, with some wretched disease that made him more fragile than the rest of us, and the senior boys were being kind to him not just because he was pretty but also because his days were numbered. Whatever the reason, it made us new boys jealous to see him getting all the attention, and privately we sulked in our rooms, looking at ourselves in the mirror and wondering what was wrong with us, inside and out.

I began to wonder if all of the houses were like this, or whether I had been put in a special place for people who were crippled in some way that didn't show in the beginning. But now we had all found each other out. Our deformities became the fuel for all our talking.

I didn't have any friends from the Dragon. There were Old Dragons here at Eton, but in the crush of new classes and houses and new friends, I hardly ever saw them. Soon their faces were like all the others, and we didn't even say hello any more.

I thought about Nightingale sometimes, although it never occurred to me to write to him. I wondered if he would ever make it here. I hoped he did, because it was tiring here the way people tried so hard to be in one group or another. They put more energy into teasing and ignoring people than we had ever done at the Dragon. At the Dragon, it had never seemed that serious. But here, I felt a coldness and a harshness that I'd never felt before. The same old Yankee jokes were different here because they really seemed to mean it.

There was no mail from home. I clattered down the stairs early every morning to see if there were any letters for me. Some days I would just stand there in front of the wall of letter slots, as if a letter might appear by magic. Then I stuck my hand in the slot and twisted it around, as if the space might only appear empty because of some optical illusion. But it always was empty. The only thing that came from that slot in my first few months at school was the dust that I wiped from my hand.

I stopped thinking about my father being sick. I just put it out of my mind. I convinced myself that no letters was a good sign. No news is good news, I told myself, and believed it.

It wasn't hard to put away my thoughts of home. America and everyone in it had always belonged to a different world, lying far away in space as well as time. Over the years at the Dragon, I had trained myself to think that way. It was either that, or go mad from homesickness. There was nothing at Eton to remind me of home, and sometimes in class I would imagine that I'd made the whole thing up and all my transatlantic memories had no more substance than the rice-paper thinness of a dream.

All first year boys were called Bugs. Sometimes they called us Tits, as well.

Second year boys weren't called anything. I saw from the start that this was the worst year to be. They had been at Eton too long to find the school new and interesting, but not long enough to have any privileges. Mostly they fought amongst each other for privileges that they made up amongst themselves.

In the third year, you could be a junior prefect, which was called Debate, although they never did any debating. All they did was patrol the corridors at night to make sure the new Bugs and Tits had their lights out on time. If they caught anyone, they had the right to set punishments. Usually they wouldn't set you work. They might swear at you for making their job more difficult, or they might unscrew your light bulb and take it with them so you'd have no way of reading and you'd also have to go into town and buy a new bulb the next day. When they did set punishments, it was usually fifty lines. They wouldn't even say what fifty lines, so you could make it up for yourself. The only time I ever asked what to write, the prefect increased it to a hundred lines for being insolent. The worst punishment they could set you was called a Georgic. It was about 500 lines and would bugger an entire weekend. The more unpopular the prefect, the more likely he was to set you a punishment. All the punishments I ever got came from one boy named Markby. He was the one who sold me The Farah Fawcett Poster, which was not a good way to make friends.

Markby was scrawny, which made you want to beat him up when he burst into your room thirty seconds after your light was supposed to be turned out and set you a hundred lines. Then he'd stand there shaking with anticipation, hoping you would insult him so he could double the punishment. People in his own block did slap him around, and whenever they felt like it. It seemed to be the rule that all you had to do was announce an excuse, no matter how far-fetched, and then you could tickle him half to death or mess up his hair or beat him with a cushion. All these slapping-arounds had given him the habit of walking with his hands criss-crossed in front of his balls. I supposed they slapped him there, too. All you had to do was shout out his name or even say 'Boo', and his hands would snap down to his Cobblers and protect them. He'd drop his books or his mug of tea or whatever he was carrying. And he couldn't set you a punishment for saying 'Boo.'

At the top of the house were the senior prefects. The Members of the Library. Everything was sacred in the Library. There was the Sacred Toaster and the Sacred Teapot and the Sacred Poster of Marilyn Monroe, her smile almost hidden behind splats of peanut butter and dried-up bits of caviar. Then Sacker brought in a thing called a Super Sandwich Grill, which let you squash things between two bits of bread and fry whatever was inside. The Super Sandwich Grill was the Most Sacred of All Things, and it made you a little nervous to see how much they adored it. Then it broke and there was much lamenting, followed by anger as they threw it around the room, making dents in the walls.

I gave up trying to understand the senior boys. Sometimes they would walk right past you and not say hello and other times they would grab you by the arms and laugh and ask if you were happy here.

Sacker already had a pot belly from beer drinking. He was Captain of the Eight, which was the rowing team and one of the most prestigious things you could be in the school. I often saw him clumping blind drunk up the stairs in his pale blue rowing sports jacket with the white silk trim and fleur-de-lis on the chest pocket. He left his razor stubble in the sink every morning, as if to show that no one else was as stubbly as him. Only Sacker could have been House Captain. It was his voice that clinched the matter, the same kind of voice as the Headmaster of the Dragon, which seemed to begin somewhere down by his knees and come rumbling up his ribs until it boomed out of him like the engine of a Bedford truck. The other thing that clinched it was that he never seemed to finish his sentences. Always his words collapsed into muttering, which made you feel as if he had just decided that you weren't worth talking to anymore.

Sacker ruled over Villiers, whose clothes were always clean and who walked off to the train station in Windsor every Saturday afternoon, wearing a silk Ascot and shoes polished by one of the junior boys. He had a woman up in London, who he always referred to as Swish Trish Delish, and when he came back from London, he had Wittingham, who was his personal servant that year. The dark green Fortnum's truck was always squeaking its brakes outside our house and men dressed almost as well as Villiers brought in hampers of food. Then the usual Viking roaring in the Library would suddenly fall silent, as they stuffed their faces with smoked salmon and brie. You couldn't put down Villiers, couldn't viper-strike at the core of what he took most seriously because he didn't seem to take anything very seriously. He was the best footballer in the house and even though he smoked so much that his fingers were stained yellow, he could still run faster than anyone else in the senior year. Sometimes Villiers reminded me a little of my dad, because he didn't seem to care what other people thought of him and because by doing only a few things extremely well, he made it seem as if he was good at everything.

There were others who made up the house that became a group of their own, even though they weren't friends or even in the same block. These were the Unpopulars, who didn't get elected into Debate or the Library, who weren't pretty or good at music or sports. They weren't even clever, which counted for a lot less than skill at sports, but it counted all the same.

Each year had one or two Unpopulars. It seemed to me that they didn't all share one ugly trait, so that you could pick them out of a crowd by the way they looked or walked or spoke. But some ugliness that they had all to themselves would push them to the fringes of the house and they would stay there, sad and angry, until they left and disappeared from Eton.

It was cruel, but you couldn't afford to get near these unpopular people. Their ugliness rubbed off on you, and soon you might find yourself out at the fringe of the house with no way to work your way back. The other thing I found about them was that most were not loyal friends. They knew they were out on the fringe, and if they thought they could get ahead by telling some gossip about you or by saying a clever thing that was rude about you, they would do it and not think twice. Then instead of them, it might be you out there on the fringe and in the cold.

So you had to have a coldness in yourself. You had to know everyone but choose only a few friends and choose them very carefully. I learned this as soon as I arrived at Eton. Of all the rules I learned and later threw away, this one I kept. If you did not know it, you could get hurt very badly at a place like Eton.

At the end of the first week, the new boys filed into the Library to take the Colours Test. Each house and team in the school had their own set of colours, for wearing on blazers and cricket sweaters and on the brims of their panama hats in the summer. There seemed to be hundreds of teams and on top of the colours, some of them had symbols like caducei or fleurs-de-lis.

In the Library they shone bright lights in our faces and threw darts at our feet when we gave a wrong answer. At first I thought it was all a joke and I laughed. But then a dart stuck in my foot and I stopped laughing.

I failed the Colours Test. A prefect hidden away somewhere in the smoke asked me what went up Judy's Passage, which was an alleyway than ran between two nearby houses. I didn't know that the answer to this joke was supposed to be Lupton's Tower, which was the main building in the centre of the school. So I failed the test and kept failing it promptly every Sunday afternoon at two o'clock until the senior boys got bored of quizzing me.

On that day Sacker looked at me with pity on his face. 'I suppose you'd better bugger off,' he said.

A lot stayed the same between Eton and the Dragon School. It had the same smells of sweat and boot polish and books. The food was the same – hard-boiled eggs on Sundays, chewy Brussels sprouts and floppy slabs of meat for Sunday lunch. The same uncontrollable anger flared up in me when I opened my window one morning and a reek of kippers ploughed into my face.

The classwork was harder. I had been in the second highest class at the Dragon, bottom of it in almost everything, but still high up in the classes. At Eton, I found myself at the bottom of the lowest class in almost everything. The idea of having good grades seemed so far away that I stopped even trying to reach them. Mostly I just daydreamed, letting my thoughts drift away over the fields beyond the classrooms like a cloud of dandelion seeds.

In sports I was bettered prepared. The Old Dragons at Eton had a reputation for being thugs, and in the beginning I was quite content to be a member of that shin-barking, nose-punching and elbow-jabbing club.

Even with my bad grades, the Dragon School had built me for this place. Much of what made sense there made sense here, even if it seemed to make no sense anywhere else. It had its own language, the way the Dragon had a language, and it was only a question of learning how things were renamed.

If I had not been to the Dragon, it would have upset me to get punished for walking around with my umbrella fastened shut. Nobody told me, but a school prefect called a Popper came up and gave me a hard time about it, saying only Poppers were allowed to keep their umbrellas fastened. He had on black-and-white hound's tooth trousers, silk piping on his tail-coat, a green velvet waistcoat, and a stick-up collar with a bow-tie. That was the Popper uniform, except that they could wear whatever kind of waistcoat they wanted, so some of them were bright blue or yellow and I once saw one with Donald Duck printed on it.

And that same day I got busted for sitting on a low stone wall in front of the school yard. Only Poppers were allowed to do that, as well. Later in the week I was fined 50p, which was all my money in the world, for going into a shop to buy a newspaper. A prefect was waiting for me when I came out. He said the shop was 'ill-advised' because they sometimes sold cigarettes to boys. I showed him that I didn't have any cigarettes but he told me it didn't matter.

I was punished for not Capping, which meant that I was supposed to raise my right index-finger whenever I walked past a teacher. It was left over from the days when boys wore top-hats and touched their hat brims whenever a teacher walked by. There were no more top-hats, I was told, because during the war when the air-raid sirens went, boys would stumble around looking for their hats rather than running for the shelters. The punishment for being caught outside without a hat was severe and the boys were so conditioned to it that they didn't think about the Germans in their bombers overhead. So no more top-hats. But you still had to pretend that you had one and you still pretended to touch the brim.

Now instead of pillow-waving dorm raids, there were Prefect raids. Markby took away my radio, which I had been allowed to own during my last year at the Dragon. I had to wait another three years before I was allowed to keep a radio at Eton.

Those things made me angry, but not upset. I knew from my time at the Dragon that sometimes rules would surface which nobody told you about. The only thing to do was obey them.

I got up early for breakfast. I didn't like coming into the dining-hall when the tables were already scattered with rice crispies and spilled tea.

Moriarty got up, too. He'd pick up his horse-racing paper every morning and wander across the road to the dining-hall. He walked like a baby, with strange, plodding steps and his Buddha-belly sticking out, so that I kept expecting him to fall smack down on his butt the way babies do.

Moriarty was almost always first outside the dining-hall. He leaned against the door while he waited for it to open, reading his horsepaper in the damp and foggy autumn mornings.

He liked to be first into the hall. There was something about being the first. For every subject, he was in higher classes than me and maybe he had a thing about being first in them, too. It was like that for some people at the Dragon School, howling with tears if they didn't get top marks at the end of the term.

It annoyed me, seeing him leaning all smug and baby-legged up against the door, every time I crossed the road for breakfast. I found myself getting up at 6.30 in the morning, just to be at the dining-hall before him and get a look at his face when he walked out of the house.

It seemed that a lot of things Moriarty did were designed to get on people's nerves. When Rupert got into one of his tempers about the Labour Party, it was usually because Moriarty had said how we were the Ignorant Privileged Class and were all born with silver spoons in our mouths. He said we had no clue how the rest of the world really lived and how Rupert had no right to make pronouncements on a hard day's work because he had never done a hard day's work. One time he asked us all to lay our hands on the table, palm-up, so we could see how there wasn't a single callus on any of our fingers, except for a permanent dent in our middle finger from years of holding a fountain pen.

I kept my mouth shut, because if I spoke for either side, both sides would come down on me for being an American. Then the whole subject would shift and they'd forget about the Labour Party.

Once the Dame, who was like the senior matron of our house, sat down at our table in the middle of one of these arguments. We all shut up straight away.

Then Rupert asked her what she thought of the Labour Party.

Her eyelids fluttered a little. Then she said 'Goodness, look at the time' and got up and left.

The Dame lived in a room between us and Mr Rosser's. It was a kind of no man's land. Every house had a Dame. I heard ours had lost her husband one Christmas Eve when he stepped out to buy a paper and disappeared. They found him a long time later, dead in a ditch from a heart attack. After that, she came to work at Eton.

She spoke with the same blustering voice that old soldiers sometimes have.

You had to call her Ma'am, pronounced Marm. It was short for My Dame or M'dame. Wittingham called her M'Tits, and not without reason. When she walked down the corridor, it often looked to me as if she had stashed two Zeppelins under her sweater.

Sometimes in the evenings, she sat on the couch in her room and smoked Havana cigars. And not just little cheroots, either. They were fat Churchill cigars as long as my outstretched hand. The smoke wound dry and sweet along our corridor, and we breathed it in through the keyholes.

Then Villiers, slumped drunk on a crumb-covered couch in the Library down the hall, would start up in a low and growly imitation-Churchill voice. 'We shall fight them on the beaches! We shall fight them on the landing fields. We shall never surrender!'

I'd heard stories about boys falling in love with the Dames, even though these women were old enough to be our grandmothers. In one house, Villiers told me, a boy named Fagan walked up to his Dame and said – 'Oh, Baby, my heart is on fire.'

Underneath the Dame were the Boysmaids. They cleaned up and guarded the communal toaster at tea time. Each floor on a house had a Boysmaid.

Ours was Mrs Sawbridge. She had a limp because she caught some German shrapnel in her leg during an air raid over London. And her head had sunk down a little into her neck, as if she kept expecting another squadron of Luftwaffe planes to carpet-bomb the school. She pushed her trolley up and down the corridor with her one stiff leg. It sounded like several things moving along at once. Squeak, squeak, thump, step.

When I first heard her speak, I thought she was making a joke of her voice. It sounded like one of those little mouth harps that had once been a craze at the Dragon. Boing Boing Boing.

We didn't have to be polite to the Boysmaids, so everyone was rude instead.

I remembered Charlotte from the Dragon, and I wondered where she was now. Sometimes when I heard Mrs Sawbridge and her trolley scooting past my door, I tried to imagine it was Charlotte, with her beautiful long legs and glinting eyes, but that took more imagination than I owned.

At first I never seemed to have time to write. It left me with a strange and churned stomach feeling as ideas for stories drifted past me like dandelion seeds in the breeze and I let them slip through my fingers and disappear. For a while, I wondered if the writing had just been a hobby, no more than a private craze amongst all the public crazes at the Dragon. But then I began to settle in to the rhythm of this new school, and found myself able to chisel out an hour here or there.

And then at night, setting out in the great full-sail schooners of my dreams as sleep veered in towards me, I knew that I would always be writing. I knew it as an instinct, whose meaning I was only just beginning to uncover, like someone peering inside an Egyptian tomb and slowly deciphering the pictures on its walls.

CHAPTER 7

I SAT NEXT to Rupert through the long autumn afternoons of our Latin classes.

We stared without understanding at a book about a man called Erasmus Rotterdamus. The book was all about how he travelled around Europe complaining how you couldn't find a good hotel anywhere and how the rooms were always draughty and then about how he drank himself stupid every night with a kind of drink called a Posset. Rupert had searched through it for some kind of codeword that he might have used to show he was actually enjoying himself. But there was nothing. Erasmus Rotterdamus pissed and moaned his way from country to country and never seemed to pay for anything.

We tried to guess how many times Mr Brundish had taught this same course. There was graffiti about him in the margins of our books which dated back to the 1960s. Sometimes he cracked a joke if Erasmus had knocked down too many Possets, but his voice stayed dull and humourless. Rupert said this was because he had made the same joke so many times that he didn't even get it any more. Rupert bet me that Brundish probably had special stars inked into his own book, showing where he should make a joke.

Mostly, Mr Brundish was furious and had no time for jokes. He would look down from his podium desk far above us, yell 'God give me strength!', and tear up his list of test questions. He would throw them up in the air and the confetti of paper fluttered down on me and Rupert in the front row. There were times I didn't blame him for being angry at us. When it came to Erasmus, we were all pretty stupid, and I hated the tough red book with its brittle pages and ink stains. Rupert and I sat watching the dreary October sky through the dusty-paned windows and could hardly see our books because it was getting so dark. But Mr Brundish made no move to turn on the lights. He seemed to like it better in the shadows.

After class, Rupert and I ran to the school tuck shop, called Rowlands. We ate powder-covered bon-bons and chips and drank Idris Ginger Beer that made us sneeze.

By now, Rupert and I were spending most of our time together. Half of this was coincidence, as we were both in the same low classes. But in our free time on the weekends, we also kept each other company, wandering through Windsor and often going all the way to the bottom of Peascod Street where there was a cheese shop. Rupert was very fond of cheese, and I would stand in the sour-smelling shop while Rupert sampled what seemed to me to be hundreds of different cheeses. I could see the shop owner getting more and more annoyed at Rupert, especially since Rupert would take so long with each sample, gnawing on it with his front teeth like a rabbit and then giving me and everyone else a lecture about that particular cheese. He seemed to know and love everything about cheese except paying for it. He would leave the shop an hour later with a sliver of this or that and then we would go to the bakery, where Rupert would prod and squeeze different loaves of bread until he had the one he wanted and the rest had been mangled.

Then we'd go back up Peascod Street, stopping at the coffee shop to buy beans. We'd stand in front of the wall of drawers that held the different types of beans, both of us drugged with the smell of roasting coffee.

Back at the house, Rupert made the coffee in an ancient pot which had to be turned upside down a couple of times for the water to soak through the grinds. This involved an elaborate swinging motion that looked to me like a dance step from an African tribal ritual. Rupert would not let anybody else flip his coffee pot, explaining that it was a very complicated operation that took years of practice. Still, he usually managed to spray me and the wall and his bed with coffee while he was busy being such an expert. I said he should buy a new coffee pot, maybe one of those that keeps the coffee warm, but he glared at me as if I had just farted instead of making a decent suggestion.

Everything was a kind of ritual with Rupert, which was another way of saying that he spent twice as much time as he should have in doing anything and always seemed to have a very long and involved reason for doing it. I saw this in the way he rolled up his newspaper and jammed it under his arm before heading across the road to the dining-hall. I saw it in the way he buttoned his trench-coat and the elaborate way he tied the belt. It was in the precise way he lopped the top off a hard-boiled egg and the way he measured out the sugar for putting into his tea, sliding his finger over the spoon to level out the measure.

I couldn't have said I was friends with Rupert yet. Couldn't have said anyone was friends with him, and he seemed to like it that way. He was too caught up in the causes that he had read about in the paper and taken up the way a missionary takes up Jesus. And the way Rupert saw things, people were always insulting him in one way or another. The people who insulted him usually had no idea what they had done wrong, and Rupert would be so appalled at their behaviour that he couldn't even begin to explain. One day things would be fine and the next he would be in a huff, and only then would you know that you had crossed the line.

Sometimes it seemed to me that Rupert was doing everything he could to become a grumpy old man before he turned sixteen. He even smoked a pipe, with no tobacco in it of course because there was no tobacco allowed at the school. Rupert, on some interior logic, agreed that there should be no cigarettes, but insisted that we should be allowed to smoke pipes or 'good quality cigars'. Fearing another lecture and possibly even an insult, I did not ask him what cigars were good.

When his three page long cigar-and-pipe petition failed to have any effect on Mr Rosser, Rupert decided that he would 'pretend' to smoke his pipe as a way of silent protest.

Many Saturday evenings, after we had eaten all the bread and cheese and drunk all the coffee, I sat in his window-sill, looking out across the school and making notes for stories, letting my mind race off and then putting on the brakes while I took down whatever ideas it had come across. Rupert lay on his bed, reading the paper, pipe jammed in his mouth and making tiny whistling sounds as he breathed through it. Rupert never asked what it was that I wrote down in my black notebook with the band of red tape around it so I could find the book more easily amongst the clutter of my desk. I think one of the reasons he did not ask was that he knew I would have wanted him to. But there may have been other grounds, and Rupert was good about minding his own business.

Another reason I stayed with Rupert was that I kept waiting for him to drop his guard, to show that he was really just like everyone else. But the guard never dropped. With Rupert, you got what you saw, and he was the only person I had ever met about whom you could honestly say that.

The first time that I had any indication of Rupert doing anything more than just tolerating my existence, was when an ice-cream van pulled up outside the Eton Library one weekend afternoon.

Boys crowded around and bought the kind of blinding white soft ice-cream with an aftertaste that tells you this stuff has not one natural ingredient. The ice-cream man was Turkish. He said his name was Roderick.

'I have a feeling this man isn't going to be around for very long,' Rupert said.

I nodded and saw how each boy moved away from the van as soon as he had bought his ice-cream. We did not know if there was a rule against people selling ice-cream on school grounds, but instinctively we thought that there had to be.

Roderick the ice-cream man may not have known that, but we did. I saw it in the grim faces of the people on the line, as if they knew they might not get served before the Lower Master came charging out of his house and told the man to disappear. In the beginning of my time at Eton, the Lower Man was the Great Red Dragon, like the one on the Welsh flag. Y Ddraig Goch, the Welsh called it. Without him, the school became only a tangle of books and stone and bronze and iron made for war or to commemorate it. He was the keeper of the gates. When strangers came, they had first to get past him, like this ice-cream man was trying to do.

It didn't take the Lower Man very long. I stood with Rupert, leaning against the huge black cannon that had been dragged back from the siege at Sebastopol by some Old Etonians and I saw the Lower Man rush across the road, still wearing his Master's gown. He looked like a huge bat trying to take off.

He scattered the boys in the line the way you can scatter pigeons pecking at breadcrumbs in the park. I hid behind the cannon, stuffing the last of the ice-cream down my throat because we could be Busted for eating food in the street. Rupert refused to hide and was about to tell me in great detail why he refused, when I dragged him into cover.

I heard the Lower Man talking to Roderick and then I heard him shouting. The Lower Man tried to shut Roderick's window and Roderick tried to keep it open. Then I heard Roderick tell the Lower Man to Fuck Off and I knew this would get meaty.

'I must say,' Rupert whispered to me, comfortable now in our hiding-place behind the cannon, 'that if you were an ice-cream man and didn't know who the Lower Man was, it still takes some balls to tell him to fuck off. Wouldn't you say?'

I agreed, surprised because this was the first time he had ever asked my opinion on anything before. It seemed to me that being the Lower Master was as much a state of mind as it was anything else. He walked fast with his head held high, eyes fixed on the horizon. His eyes were the kind of blue you only get from an electric current.

Roderick stayed for a while longer after the Lower Man had gone away. Now and then, his giant Afro'd head would poke out of the ice-cream van's window, past the neon-coloured list of Mivvies and Lollies and Cones. He couldn't figure out where all the boys had gone. Maybe he saw me and Rupert, peeking from around the Sebastopol cannon, but not daring to cross the open space of ground between us and his van. He saw others, too, looking down sadly from their rooms, as sad for themselves as they were for Roderick. Because nobody told the Lower Master to Fuck Off without seeing that Great Red Dragon rear its head, unleash its bayonet claws and furnace-breath and come toward you in its armour-plated skin.

A while later, I read an interview with the Lower Master. In it he said that when he was away from the school, he sometimes didn't tell people that he taught at Eton. Instead he'd only tell them it was a school near Windsor. I was sad when I read that, because not to say you were at Eton was to be ashamed of the place, and of all the people who should not have been ashamed, the Lower Man was first on my list. If I had been the Lower Man, I would always have said I taught at Eton. And if the people who asked me didn't like it, then I'd have given them the same glacier stare that he saved for people like the ice-cream man. It was a stare that could shatter your face.

Finally when it got dark, Roderick slid his window shut and rode away, ringing his ice-cream bell on the way back up to Slough. We figured that was that.

But Roderick was back the next day. Same time. Same place.

Rupert was impressed. 'Either this Turk is very ballsy or he's stupid in a way that, as the Reverend keeps saying, "surpasseth all understanding".'

I got in line with Rupert and we had a petition shoved in our face before we could buy any ice-cream. At the top of the page was – Stay Rodrick at Eton!!!

The boys in front signed and then Rupert signed and I signed, too. I paid for my soft ice-cream and turned to leave. Then something caught my eye. It was the names on the list.

I read – Winston Churchill. Joseph Stalin. George Orwell. Someone had signed the Lower Master's name. Rupert just wrote – Pavarotti. And then, in big, easy-to-read letters, I read – Paul Watkins.

'I'm dead, aren't I?' I asked Rupert on the way back to house.

'Quite possibly.'

'You're a cold-hearted bugger, Rupert. *Pavarotti*.'

'I would have thought you'd try for an American hero, like Al Capone or Billy the Kid. Would you like a game of chess when we get back to House?'

'Chess? How can you talk about chess when you know I'm about to get dragged up in front of the Lower Man? He'll probably breathe fire on me and there'll be nothing left but ashes.'

'Yes, but there's nothing you can do about it now, so you might as well get in a good game of chess before the axe drops.'

We did not have long to wait. Markby walked into my room in the middle of the chess game. 'Rosser wants you.' He was grinning like a skull. I wanted to kill him.

Mr Rosser called me into his study. He had a xerox of the list on his desk. He pushed it around with his little finger, the way a cat pushes around a bug that is pretending to be dead. 'Now, Watkins. What's all this about you signing a list? The Lower Master is very upset. He said he wants to know exactly what is going on here.'

I told him I didn't know. When he flipped up the list for me to see, I said it was some kind of joke. Then I screwed up my eyebrows. 'I hope I catch the person who did this to me, sir.'

Mr Rosser's eyes opened wide. 'I say,' he said. And then again, 'I say.' He seemed to be paralysed, as if I could go away and come back tomorrow and there he'd be, eyes wide open, the list still in his hand.

But he snapped out of it. 'I should jolly well hope you do catch them. Give them a good wallop, too. We can't have people signing any lists of a bloody Lolly Man from Slough.'

When Rupert heard the story, he set down his paper and sat back in his comfy chair. He tugged the pipe out of his mouth. 'That was fairly inspired.'

'*Fairly*? Oh, Rupert, now don't get all gushy on me.'

He reached out his leg and jabbed me in the thigh with the toe of his highly polished shoe. 'Things would be boring without you around.'

I knew he liked me then, and could not stop the smile from spreading on my face. Being jabbed in the leg by Rupert was as close as I had seen him come to an expression of Maximum Joy.

Sometimes I couldn't sleep at night, especially after drinking coffee with Rupert all evening. So I'd write stories in bed by flashlight under my blankets, while Markby stalked the halls outside like some rubber-legged Vampire. I wrote on scraps of A4 writing paper and kept them in a file.

At the Dragon, the writing had seemed more like a game. When its newness wore off, I treated it like a hobby. But now I began to feel as if I needed to keep writing. I needed the escape it gave me, from the pasty face of Erasmus Rotterdamus, from failing the Colours Test, and from that damn record the Library kept playing over and over again.

It was the only thing at this place that I did for myself. Everything else seemed tied into my failing grades and the constant struggle to be popular.

There were no girls at Eton. Once in a while, a housemaster's daughter studied at the school, but that was rare. I did not hear girls talked about very much. They remained more beautiful ideas than anything that actually existed. Even to dwell on them woke something inside us that we tried to keep asleep. It rushed through our senses in the way I imagined it might be to breathe the white dust of cocaine.

Rupert and I almost never spoke of girls. He seemed to avoid the subject entirely.

I couldn't imagine Rupert with a girl, or with a boy, either. He let it be known that, as far as he was concerned, sex was a grubby, clumsy business and he had better things to do.

But being clumsy and grubby was just fine with the rest of us, and sex of any kind at all looked good to Wittingham. By now, everyone knew that Villiers was in love with him, and Villiers often took him to restaurants in town where they ate truffle pâté and roast duck and drank the orange-labelled bottles of Veuve Clicquot champagne. We asked Wittingham if he was in love with Villiers and he said no, but none of us believed him. They were serious about each other. The truth was that no one seemed to find it particularly strange that Villiers could be in love with Swish Trish Delish up in London and also with Wittingham here at school.

And it was the same for Wittingham. One day, I walked into Wittingham's room and found Villiers lying in bed with him. They were reading the paper together. Villiers ran his fingers through Wittingham's hair and Wittingham pretended not to notice.

Another boy named Elliot also fell in love with Wittingham and wrote him a long letter to say so. Wittingham threw the letter away, and somehow Manson got hold of it. This was about the worst thing that could have happened to the letter and to Elliot. It took weeks for the gossip to die down.

There was a joke running around the house that Wittingham and Villiers wore each other's underpants, except it wasn't a joke. Wittingham had once shown me Villiers' nametag on the boxers he was wearing.

There were a lot of things I used to think were jokes, and laughed about and thought crude. Villiers would slap Wittingham on the butt and then Villiers would slap him back. It was all a joke, but people would laugh a little too long and sometimes I'd see them winking at each other. Then they'd start laughing at me.

I'd heard the rumours about what they did together, but really I never believed them. The whole business started to get on my nerves.

Rupert had all kind of theories about this, the same as with everything else. He said that at school, it was far too risky to mess about with either boys or girls. The safest thing, he told anyone who would listen, was to bury your face in a porn mag and hope that you didn't get caught.

There was a boy named Harrison and he was the Porn-Mag King. His tail-coat might have fitted him when he first arrived at school, but now he had grown out of it and the seams were splitting as his back grew broader and his sharp elbows jabbed through the black cloth. It seemed to be held together with safety-pins.

People said he had hundreds of magazines, some of them so rude that they weren't even printed in English and others even ruder with no writing on them at all, just pictures.

Any brain-twisted, tied-up, whipped, threesome, foursome, two men and a woman or two women and a goddamned fire-hydrant fantasy that you could think up, Harrison would have the right magazine for you.

He carried a black brief-case, which was unusual since most of us just carried our books in our arms. I heard that the brief-case was what he used to transport mags from one house to the other. He couldn't afford to have too many strangers coming to his room, so he made house calls like a doctor. Some people called him Dr Love.

He was one of those boys you could stare at and he would know you were staring at him, but he would never catch your eye. I wondered if maybe it was a lie, that someone had stuck him with the Porn King label and made his life a misery.

But then when I saw him again in the street, shifty-eyed and his hair slicked back with something that made him smell like an old coconut, I knew it had to be true.

Now and then a porn mag would find its way down through the ranks of older boys to us at the bottom of the house. They were the tamest, dog-eared old magazines with fuzzy pictures and political articles thrown in, so a person could try the lame excuse that they were only reading it for the articles and have some fool-hope of being believed.

It was always Wittingham who seemed to get hold of them first. He and Manson and I all had tea in my room every day. We would be sitting huddled over my desk at tea-time and Wittingham would suddenly get up and shut the door. That meant either drink, smoke or sex. Nothing else was worth closing the door for. He would pull the magazine from his tail-coat and grin with his eyes narrowed into slits.

Sometimes it didn't matter what the pictures were. It was just the knowledge that this was a porn mag, that didn't try to pillow any naked flesh in lectures of true love or fidelity. This was straight-up Tits and Bums.

You couldn't afford to look too desperate when Wittingham pulled out a mag. If you let your eyes bug out of your head, or grabbed the mag and ran out of the room as Manson had once done, soon enough a boy at the very top of the house whose name you hardly knew would be pointing at you and whispering the gossip to one of his friends. And with their laughter would come the tightness of shame in your throat and the blood boiling hot in your face.

So you had to wait until everyone else had finished pawing it. Then you might pick it up casually and say something about how you had seen a lot worse than this. I once told Wittingham that I had seen a mag with five women and a zebra and he offered me money if I'd show him the pictures.

It was no good offering money for a mag. Even if you could keep up the face of not-caring about it and the lie that you had seen a lot worse, if you handed over cash for one of these ratty old things so creased it looked as if a spider had made a web over the pictures, then it showed you were more desperate than anyone. Because handing out money meant that you owned it and you wanted the women for yourself, almost as if they were real.

After you had casually asked to borrow the mag off Wittingham, you could look at it after lights out and after Markby had finished his rounds. It was terrible to be caught with a porn mag. If you were caught by a boy, it usually didn't go much further unless it was someone like Markby. He would take you downstairs and dump you in your pyjamas at Mr Rosser's study door.

Worst of all was if Mr Rosser himself caught you. He never tried to catch anyone, and I think it was more embarrassing for him than it was for us, but sometimes he'd walk right into a boy's room and find him ripping out from the back of a mag the price list for turbo-powered vibrators, with names like The Orgasmatron. Not that the boy meant to buy one, but perhaps it was the only page left where the print was still legible.

I almost got caught one time. I think I *was* caught, but for some reason Rosser let me off the hook. Maybe he was tired that day. He burst into my room with a big 'Hello' and I only had time to stuff the magazine under my pillow. He sat on my bed and talked to me about my work, hands folded in his lap, while I nodded fiercely and agreed with everything he said, knowing that if I moved at all, the magazine would rustle under my pillow.

When he left the room I collapsed, because the blood had run out of my elbows and my hands had fallen asleep. That was when I noticed that a whole page of the mag was sticking out from under the pillow. It said – 12 weeks of *Yes, Please* Magazine for Men for only 7.95. Over Half Off The Newsagent's Price! It even offered a free calendar with every subscription. With All Your Favourite *Yes, Please* Girls, it said.

I got down on my knees and beat my head against the floor.

I figured I would be thrown out, the way I had already seen one boy go, for his third time caught smoking in a month. His sheets were stripped and mattress rolled up and tied at the end of his bed. Desk emptied. Posters ripped off the wall so that all that remained were the corners, stuck with blue putty on the paint. Parents notified. I would rather had been shoved up against the wall and punched senseless by the Headmaster himself than have my parents told about me looking at *Yes, Please* magazine.

Rupert said it served me right.

I plucked that stubby little pipe out of his mouth and threw it out the window. It stuck like a bulb-ended arrow in Mr Rosser's flower bed.

'I suppose I asked for that,' Rupert admitted.

Nothing happened to me about the *Yes, Please* magazine and slowly the fear left my bones, but a week later Mr Rosser gave us all a lecture in prayers about pornography. He said it was a Plastic Primrose and not the real thing at all.

This much we already knew.

He talked on for a long time, but I didn't hear what he said. The words Plastic and Primrose kept echoing in my head. I tried to picture it – a plastic flower faded in the sun and stuck in some old bud vase on a dusty window-sill.

On my way out of the prayers room I heard Villiers say – 'Well, if he'd like to hand his wife around for a quick one twice a week, he wouldn't have a porn mag problem.'

'Yeah,' Sacker said. 'And not even the whole house, mind you. We could make it a Library privilege.'

'If you want to call it that.'

There was a porn mag epidemic. They appeared in the house like locusts. We even started calling them Primroses.

One day at tea, Wittingham shut the door and talked about going to Harrison. We all slapped down a pound to pay for the worst, most porny porn mag in Harrison's collection. We drew straws and I lost. I said the whole thing was rigged, so we drew again and I lost a second time.

'Go for the one with the biggest tits,' said Wittingham.

But Manson wanted to see people tied up.

'I just assumed any healthy person would want to see the biggest tits.' Wittingham took his pound off the table. 'I'm not paying if I don't get to see big tits.'

So it was big tits.

I had to find Harrison and ask him. I said I wasn't going straight to his room like some porn addict and everyone agreed that would look bad. I'd find him on the street and ask him there.

It seemed as if Harrison used to be everywhere, but now he had disappeared. I kept my eyes out for his black brief-case and the stench of rotten coconut, but he had vanished.

Each day at tea-time, the door would be slammed shut and all eyes turned towards me. I'd be grilled about why I hadn't found Harrison. Wittingham said that if I hadn't tracked him down by the end of the week, I'd have to go to his room.

'Or we'll make up some rumour about you and spread it,' Manson said. That was Manson's way of doing business.

The next day I saw Harrison walking off the Rugby fields. His game had finished at the same time as ours.

Harrison had on his house colours, black and red with a skull stitched to the chest. His knees were bloody and pasted with mud. He walked by himself, eyes fixed on his boots.

I walked beside him for a while, swinging my legs out to keep pace with him. My heart was trying to kick its way out of my chest. 'Are you Harrison?' I asked him.

'What do you want?' He didn't even look up.

'I got three pounds and I want a porn mag with big tits. The biggest you've got.' Wittingham had made me promise to say that part.

Now he looked at me. 'Who are you?'

I told him my name was Manson.

'What house are you in?'

I told him.

'It'll cost you more than three quid.'

'More?' I shouted, not able to help myself. 'That's a lot of cash!'

'It'll cost you six.' Then before I could snort at him again, he added, 'I've got just the one for you.'

It was set up for me to meet him out behind Bekynton dining-hall at seven o'clock that evening. By then it would be dark.

Manson and I made Wittingham cough up the extra money.

Dead leaves blew down the alleyway as I waited in the dark for Harrison. Boys shambled into supper, hands in pockets, looking at their shoes. There had practically been a riot the day before, when we were served Spam Fritters twice in a row. There was not much you could say about Spam Fritters, except that it seemed rude even to have served them once. So today the cooks were trying to make up for it, and had promised Gourmet Food. On the menu board, I read – Chiken Vol Or Vent and Cauliflower Cheese Au Gratin.

I stayed hidden in the shadows at the side of the building, lapels

pulled around my throat to hide the white of my shirt. I was thinking Harrison might have set me up and at any second bright lights
would shine in my face and I would be thrown to the ground by
some Popper.

But Harrison showed up. I smelled him before I saw him, the
washed-out reek of some Tropical Paradise.

He stuffed the mag in my hand. It was wrapped in a copy of the
New Statesman. Then he grabbed the cash and disappeared across
the fields.

I had to admire him. *Across the fields*. I knew that meant a detour
almost into Windsor and then up the High Street back to his house.
This man took no chances and I knew how he had stayed in business long enough for everyone in the school to know he was Porn
King. I saw him head out through the tall grass, moon on his back
like a cloak.

It turned out the magazine was even called *Big Tits*, as if they had
read Wittingham's mind. But all I felt for the women was sorry.
Their ledges of breast were so big that I knew the only place safe for
them in the world was tucked inside the pages of *Big Tits* magazine.
They all looked so uncomfortable. I didn't even see how they could
walk upright.

I thought about Rosser and his Plastic Primroses. I realized he
was wrong about it not being real. I had never considered before
that these women actually existed. I knew they were people, but I
had no sense of them maybe living close by and doing anything
except writhe on fuzzy carpets for the camera. I thought of how
these women must get to thinking sometimes that God had
dumped on them and made them only fit for being drooled on and
pointed at. You couldn't live a normal life with breasts like that, and
I felt sorry for the ones that wanted to.

The next day at tea, the door slammed shut again.

Manson said it had to be trick photography. He wondered if they
could even be real.

I said I felt sorry for the women and Wittingham told me to shut
up. He didn't want to hear about it and he didn't want them to be
real. They were fine being Primroses as far as he was concerned.

'You'll probably get caught,' Manson told me. 'If they ever bust
Harrison, they'll make him say all the names of people he sold
mags to.'

'Then you'll be in deep poo, because I gave him your name.'

The blood drained out of Manson's face as if I had just pulled the plug on his heart. His lips turned blue with the shock. For the next couple of weeks, Manson spent his free time in his room. And in the street he carried an open umbrella, even when it wasn't raining, hiding under the dome of black cloth.

Another sex lecture.

'Bloody uncanny,' Rupert muttered to me, as we shuffled into the biology room. 'Are you sure you didn't tell anyone about buying that magazine off Harrison?'

'I swear I didn't, Rupe.'

'Bloody uncanny.'

'Yes, Rupe. As you said.'

'Do they honestly think we don't know about sex yet?'

'I think it's just to make sure, Rupe.'

'Damn silly business, if you ask me.'

'That's the thing, Rupe. Nobody is asking you.' It was the first time I lost my patience with Rupert. For someone who thought that sex was clumsy and grubby and to be frowned upon, he talked about it far too much.

On the wall of the biology room were charts of human bodies, showing the lines of muscles and veins that ran beneath the skin. The body stood with its hands held slightly out, as if waiting for an explanation why someone had ripped off its flesh.

An old man walked in through a side door and at first we thought he was one of the cleaners who had got lost.

But this was him. The famous Dr Twombley. Even the mention of his name to Sacker or Villiers would send them into spasms of joking and laughter. They would stagger around in the corridor, pretending to be blind and humping doors or dustbins.

Dr Twombley drew pictures almost as badly as Ma Woods back at the Dragon School. He sketched two stick people lying on top of each other and then turned to face the class.

Nobody could see through glasses that thick. It was not possible.

'Why,' he waved the chalk at us, as if he thought he was still facing the board and was trying to draw another diagram, 'do you suppose people lie on top of each other when they are having sex?'

There were a couple of answers to this, but saying the wrong one could get you dragged up in front of the Headmaster, so we all kept quiet.

Dr Twombley drew the answer in the air with his chalk, speaking slowly so the writing would keep up with his voice. 'So they can talk to each other!'

I saw a look spread on Wittingham's face, but it was too late to stop him. 'But, sir. Surely if you just raised your voice a bit, you could do all the other styles and still talk as much as you wanted to.'

Wittingham spent the next couple of hours on punishment duty, which we called On the Bill, picking moss from between the flint cobblestones of the main school courtyard.

'He should have known better,' Rupert told me.

I agreed, but I knew we were both secretly jealous.

I was coming bottom in all of my classes. I was trying as hard as I could but nothing helped. It felt as if I was at the controls of a plane going down in flames with no way to pull out of the dive.

In maths, my first text came back and at the bottom there was only one word. The teacher, Mr Wise, had written – Absurd.

The subject never had made sense to me. I squinted at the yellow and red pyramids of numbers squiggled on Mr Wise's overhead projector and could only think that back home, the leaves would be changing colour now that it was October. The poison ivy would be all shades of red and the maples would be gold and you could look out on the calm New England landscape and see whole valleys seeming to burn with the shades of changing leaves. I kept it to myself like a secret, but also because the leaves didn't change beautifully over here in the autumn. They just turned brown and fell off, and under the jagged-leafed trees, you'd see the spiked balls of horse chestnut cases and the polished mahogany brown of the chestnuts. At the Dragon we would have gathered them all up, but here nobody played Conkers, and the chestnuts were left to be trampled or washed down the gutters in the first hard winter rain.

My mind kept slipping, like a car whose gears have worn out, on the tests that Mr Wise handed to us in the strange purple writing of his copy machine. He always looked a little desperate, because we were the bottom maths class at the bottom of the school. It was, Rupert told me, the equivalent of a leper colony, where people were put who could not be saved.

When I should have been doing my homework, I wandered out across the empty playing fields in my ratty Soviet greatcoat, seeing the heavy-bellied jumbo jets on their way in to land at Heathrow.

Just as I could write a story but not know what made it easy for me, the numbers were also a mystery. I barrelled away down the corridors of my day-dreams, while Mr Wise begged us to see what he saw. He liked numbers, and sometimes when he strode into class, I knew he had convinced himself that if he could only make us see it his way, then we would all come to love mathematics.

He would keep up his brave face for a few minutes, but then it would collapse as we reminded him that we were the lepers of his trade.

I wished he wouldn't look so sad about it, as if he took everything personally. I wanted to say if he thought we were bad at maths, then he should have seen Nightingale back at the Dragon.

Nightingale did show up eventually. He had finally passed his Common Entrance exam, after three tries and going to summer school.

I laughed when he burst into my room. Rupert and I were sitting over a backgammon board, and I was winning all his pocket money. I laughed at Nightingale because he looked the way I must have looked when I first arrived. His uniform did not fit him properly. He could have pulled his trousers up to his tits and still had room to spare. The black cloth of his tail-suit gave off a glow of newness and he hadn't yet had time to ink in any of the white pinstripe lines on his trousers.

I introduced Nightingale to Rupert, who nodded hello and said he had some work to do before the next class. He knew he'd just be in the way while Nightingale and I talked about old times. Once he had passed Nightingale and reached the door, he turned to me and took the pipe out of his mouth. He raised his eyebrows as if to say 'Is this the kind of Wally you went to school with?' Then he was gone, his Lobb shoes creaking down the corridor.

The first thing Nightingale said to me was 'Why's that bloke got an unlit pipe stuck in his face?'

I tried to explain but gave up. Nightingale wasn't interested. He talked fast, calling the other new boys in his year idiots and trying to drag up some shreds of Dragon School gossip.

He tried some of the old jokes, using them like passwords among friends in this new and enemy land. He talked himself into a sweat and then slumped down on my bed and asked me what was new.

I'd been afraid to admit it, but I wasn't looking forward to him coming over. At first I didn't know why. It just made me uneasy to hear that he was in town and to know he would soon be swinging by. But as I watched the blur of his mouth and the same old way he wouldn't look me in the eye when he talked, I knew it was because I had changed since I left the Dragon. I had changed in a way that left the old school and Pa Winter and Pa Vicker and Cuddly and even Nightingale behind. That part was over and gone.

Then, like someone pulling a trump-card at a poker game, Nightingale reached into his pocket and held out his clenched fist.

'What is it?' I asked him.

As his fist slowly uncurled, I saw he was holding the old Indian arrowhead that I had given to him years before.

'Remember this?'

I smiled and took the arrowhead. I tested its point against the heel of my palm. 'Still sharp.' Then I gave it back but could not look him in the eye. I thought to myself – How can I ever explain that it's all over?

So of course I didn't. I faked that we were still the best of friends, knowing that in a couple of weeks, the schedule of our work, with him already so far behind, would get in the way of us seeing each other. There was too much that he had to learn which I had learned already. I hoped it would all happen gently, and that there would be no time for anger or even hatred to rise up between us.

It didn't take long. He drifted away and I saw him now and then. A couple of times, he and Rupert and I went wandering through Windsor together. I never would have thought that all the time we'd spent together could end. For a while, I just assumed that the two of us would grow old and die together. The truth was, I'd never thought much about the future at all, with Nightingale or without it. But the time did end, and by the time I realized it, it had been over already a while. Nightingale and I were still friends and still told the old jokes sometimes. But we had to put aside the way we used to be – almost in love in a way that did not touch.

Rupert had a whole box of Cuban cigars. His father had bought them Duty-Free and given them to Rupert, saying he should hold on to them for a few years, because they would improve with age. Rupert had owned them for less than a day when he decided that we should smoke them in my room on a Saturday night, when everyone else would be downstairs watching TV. Nightingale was not invited. Rupert said it would have been too risky to bring him over from another House after dark and then try to smuggle him out again. Rupert was relieved when I didn't argue. It was clear that the two of them didn't get along. It seemed to be that old friends almost never got along with new friends.

The cigars made a lot of smoke, which we tried to blow out of the window, but most of it billowed back into the room. We choked ourselves because we thought we were supposed to inhale them, the same as with cigarettes.

Then the door burst open and a silhouette filled up the doorway.

I threw my cigar out the window and froze.

Rupert said 'God' very quietly.

When the smoke had cleared, we could see that it was Villiers. He was grinning at us.

I slumped down onto the floor. 'Oh, Jesus, I thought you were Markby.'

'Those smell like Havanas.' Villiers said.

'Romeo and Juliets.' Rupert held out the box as if it was a sacrificial offering.

'Where the hell did you get them?' Villiers held the box up to his nose and sniffed and closed his eyes in ecstasy. 'These cost a fortune.'

'Have one!' Rupert tried to smile but only grimaced like an idiot. 'Have several.'

'Thank you.' Villiers lifted out a handful, leaving behind only two of the fifteen cigars that had been in the box. 'Next time, smoke out by the river-bank.'

For a second after Villiers had gone, Rupert and I sat very quietly, waiting for the clip-clop of Markby's feet along the corridor. When nothing happened, we grabbed my aerosol deodorant and sprayed it all over the room, trying to hide the smell. We turned out the light, then gargled with mouthwash and spat it out the window.

The lights flipped on in the Library next door. Rupert and I ducked down again.

A second later, we heard Sacker's booming voice – 'These are *Havanas!*'

'Romeo and Juliets,' Villiers said, with a tone of superior wisdom.

Then there was the scrape of a match along the wall. After that, it became very quiet, and the sweet Cuban smoke drifted out into the night.

I saw Rupert smiling at me in the dark.

The next day, we had a smoking lecture.

'Good Lord, this is uncanny.' Rupert gave me the Beady Eye as we walked over to the Farrar Theatre.

'Well, it's nothing to do with me, Rupe. Honest.'

'It's the strangest damn coincidence I've ever come across.'

On a huge movie screen, a doctor showed us lungs which he said he had personally cut out of dead people. They were pink if the people hadn't smoked, but if they had, the lungs were black and filled with fluff like cottage cheese.

I heard that you could be caught smoking three times at Eton before they'd throw you out. And you had to be caught red-handed, not just smelling of tobacco. You could be thrown out for drinking at a first offence, but they usually gave you a second chance.

Cheating could get you thrown out, but I never knew anyone who cheated.

Being caught with a girl in your room would almost definitely get you expelled. But if they caught you in bed with another boy, I heard that the worst they'd do was send you to a psychiatrist. That's just the way it was. I thought perhaps that the shame of being caught with another boy might have been considered punishment enough.

There were punishments for everything at Eton. If you showed up late for class, they'd put you down on a list of boys who had to be at the School Office at six in the morning to get your name crossed off a list. The teacher always checked to see if you had your pyjamas on underneath your tail-suit, in case you were trying to sneak back to bed.

If your work was bad, the teacher would rip it down the middle and make you take it to the housemaster.

Expulsion meant having to leave fast. They gave you a couple of hours to be gone from your room. The first people I knew who were expelled from Eton were a couple of boys from the Dragon. I heard it had to do with drugs, but no one knew the details. People said they had been beaten by the Head Man on the ancient Beating Stool.

I didn't believe that there really was a Beating Stool, but Villiers swore it was true. He said it had been donated by some Old Etonians and that it was like an upside-down chair and also that the Head Man beat you with a thin cane like Charlie Chaplin used to carry. If you had been really bad, the cane would first be thrashed against a table and split, to make it hurt even more.

It made me shiver even to hear about it. I'd rather the Head Man just punched me in the jaw than go through all that ritual of stools and canes.

Manson told us that his father had been beaten several times when he went to school here, and had scars across his butt to prove it.

The first time I thought I might be beaten was in a physics class when I broke the Ripple Tank that was used to show refraction.

'You did this on purpose!' Mr Bixby looked down at the machine, which was still humming and wobbling back and forth, but not making ripples any more. Mr Bixby was a small man. I always wanted to pat him on the head as he walked past. He seemed so angry that I was afraid he would try to have me sent to the Head Man. I thought of the wound stripes that the cane would leave behind.

'On purpose!' Mr Bixby yelled again.

'No, sir. The bobble just came off by itself.' It was a little thing like a styrofoam ping-pong ball, that was attached to a metal stem. The stem wiggled and the ball made ripples in the tank.

'Well, it's never done that before.' He kept staring at it, as if he expected the machine to pull itself back together. 'Go and find the ball and bring it to me at once.'

The ball had bounced across the floor and stopped at Rupert's feet. He had picked it up and put it in his mouth and was chewing on it now. By the time I handed it back to Mr Bixby, there were teeth marks all over the styrofoam.

'The whole thing's ruined!' He threw the ball away.

Rupert went and fetched it and put it back in his mouth. He was always chewing on something. His lips were stained permanently blue from ball-point pens that had been gnawed down to the ink. He ate paper and erasers. Even his ruler had been nibbled. He said it helped to keep his mind off smoking, because Rupert had recently given up on his empty pipe protest and had started to smoke cigarettes. They smelled less, they were easier to carry and if you ate half a box of Altoids mints afterwards, it would pretty much deaden the smell on your breath.

At a school where smoking was forbidden, and considering what an earful Rupert had given me about how he did not like cigarettes, I was amazed at how many he put away each day. He smoked behind the dining-hall and out in the playing fields and up in Slough and down in Windsor. He smoked up on the roof of the house in the middle of the night. His favourite were German cigarettes called Roth Handle. They gave off thick white smoke which smelled a little of perfume, and I began to notice that Rupert himself smelled a little of this. His room had a dry mustiness that came from the tobacco.

Mr Bixby made me stay behind after class. 'You're going to be charged for a new Ripple Tank.'

'How much do they cost, sir?' I forced myself not to pat-pat his head.

'I don't know. I'm sure they are very expensive.'

Rupert waited for me outside. He hugged his books to his chest. Nobody carried satchels. I had arrived at school with a little brief-case. It had loops for pencils and a built-in calculator. In my first class, Mr Brundish had asked me if I was commuting in from the city, which doubled him over with laughter at his own joke. So that was it for my brief-case with the built-in calculator. Now I used it to hold food that I'd scavenged from the dining-hall or the Library.

Rupert and I wandered back to house for tea. It was getting dark and, across the river, the battlements of Windsor Castle were like dulled teeth against the purple sky.

'They'll kick us out if we fail our exams,' he said.

For both of us, the classwork had been too difficult from the start, and you could only laugh it off for so long.

'What will you do if you get sent away?' I looked around at the darkening buildings. I began to wonder if I could survive at Eton. I didn't want to be here, but I didn't want to be sent away either.

'I don't know. If you get kicked out of this place, it will stay with you the rest of your life.' Rupert flinched as the first of the yellow-orange streetlamps popped on above our heads. He didn't seem worried at the thought of being kicked out. Instead, he acted as if everything was just beyond the reach of his control. He put himself in the hands of his own private God and let himself drift on the breeze.

But I was not like Rupert and I worried about a lot of things. Too many things, Rupert always said. I felt now as if I was standing at the edge of a cliff with the wind trying to carry me over. If I stayed where I was any longer I would fall. I could not allow myself to be kicked out. I would slam the door on the gateways to my day-dreams and I would not dream again until the coast was clear.

CHAPTER 8

TIME AND PEOPLE seemed to slip past, as if there was a layer of oil between me and them.

There was still no mail from home. But I continued to think that no news was good news. I didn't even check my letter slot anymore.

Even with my Imperial Decree not to sit around day dreaming, my grades were still spiralling down. I didn't let myself watch TV, for the two hours a week which were allowed to us on Saturday evenings. I punished myself by saying that I could not go across the bridge into Windsor, gating myself the same way the headmaster might gate a boy. I even put away my miniature radio, and on Sunday evenings when I usually listened to a run-down of the record charts, I sat at my desk in silence and stared and stared at my lessons.

It helped a little, but not enough. All my tests came back ripped down the middle. The stories I wrote in my spare time turned cruel and ugly. I became afraid of sitting down at my desk with a stack of blank A4 pages. I didn't know what was happening to me. I had spent so much energy teaching myself to write and having the writing become a part of each day, like brushing my teeth or getting dressed. But now I taught myself to stop, because I was giving life to nightmares, which unravelled cackling and hideous from the gold nib of my Parker 51.

One Saturday afternoon, when Rupert and Manson and Moriarty had all gone down to Windsor, I found myself wandering through the biology labs. They had a similar smell to the labs at the Dragon, except here the smell was stronger. It was a smell of dead things preserved and locked in glass jars. It was the ranks of African animal heads, stuffed and with glass eyes hammered into their skulls. They hung on the walls of one classroom. Their corkscrew horns gave me the feeling that these animals must be extinct now.

The strangeness of their faces and their fur didn't seem to belong in the world any more.

I looked in a glass case where a shrunken head from South America was on display. It had long black hair and its eyes and mouth were stitched shut. There was also a three-footed duck and a two-headed cat.

Normally I would never have gone near an empty classroom. I had the sense of being watched, and not just by the glass-eyed antelopes beheaded and leaning as if through the plaster of the biology school walls.

There was something wrong with me. It was as if a part of my brain that could not speak had led me here to these freaks in the glass case to warn me of the trouble. That night, long after dark, I found myself alone in the bathroom, washing my hands over and over, until my knuckles were streaming with blood.

At first, I thought it was just the toughness of being in a new place. But now the newness had worn off and I realized that it was something else. It muffled me and left me staring empty-eyed at the swamp-green walls of my room, when I should have been out in Windsor, or writing, or rebuilding an old Triumph motorcycle at the School of Mechanics or playing sports, the way other Etonians did.

I knew what it was. I knew, but I had shoved it so far back in my mind that the thing still managed to surprise me when it reared up and showed its river-ghoul face.

It came at the half-term holiday, when I went out to see my relatives.

The winter had closed in on Wales. I sat by the coal fire, hearing the wind tug at the white stone chips embedded in the outside walls. I saw the grey-beard rollers coming in off the Irish Sea and smashing into the cliffs of Dinas Head. The waves exploded and threw spray almost to the tops of the cliffs.

There was nothing to do. The streets were empty and grey and fields that in summer had glowed purple from heather and yellow with gorse now were wind-flattened and dull. I wondered what the hell my ancestors used to do in this place when the winter clamped down on them in their thatched-roof huts.

I went up to the attic and rummaged in old trunks. I crawled far along the rafters, hearing the rain much louder here. There seemed to be a rhythm in it, a code trampled out on the slate roof tiles –

something desperate called to me in a language that I could not understand.

The phone rang downstairs and I heard the high-pitch of my aunt's voice, the special rising pitch she only used when answering the phone – 'Fishguard 2906.'

I popped open a trunk. On top of some old clothes was a picture of my father. He was young in the picture and I wondered how it had got up here, since he wasn't related to them. I took the picture out and turned it over in my hands a few times. Then I put it back and closed the trunk.

It was my mother on the phone. My father had slipped into a coma. Slipped. She used the word slipped, as if it was only a slight accident and he would pick himself up and dust himself off and walk back into his life. But I did not think of the word 'slipped'. I thought of a long silent free-fall, like a sky-diver whose parachute has failed to open. I saw the helpless drifting of an astronaut whose cable has come loose from his space ship.

My mother spoke in a wobbly voice that made it sound as if she had hiccups. The news snuffled into my ears over the transatlantic line and I barely heard it. I barely listened, either.

I took an early morning bus back to school. My uncle John and I stood in the rain while we waited for it to arrive. We couldn't think of anything to say. I turned to him once, and saw his face peeking out of his duffel coat hood. I could see the grim flat line of his pressed-together lips, and it told me more than I'd heard on the phone.

All through Wales, it was just the driver and me. At first, before dawn, the land outside was total black, as if the windows had been painted with it. The bus ride took all day. At noon, the driver stopped at a cafe to get a sandwich. I stayed on the bus.

While I was waiting, I heard a cracking noise in the seat behind me. It sounded as if someone had taken a stalk of celery and twisted it until it broke. The noise was so clear and loud that I jumped out of my seat. I looked behind me, and then I looked all around the bus, but the place was empty.

When I reached school, I was carrying my suitcase up to my room. One of the senior boys poked his head out of the Library and said he was sorry.

I didn't get it. The whole business was shrieking in my face and I didn't get it.

Then Mr Rosser called me into his study and made me get it once and for all. He set a mug of instant coffee down in front of me and told me my father was dead. He asked me how old my father was. I figured it out and told him – forty-two. Mr Rosser had a tough time talking about it and when he talked about his own father getting hit by a car and dying, I watched his face burn red and his breath run out in gusts. He said I was going home tomorrow, but would come back at the end of the week.

I sat on my bed and cried into my pillow while Sacker leaned against the wall with his hands in his pockets. He squinted at Farah Fawcett on the wall and at my collection of stale toast, which I brought over from the dining-hall and ate when I got hungry in the middle of the night.

The Dame drove me to the airport, where I met my brother, who had come down from the Dragon. We flew back for the funeral and didn't talk much on the flight.

Even more than the fact that I was going home to bury my father, there was something out of balance in going home at this time of year. I used to imagine that the place closed down when I wasn't there. I thought of Narragansett sinking into a kind of hibernation, deep in winter sleep with fog pillowing the bay and dew resting heavy on the branches.

And that's how it was when I reached home.

My father had died in my bed. His death certificate was lying on my bedside table. He had died at seven in the morning, which was exactly the time I had heard the strange twisting and cracking noise on the bus, five hours ahead on British time. All around the room were rubber tubes that had been used for when people gave him injections and brown bottles of morphine with instructions written in Spanish.

My aunt was there. She helped to look after my mother.

I woke up early the next morning because of jet lag. I walked out into the fog and stepped along the low-tide sand. I couldn't see more than a few feet in front of me. This didn't seem to be home. I moved through the mist as if trapped in a bubble, with muffled sounds and the clammy air around me.

At the memorial service, I read from St Paul's Epistle to the Romans. I didn't crack up as I read. I'd worried that I might. Pale light streamed through the windows and it was cold in that church with the little green door.

After the service, I stood with my mother and brother and shook hands with people coming out of the church. I saw fat tears on the cheeks of my father's friends. The research ship that had carried him down to the Antarctic and up to the ebony-coloured beaches of Iceland rode out into the bay and flew black flags.

And then I was back in school, the whole trip less real than any of the half-dream voyages I'd made from my iron-rail bed at the Dragon, or the fold-up sagging mattress here at Eton.

I realized now that this was what had haunted me all through the summer and the autumn.

In the time that followed, I grieved for my father in ways far more painful than crying. Each time my thoughts grew quiet, the grief would rear up like a gargoyle and show its hideous face. It sought me out in the dark and woke me from my sleep. For the first few seconds, I'd feel calm, but then the gargoyle would return and sadness carved through my stomach.

It tore me to pieces until I felt like the Straw Man in *The Wizard of Oz*, after he had been attacked by the flying monkeys. For what seemed like ages, I lay there with my stuffing hanging out, long after the point where people stopped feeling sorry for me and just went on with their own lives. Then I realized that the moment had come when I would either be crippled for life by this or I would have to move on.

Long before he had passed away, I dragged around the skulking shadow of my father's death. But now I began to shrug off the shadow, one grey layer at a time. Slowly the numbness began to recede. It pulled back like a tide.

One rainy afternoon in the middle of a Rugby game, I broke from the scrum and had my arms raised to catch the muddy ball. The pink and blue quarters of my Rugby shirt were splattered brown from sliding in the dirt. My boots were clods of wet earth and rain had plastered the hair back on my head.

I was watching the ball. It cart-wheeled down towards me. Flecks of soil spun off its leather sides. I could hear the thump of boots along the ground, as people from the other team closed in to knock me flat as soon as I had hold of the ball. The sky was eggshell white.

Then suddenly, for a fragment of a second, all sound and movement stopped. I felt the last veil of shadow rise from deep inside me. It blew into the wind and disappeared. My head was clear now. For the first time in months, I could think straight.

Now that the shadow had gone, my father seemed to tumble far into the past. I remembered pieces of sentences, the way he used to say 'Hello Chaps' to my brother and me when he came home from work. I recalled the expressions on his face, the awkward pursing of his lips as he leaned down to kiss me goodnight. I remembered his sailor's hat and his shredded blue anorak when he took us out sailing, but these things did not add up to a whole person.

My father had gone Super Nova. Bright meteors of the explosion spread out through my mind. For the rest of my life, the meteors would be finding their way in from distant orbits. They'd burst open and make me remember the things they had been hiding. Memories would flare up clearly and return me for a moment to the time when he was alive. Then the picture would burn out, as quickly and unexpectedly as it had appeared. My father would never be whole again. From now on, there were only meteors.

The Rugby ball slammed down into my arms. My muddy hands held it against my chest. I dodged the people closing in on me and dodged again and ran and passed the ball.

It was as if my father himself showed me that I had to leave him behind. He showed me in a way that I knew could only have come from him – in the hurling of a ball towards me, a ball that I could catch to win the game.

When the last long falling-and-then-rising tone of the whistle blew to finish the game, I still had energy to spare. I took the ball and ran with it back to the house. I kept throwing the ball up and catching it, and people made way to let me pass as my steel-studded boots clattered off the fields and onto the road.

I quit staring into space, at the trophy-head animals in the biology labs, at my green-painted room and at the brick wall six feet from my window.

I became restless to see what was beyond Eton and Windsor. Some free afternoons, I got on the train to London, more for the ride itself than for anything I wanted to see in the city. It was the sense of movement that I wanted. It made my heart beat faster. I'd stand in the space between carriages, open the windows and feel the speed of the train shudder up through my body. Once the train arrived at Paddington Station, I wandered through the crowded streets around Covent Garden and Piccadilly, feeling the movement of people around me like the flow of running water. I thought of them all streaming back to their homes in the city or to the sandy-coloured buildings of the Cotswold country, to the treeless hills of west Wales or out across the water to foreign countries. I wanted to follow all of them. I wanted to see everywhere and know everything at once.

I began to write again. The nightmares had gone. The stories moved in the clean black and white of ink onto page. Soon I was back to writing every day.

It used to be that I bulldozed through my classwork and sometimes it worked out and sometimes it didn't. Now I taught myself to study. Before, I had never really known how.

I was ashamed of coming 235th in the overall exam places, one place short of the names listed in red which were the names of people failing. My teachers had stopped being angry with me and writing 'Absurd' on my reports. Now they were giving me sympathy. I got o out of 50 in a maths test and Mr Wise wrote – 'Don't give up.' It was more than I could take.

To teach myself, I used three marbles. They were beautiful Victorian spirals from my collection at the Dragon. I rolled them in my hand, grinding one against the other. This stopped me from day-dreaming while I read through my assignments. When I had to memorize lists and names, I took the first letter of each important name and piled them all together to make one long word that looked like nonsense. I chanted the word until I knew it. Then in the test, I would write down the word and fill in the names around so that it looked like a crossword. If I had to learn dates or equations, I matched them up with songs. I sang the Periodic Table in physics to the tune of 'I Can't Get No Satisfaction.' I could list most of the important dates in World War One by singing them to 'Home, Home on the Range.'

In the next set of exams I came 35th and for the rest of my time at Eton, I never came lower than that.

I didn't stop the day-dreams. I needed them to blow out the pressure that I could feel sometimes at the base of my skull when I'd been studying too much. Instead, I wrote the day-dreams down and hammered them into stories. On paper, I forced them to make sense, instead of bloating into nonsense like a reflection in a Fun House mirror.

I used them in my English classes and when there were no assignments that I could use them for, I'd hand them in anyway. It never seemed to tire me out, the way the Lesson Chanting could or the Learning Songs or the body-slam tackles in Rugby. And there were always ideas for stories, triggering like muscle reflexes off newspaper articles or songs or people I saw in the street. Eventually I couldn't read other stories without the reflexes coming in so fast that I had to stop reading and get on with the idea that had popped open in my head.

Once I dreamed that there was a dark red river flowing just above my head. It was the river of untold stories. All I had to do was reach up and touch the river and the stories would pool like blood in my hands. I knew in my dream that it was a timeless river and easy to reach if you knew it was there. But that was the great secret. You had to know it existed.

I wrote it all down in the middle of the night, while a lightning storm burst so viciously overhead that it set off the fire alarms. As I wrote, I thought of the javelin that had sailed from my hand long ago at the Eagle House athletics meeting and the angels that carried it up. I'd had the same feeling back then, that it was a strength I could use if I only knew how.

It was like the voyaging I'd used to take me back home in the night.

Now I began to voyage all over the place, leaving like the humpback jumbo jets that rattled my window-panes as they thundered overhead.

One place I voyaged to more than I wanted.

We were studying the Great War in History class. We concentrated on the Western front, on Ypres and Passchendaele and the Somme.

We watched a documentary in which a man in a raincoat was walking across a field in the rain. 'This place,' he said, 'was where five thousand men rose up out of their trenches on the first of July 1916 and ran at the German trenches.' He walked towards the camera, surefooted in the muddy field. The camera kept backing up, as if it was afraid of the man. He pointed to the ridges in the earth to show where the trenches had been. He rummaged in the dirt and pulled up the remains of a British helmet. He said that on this field and in others not too far away, twenty thousand men had fallen in the first six hours of the Somme offensive.

There was something about the way he walked across that field. It was the way I used to walk back from the river-bank at night, to supper at the Dragon School. It was a walk that wanted to break into a run, as if he was being followed.

It was the sinister calmness of the trees and fields as the camera panned across them. They were calm to the eye, but there was something else, something that it did to me in my bones, that was not calm at all.

That night, we were given poetry to read. It was poetry written by soldiers who had been in those fields and some of them had stayed. Blunden, Owen, Sassoon. At one point, I slammed the book down on the desk and yelled at Farah Fawcett – 'Who the hell could write poetry about a place like that?'

I couldn't get it out of my head. I found the poems repeating in my thoughts, even though I had not tried to learn them. The walking man stalked through my dreams, always on the verge of running and the blindness of fear taking over.

I felt called by that land. It was not one human voice or even a voice from the ground itself. It was thousands of voices, human and not human, all whirled into one vast whisper that in one sense I could not hear and in another sense was deafening me. It blew in a mist across the water and up the crooked walkway of the Thames and came to me. And once the whisper had arrived, it would not leave until I followed it.

That half-term holiday, I did not go to Wales. The restlessness in me had become too great, and whereas before I did not have the chance to travel and did not even know where to go, now it all seemed to fit into place. I sold my stamp collection to Moriarty, too impatient to be angry at how much he ripped me off by using stamp values from a long-outdated Stanley Gibbons catalogue and thinking that I didn't notice.

I bought a ferry ticket across the Channel to Belgium. I borrowed an old rucksack and a tent from a senior boy who was in the Officer Training Corps.

Then I left for Belgium. It was a night ferry from Dover. I stood on deck, watching the lights of Ostend grow larger, seeing a Ferris wheel from a fair turning loops in the pitch black.

In the purple-grey light before sunrise, I stood on a railway platform with people crowded around me and on their way to work. I heard them all talking but couldn't understand one word of their Flemish.

From Ostend, I took a train to Courtrai. A fat man in a blue and red uniform wheeled a cart up and down the aisles, selling food and mumbling the menu as if he was singing a song. I could tell when he was about to begin his list again, because he would sigh out the word – Toblerone – which was a kind of chocolate with chewy bits in it. The Belgian coffee tasted stronger and there was no tea for sale.

It was a clean feeling and a pure feeling to be on my own and far away from home. There were no teachers prowling the corridors in their crêpe-soled desert boots, ready to catch us with cigarettes and the little bottles of Belgian liqueur that the fat man sold from his cart. I found myself checking the things in my pack, testing the strength of the canvas straps and counting my money over and over.

It was June and the fields were clotted with morning fog. I saw a farmer out ploughing his field in an old tractor, seagulls swooping down in his path like a constant shower of wedding confetti. The sun was a ball of cantaloup melon in the trees.

The mist burned away and I watched the same blinding green as the English countryside unravel beside the tracks.

In Courtrai, I bought a bottle of wine that was older than me. I stuffed it in my pack and rode the bus to Passchendaele. It was a red brick town that looked as if it had been put up in a hurry. I didn't see anyone in Passchendaele. It was as if they had all left. I didn't have enough money for a hotel, so I spent the night in a little patch of woods, not far from a memorial to the Canadians who had died there. All around were barley fields, which shifted in the wind and made a sound like rushing water.

I cooked a tin of spaghetti on a portable Hexamine stove and listened to the cuckoos out in the barley. There were three Holstein cows that a farmer had led into the wood at sunset. I stayed very still while the farmer was close, then slowly allowed myself to breathe again, as he shuffled away down the road in his huge and muddy boots. The cows wandered over and stared at me, with the same wide-eyed expressions that the boys had on their faces on my first night in dorm at the Dragon School. They came closer and closer, pretending just to pull up tufts of grass, but really they were sneaking towards my spaghetti. So I jammed my heel in the ground and watched them trample back out of range, swinging their tails over manure-splattered butts.

For the first time in my life, nobody knew where I was except me. It felt strange and drifting and I read the book of poems before I fell asleep.

The dew settled quickly after the sun had gone. I watched it billow along the road, breaking everything into the grey particles of twilight. Then it crowded around the trees of my little wood. The cows stood still. Their black-and-white flanks seemed to disappear in the mist.

I saw the dew bead up on my tent and when I touched the fabric on the inside, the dew poured through. So I had to sleep curled in a ball, trying not to touch the sides.

I woke up later and thought it was raining, but it was only one of the cows, who had decided to pee on my tent. It didn't make any difference when I clapped my hands or told her to bugger off. The cow had started and there was no way to stop. Then she stuck her nose in my mess-tin and licked up the last strands of spaghetti.

All night, the sound of the cuckoos echoed through the mist. I imagined them sticking their heads up above the barley, chirping and then ducking down for cover.

In the morning I walked the Menin Road, past the neat white-slab graveyards of the war dead. Hundreds of times, I read – A soldier of the Great War. Known unto God. I had been told that the reason so many soldiers could not be named on their graves was that they had identification discs that were made from pressed paper, which dissolved sometimes when the soldiers were still alive. I also knew that men would sometimes remove all identification before trench raids. And I knew that in this place of mighty silence, there had once been the noise to ruin all hearing of cannon-blasts that shattered men's bodies into pieces that could no longer be named.

The rucksack straps rubbed my shoulders raw and its steel frame dug into the small of my back. I felt blisters bubble up on my feet, then burst and start to bleed.

It took me most of the day to reach Ypres, where I sat in the town square, eating bread and cheese. I took off my boots and wiggled my pale toes in the sun. I read in a guidebook that in the Middle Ages, people threw cats from the tower of a huge building called the Cloth Hall. They thought the cats were witches. I looked squinny-eyed at people passing by.

Before evening, I moved on to the village of Zillebeke, and found the Zillebeke Brook which Blunden had written about in a poem. It wasn't much to see, and looked more like a drainage ditch than the fast-running and rock-bottomed brook that I had imagined.

I pitched my tent near a pond and ate apples and chocolate for dinner. People fished with bamboo poles and bobbers in the pond, pulling out little carp, which they tucked away in canvas bags. One old man asked me something and when I shook my head and spoke to him in English, he pulled out a cigar and gave it to me and slapped me on the back.

As the evening mist returned, I sat on the wall of a little grave-yard and smoked the cigar. The graveyard had a few of the same white slabs of soldiers killed in the war. In the fading light, I looked across at one of the graves and what I saw made me cry out and jump back. Goose-pimples pulled at my flesh. At the top of the stone was the Eton College motto – Floreat Etona. The name on the stone was the same as a boy I knew at school. Albert Jenner-Smith, Welsh Guards, died at the age of 19, September 1915.

For a long time I only stared at the grave, thinking that it was this I'd come to see. I knew the voyaging to this place would stop now. The nightmare Walking Man would disappear and the chant of the poems would not echo in my head. I remembered slamming the book down and asking who could write poems in a place like this. Now that I was here, I thought – Who could walk across a field in Passchendaele, seeing in the poppy-crowded ditches a constant line of rust two inches down, and tripping over pieces of metal twisted like crippled tree branches – who could do that and *not* write a poem about it?

I didn't sleep. I sat on my haunches at the edge of the Zillebeke Brook, feeling the dew settle heavy on my clothes, and I waited for the night to go away. I remembered my uncle telling me about a time when he visited a graveyard of Welsh soldiers from the Great War, somewhere in France. He said that as soon as he walked into the graveyard, he felt something angry surround him. It welled up out of the ground and whispered to him – 'Get out.' It had terrified me then to hear that story and even now it made my skin crawl. But I didn't feel any anger rushing like a gust of wind out of the dark towards me. It was almost the opposite. I felt a kind of gentleness surround me in the mist. It was a sense of being looked at by kind eyes and protected from harm. When I thought about it later, of all the things I could recall in every detail, I could not bring back that feeling of being protected or the gentleness that seemed to me more than just the mist drifting past my face and resting on my back like a blanket of tiny pearls.

I didn't remember much of the trip home. I hadn't washed in a few days and it didn't bother me, but I was afraid it might bother other people. My stomach was messed up from too much chocolate and coffee. I didn't know anything about nutrition and I would not have been able to figure out a balanced diet for myself. Always, I'd just eaten what was put in front of me, except kippers.

The next thing I knew, I was walking back from Slough in the rain. Then I was lying on my bed, too tired to sleep or to wash. Already the time spent away had formed itself into a bubble in my head. I knew the pictures would replay themselves gradually over time. I could pull them out and study them the way we used to pull out the trays of rare butterflies in the Dragon School Museum and see how their long-dead wings suddenly caught sunlight, as if they stored the light in all their bands of colour. You couldn't put a price on it. Already I was anxious to leave again, to pack up my tent and set out early in the sunny morning with my rucksack on my back, alone in myself and my thoughts. If I'd had any money left, I might have left right then.

Carter House always had a fire practice on the first night back from half-term. The longer you had been at the school, the further up you moved in the house. The top floor had a narrow passageway and rooms that collected the sun. On the top floor, they wrapped socks around the hammers of the fire-alarm bells. Otherwise they were deafening.

So now when Mr Rosser set off the alarm, all we heard from upstairs was a frantic Thup Thup Thup as the sock pummelled the bell.

We gathered outside in our dressing-gowns, hugging our ribs to stay warm, while the senior boy called out our names. I was impatient with the list of names and the rule of where we had to meet and just then I was fed up with every other rule at Eton as well. It was a way I had never felt until then. It rose up inside me and I had to beat it back down, because there was work to be done.

For the first time, I began to wonder why my parents sent me to school in England. It seemed a little strange that I would have waited as long as I did to wonder, but in the past, it had not occurred to me to ask. It took all my strength to get used to travelling back and forth across the ocean, to speaking American sometimes and English at other times. I trusted that my parents had figured it out long in advance, and there seemed to be no point in asking why. We never sat around at the Dragon, trying to figure out what we were doing there. We didn't think like that. This was something I was never able to properly explain to adults in

America, and it was only in America that anyone ever asked. But American friends who were my own age understood. When you are young, you do not spend your time trying to figure out why you are in a certain place and who to blame for it or who to thank. You just know that you are there and if you are sad, you try to make yourself happy and if you are happy then you keep things as they are.

My father didn't go to Eton. He quit school at seventeen and went to work in a factory that made aeroplane engines. He hated it so much, he went back to school, and on to university at Leicester, where he met my mother. He became a geophysicist and they moved to Canada straight after they got married. They lived in Alberta and froze their butts off. They worked their way south to California, and from there to Florida, settling finally on the shores of Narragansett Bay.

Sending me to the Dragon School and then to Eton was a way of making sure that my brother and I didn't end up back in the kind of situation in which my father had grown up. I also knew that the people who had most intimidated my father were the Old-School types that Eton produced in more refinement than perhaps any other place. I wondered if there wasn't some strange sense of revenge in a man sending his own sons to the very core of what had stood against him in his life.

My mother said that Eton was the best and that was why they sent me there. And when all the objections had been raised and exceptions noted, she told me, it was still the best.

I didn't know if it was true because I had never been to any other school. I didn't know anything about how it might be in a state school and all I saw or knew of other private schools were their Rugby fields and athletics tracks when we came by to compete. I had no way to judge and because of that no way to argue. I only knew it was so different a way of life, that unless you tried very hard to cross back and forth between the two, it would be hard to understand how other people lived and why they might hold a grudge against you.

I thought that my father's family probably held a grudge about me being sent away to private schools. It was a grudge or some other word for anger, because my father had said they disapproved. I almost never saw them and rarely heard my father speak of them. After he died, I never heard from them again.

The last I saw of someone in my father's family was my great-uncle Bill, the baggage porter at Heathrow. He had a big square head with a dent in it, which my father said he had got fighting Rommel in the desert.

When my brother and I got off the plane in England after the funeral, my uncle Bill was waiting. He stood there in his blue and red uniform, leaning on his trolley, and he was furious. He had not been told about my father dying, because my father didn't want anyone to know. It was their fussing and sympathy he didn't want. I saw my uncle's face grow red with anger and all I could do was hand him a xerox copy of the obituary that had appeared in the paper.

Sometimes after that, as I waited for a flight back to the States, I'd catch sight of a porter in his red and blue uniform, almost lost among the crowd of people at Terminal Three. I'd run after the man and catch up with him, but it was never my uncle Bill.

What I understood without having to ask was why my parents had to send me away to boarding school at the age of seven. The system had so many of its own rules and so much of its own logic, that you had to start in it as early as you could. I saw for myself what happened to people who came to Eton without having gone to a school that specifically trained them for moving on to a place like Eton. The ones I saw did not fit in, and the few Americans I knew who tried appeared to me as no more than tourists. They left angry and confused, because they saw brutality and prejudice and rules that seemed to make no sense, and I knew that the confusion would probably dog them for the rest of their lives. What lay behind it was the mistake of thinking that because these people spoke the same language, they were the same people. It could have been said that people were basically the same everywhere, but there were always subtle differences, and never so subtle that the differences could be ignored.

You could not go just half the course. It was hard enough, at times, to go through Eton at all. But to go there without being prepared and trained for it must have been something like it was for Alice, when she tiptoed through the Looking-glass.

My brother came to Eton, but he didn't stay for long. I saw even less of him here than I had done at the Dragon. He did as badly in his work as I had done when I first arrived. After a year he asked to be sent home. It looked as if he might be asked to leave anyway. So my mother took him out and brought him back to America.

From then on, he studied at Phillips Exeter Academy in New Hampshire.

After he left, I realized that he had always been closer to America, and I knew he would be happier there. I missed him, although I never told him and we never would have talked about a thing like that.

I began to wonder why I had never asked to be taken back to America. The truth was that, despite my constant drifting home across the water in my day-dreams, I didn't think of quitting school in England. If I'd quit, I would have felt as if I'd been beaten. And besides, even though I had begun to question things around me, I was comfortable here. I was moving up in the school and I was starting to enjoy myself. Time seemed to pass more quickly now, and I knew that the rhythm of the school had finally begun to work in me.

I told Jenner-Smith about the grave I'd seen in Flanders.

For a moment, he looked as if he hadn't understood. Then his face brightened up and he said – 'That must be my great-uncle Albert.'

I asked him if he could tell me about the man, but Jenner-Smith had nothing else to say. He didn't seem interested. It had as much effect on him as if I'd just pointed out his shoe-lace was undone.

So we shrugged at each other and walked away in different directions.

A rumour appeared like a thunder-cloud. I heard people snicker that I was spending my time in old cemeteries. One day in lunch, Manson leaned across to me and asked if I was going to be like the poet Thomas Gray and write an Elegy in a Country Church-Yard.

Jenner-Smith must have told Manson, and Manson had started the rumour. Now he sat back and laughed and drummed his fingers on the salt-strewn table.

I did not trust Manson. Gossip streamed from him in such quantities and in such viciousness that there was no way to hide from it.

I wasn't wise to this at first. We would all be sitting at our table in the dark corner of the dining-hall and he would lead someone into a conversation. With me, it was always something to do with America. The guns or the cars or the women. And he would lead me into a word-trap, where I'd say something stupid. Then he would laugh in a loud croaking voice that seemed to come from a blackbird, and while I scrambled to talk my way out, there would be only the laughter of Manson and the others, who laughed mostly out of relief that Manson hadn't picked on them.

It was a relief for me, too, when he picked on someone else. I felt it like a shower of cold blood down through my chest when Manson turned his blackbird laugh on Moriarty or Rupert. With Moriarty, it was always something to do with him not being coordinated and the spluttering way that he talked and what was he doing at Eton if he hated everything it stood for? And with Rupert, it was how boring a life he lived and always a jab about the Labour Party, which was like waving a red flag in the face of an old bull. And Wittingham was such an easy target, with his Pretty Boy face that was quickly getting not so pretty as he turned into a man, and his Porn Mag Lust and Nouveau Yankee Image and bleeping, soldered-together universe inside his room, that Manson didn't even bother with him any more. The truth was that Manson was in love with him, in a hopeless way that served as his own punishment for the ugliness he dealt out. He dragged that love around the way Marley's ghost trailed the chains of his greed, and this love was the fuel for his anger.

Late one Saturday night, when Rupert and Wittingham and I were playing cards and drinking vodka, the door burst open and Markby rushed in, saying we were busted for drinking. He searched the room, but we had kept the vodka hidden under the floorboards and he forgot to look in that place. He ransacked the room and found nothing. Then he got furious and left.

For a while, Rupert and Wittingham and I just stared at each other. We looked around the room, which seemed to have been swept by a tornado. Then Moriarty ran in and spluttered that he had seen Manson talking to Markby, and it was Manson who tipped him off about the vodka.

I had been afraid of Manson, just like everybody else. None of us felt sure enough about ourselves that he could not find a chink in our armour and dig in with whatever sharp words he could find. But lately I'd noticed that his spell over me was growing tired. I didn't care what he said about America or any other damned thing.

He had found a brother in Markby, the two of them itchy-fingered with the thought of making other people miserable to fend off some misery in themselves that was nobody's fault but their own. And with this plan of his to bust us for drinking, Markby used like a greedy policeman, Manson's spell slipped off me forever. In its place, I could only find anger. So I went looking for Manson. I realized that for a long time, I had been looking for an excuse to get in a fight with him, because I knew I would win. Just then, I didn't care if I won the fight or not, because at least it would be the end of sitting there and taking it. And this fight would be different from any fight I'd seen or been in at the Dragon, because now I had the strength to hurt him properly, and unlike any time at the Dragon, that was what I meant to do.

I didn't find him. I heard later that he went and hid in the squash courts.

But after that, I always made sure Manson was on the opposite side in any game of sports. There were times when I had fouled people at the Dragon, but mostly it was by accident. Now I fouled Manson whenever he came anywhere near me, and I knew enough to make it look as if no foul had been committed.

In the Rugby games that we played in the sleet and thrashing rain that spray-painted our bodies with mud, I sent Manson down. If he ever got hold of the ball and started to run, I slammed him to the ground and let my body crash down on his ribs.

In the scrums, when we were all tangled together, I raked my steel-studded boot across his shins so that he couldn't even hobble off the pitch.

It became my speciality to punt the ball into his chest, and see the shock on his face as the air jetted out of his lungs.

It was all legal, loopholed in the vicious rules of the game. I never got sent off the field for unsportsmanlike behaviour. I never said a word about my private war on Manson. Since the time when I'd gone hunting for him, I kept the anger to myself. It seemed the best way to pay back Manson's waterfall of constant mockery was to give him only silence in return.

Slowly, he began to understand, and I never had trouble again from Manson. In time, we even became friends, although it was in a crippled and untrusting way that could only have passed for the weakest kind of friendship.

I found myself less in need of friends now than in the past. I was standing on my own these days, and in a way that I found hard to explain; needing friends less to support me gave me the chance to be a better friend to them.

CHAPTER 9

THE SILENCE I had drawn around me became comfortable, and for the rest of my time at Eton I was quieter. I kept more to myself as term blurred into term and worked harder at writing my stories. On the pages of A4 notebook paper, I invented people I wished were alive and around me, and we struck out together on the adventures I hoped one day would come true.

Sometimes, after half an hour of staring at a blank page and coming up with nothing, I'd find myself as if in a trance, walking around in circles in my room. I'd feel guilty about not having written anything that day.

Over time, I came to value the guilt. I made myself feel so bad if I slacked off that it was easier to write, even if I didn't want to. I wouldn't let myself get up from my desk until I had written, or at least sat there and stewed my brains trying to figure out a story.

I carried a notebook with me, because I found that the best ideas always came when I had no way to write them down. Often I would be lying in bed, my body going numb as I drifted towards the precipice of sleep, and I would think of the simplest, best idea, one that could keep me going for months and on through the holidays. It was such a clear idea, that I knew I would remember it in the morning.

But in the morning I remembered nothing. I lost so many ideas in this way, seeing them drift into the dark like dandelion seeds and fooling myself that I could bring them back. So I tied a pencil on a piece of string to the rail of my bed and when the ideas came, all I had to do was scribble something on the wall and I'd see it in the morning. Sometimes the scribbles were so vague that it took me several hours to find out what they meant, but it was better than nothing at all.

I returned again and again to the river in my sleep, the blood-red tide that I had dreamed about before. I went there the way an animal on the Serengetti Plain would go to a watering-hole, alone in the dark. I wondered if this river belonged to other people, too, and I felt sometimes as if I had been shown something I was not supposed to have seen. Some strange curtain had billowed out in the wind and let me see the river.

When the best ideas came, they came simply and without effort. The harder I thought about stories, the more tangled I became in them until I could make no progress at all. Then I would give up, sling on my heavy pale-grey greatcoat with the red lining and head into Windsor. But half the time, I never made it. As soon as I had given up, and set myself loose from the story, it would suddenly reappear in perfect focus, with all the problems solved so simply that I felt stupid for not having worked them out before. I'd spin around on the steel-lugged heels of my shoes, go back to my room and work on the story some more.

Often when I got stuck with a story, I would walk down by the Thames to clear my head. I stumped along a flint-hard path that ran beside the river. I carried a walking-stick that I had cut from a tree and shaped with my old Swiss Army knife. I kept it hidden under an arch of the brick railway bridge that crossed the fields.

A man came up to me on one of my long walks. He was dressed like a tramp, the dirt on his elbows polished shiny black. But he didn't talk like a tramp. He said he had worked at Eton and he made it sound as if he'd been a teacher.

I didn't answer him back except to say hello, but I didn't run away, either. He did not seem to mean any harm. I thought he just wanted to talk, and soon he would go on his way.

He said he always walked along the river-bank, especially in the summer. Then he began to list all the different kinds of trees and flowers, giving their Latin names, even giving the shapes of their leaves and saying if they had any medicinal value.

I figured he must have been a biology teacher. Maybe he had spent so many years in a wing collar and bow-tie that now he was rebelling in his retirement by wearing filthy clothes.

We came to a bend in the river, where trees grew thick and the sound of the motorway up on the embankment came down on us like thunder. Suddenly the man ducked into the bushes. 'Quick,' he hissed. 'Quick! Here!'

I stepped a few slow paces into the darkness of the covering trees.

He stood in a little clearing, only a few feet away.

'What's the matter?' I asked him.

He stepped towards me, smiling. 'Come here and take your clothes off,' he said.

Before, I might have been afraid. God knows, I might have been so scared that I'd have done what he asked me to do, just because he was an adult and I was not and I was used to doing as I was told. But now I didn't even let him finish his sentence. I smacked him on the head with my heavy walking-stick. I felt the branch connect against his skull and saw his eyes close. Then I spun around and ran back to the house.

I told Wittingham about it and he rushed to find Moriarty. Then they both sat me down in Wittingham's room and shut the door. Moriarty made me tell the story again. All the while, their eyes stayed wide. Then I told them about smacking the man on the head and they boomed with laughter.

When I had finished the story, they told me it was a man called Captain Andrews. Wittingham had heard the whole story from Villiers ages ago. Andrews used to be an Army officer, but then he quit the service or was dismissed and had turned into a tramp. A few years before, they didn't know how many, Andrews had snuck into a boy's room and buggered him. But then he was caught and sent to prison. They didn't know the details. It was some black foggy legend that had been passed down from boy to boy and got blurred in the telling.

But now he was out again. They spoke as if a werewolf had come stalking through the fields.

For a long time I didn't go out to the river. I worried that I had killed the old man, but I was afraid to check. I imagined his bones bleaching in the clearing, with the constant rumble of the motorway booming down. I had dropped my walking-stick, but I didn't remember where. Now I was afraid that the police would find it and know this was the murder weapon.

Eventually, I persuaded Rupert to come with me to see.

Rupert was grumpy about it. The only way I managed to persuade him was by saying he might get a look at a dead body. He still grumbled, not wanting to exercise any more than he had to. But he put on his welly boots and his Barbour jacket and a heavy white wool turtleneck sweater and then stood in the hallway, looking as if he were about to go exploring in the Himalayas. He clapped his hands together. 'Are we going or not?'

There was no body. The clearing was damp and evil-looking, as if it really was the hiding place of a werewolf. But no dead man.

Rupert didn't speak to me all the way home. He could have spent the time drinking Blackthorn Cider at Tap, and he wasn't likely to forgive me any time soon.

Tap was a pub for Etonians only, in an unmarked house half-way down the High Street. You had to be sixteen to get in. It was a sign that you were moving up in the school, and perhaps the biggest privilege that you could be sure of getting.

The walls of Tap were dark brown and drank up the light. It stayed crowded in the evenings, and people lined the staircase that led up to the second floor. There was a garden out at the back, where you could sneak a cigarette before the Poppers hunted you down.

We sat shoulder to shoulder, with heavy pint mugs in our hands. I drank the musty-smelling Blackthorn Cider and watched the barman, who had one thumb missing and said he was a member of the Fascist National Front.

I said I was surprised that I hadn't heard about the Andrews thing before. Rupert shook his head. He told me the school was very good at keeping scandal quiet.

'Well, usually,' he said and nodded at an empty chair in the corner of the room.

That chair was Ziggy's chair. Ziggy was one of the scholars, and called Ziggy because of the David Bowie song about Ziggy Stardust. Our Ziggy had so much dandruff raining down on his shoulders all the time that people took to calling it Ziggy's Stardust. He was one of the cleverest boys in the school, but he couldn't play sports and never seemed to wash and it was rumoured that he even had trouble doing up his own shoe-laces.

There was a time when it seemed that anything that happened at the school was finding its way into the press. Some Lord would be caught smoking and you'd read about it the very next day. For a while, the school couldn't plug the hole. They didn't know where it was coming from. Then somebody at the newspaper must have been threatened because the school found out that it was Ziggy. He was always sitting in Tap in that same chair, all snot-faced and greasy-haired. People used to pile their raincoats on him as they went past into the room and he barely moved. He just sat there with a mug of beer and stared at the floor. But all that time he was listening. He picked up any threads of gossip, and if you were going to hear it anywhere, you'd hear it at Tap. Then he called a newspaper in London and sold the information. Not cheaply, either, I'd heard.

Ziggy disappeared from school so fast that the only thing to remind us that he had ever been there was the faint smell of body odour that he left behind on his chair.

So now that chair was Ziggy's chair, and unless you wanted people calling you Ziggy and dumping their wet raincoats on you, it was best to sit somewhere else.

You couldn't buy hard liquor at Tap, only beer or cider, so Rupert kept a stash of Slivovitz plum brandy. He was so nervous about being caught with it, that he hid the bottle in a stream called the Jordan, which ran across the playing fields. He'd sneak out in the evenings, and dig the bottle out of the mud. He slugged back the clear burning liquid, while river-slime poured down his sleeve.

One time the Jordan froze, and he beat his knuckles bloody on the ice, trying to get to his Slivovitz.

A couple of months after my sixteenth birthday, Tap was moved to a new location, in a new building closer to school. It was lighter and smelled of new paint. The bar and the chairs and tables were all shiny with polish, instead of dulled and waxy from spilled beer and palm-sweat the way it had been in the old building. I missed the old place, even though I barely got to know it.

As Rupert and I walked back from Tap, a truckload of men drove into the town. The men wore black wool coats called donkey jackets, with orange panels on the back. They were the kind road repairmen wore so they could be seen by people in cars. A man with a spider-web tattooed on his elbow leaned out of the truck while it was stopped at a light and spat on me and Rupert. Then he beaned me on the head with a can of Carlsberg Special. They said they were members of the Socialist Workers' Party and they were demanding their rights.

I said that between Rupert and me, we didn't have any rights to give them.

Rupert trod on my foot to get me to shut up.

The light changed and they drove off, angry faces squashed against the back window.

Rupert went and fetched the can of beer. It was still unopened, so he tucked it in his pocket. 'Typical,' he said. 'These bloody Oiks come trundling into town talking about Workers' Rights and how they have no money and then they go about throwing cans of the most expensive beer on the market. And *unopened* cans as well!' All the way home, he kept muttering 'Typical.'

I had no trouble seeing why those men hated Eton. But I had a harder time understanding why some people who went to Eton said they hated it.

They were mostly the Fakes. The ones who really did hate Eton left, or got themselves expelled. The others just stayed behind and complained. They'd wear their tail-coats all week, then slip into a donkey jacket and Doc Marten bovver-boy boots and head up to London to pretend they were poor and downtrodden. I heard some people say it was Doing-The-George-Orwell-Thing.

A group called The Jam had a song called 'The Eton Rifles'. In it, they asked what chance a person had against a tie and a crest.

'Truth is,' Rupert said after hearing the song, 'not much of a chance, if you tangle with the wrong tie and the wrong crest.'

Seeing those men and the anger on their faces made me realize that going to Eton could make you a stranger in parts of your own country. You could be treated with the same uneasiness that met Americans who came to England and tried to fit in.

I knew a few Americans who tried this. They saw England from a distance and fell in love with the castles and the titles, so they packed up their money and came to England, trying to slip into the ranks. But the English more than anyone could spot a foreigner. I once heard that no enemy prisoner ever escaped from England during the last war, partly because it was an island, but also because the English could pick out the slightest trace of a foreign accent or the most tiny irregularity of clothing.

If they were rich enough, some Americans worked their way into what they considered the right clubs and attended all the right parties. They let their words grow rounder with the English pronouncing of words. They bought suits from Gieves and spread-collar shirts from Turnbull and Asser and had their shoes custom-made at Lobb: the same clothes that Rupert borrowed off his uncles. But to the English, they were always just the Posers.

The English might never mention it, and so the Americans might think their Euro-camouflage was perfect. They might think of them-selves as transatlantic chameleons, owning the best of both worlds and the respect of the English, which they valued more than any-thing else. But they never got it.

The reason they never got it was because they didn't understand one thing, or if they did understand, then they pretended to ignore it. The thing was that in America, you can start from nothing and if you make enough money, you can work your way to the top of society, all in one lifetime.

But it wasn't the same in England. Your family had to be old, and old in a way that Americans found hard to picture, because it was an old which was hundreds and hundreds of years older than the founding of America itself. To reach the social top, there were so many traps and passwords to be spoken, that people who tried often got lost in the maze and looked foolish.

But you could also look pretty foolish being an Etonian down at the Globe pub in Fishguard in South Wales. It was a key to some places, but it often got the door slammed in your face as well.

There was no grey zone. You either were or you weren't. It was as clear as the black and white of our tail-suits. And even out of school uniform, I heard people say that you could spot an Etonian at a hundred yards just by the way he carried himself. Usually it was true.

It seemed that all of us were beginning to ask questions that we had never asked before. Even Rupert, who at first mistook his confusion for some kind of insult, but he couldn't think who had insulted him. To balance this, he decided to take offence at everything.

Wittingham got tired of ties and crests and his family in Moreton-in-Marsh. He decided that he was really an American. Something had just clicked inside him. He told me about this one morning on our way over to breakfast. I had the feeling he had woken up especially early so he could corner me at breakfast and tell me his story with no one else listening, except perhaps for Moriarty, who didn't matter anyway.

I looked him in his ex-Pretty Boy face and thought – This is a trick. You and Manson have conjured up some complicated joke to make me look stupid. So I gave him the Beady Eye and said nothing.

But for weeks after that, he spoke to me in a badly faked American accent and kept a pencil stub in his mouth as if it was a cigarette.

I could never tell whether or not he was kidding around. Manson said wouldn't it be a better idea to pretend he was Japanese, since weren't they the ones who made all the electrical gadgets that had turned his room into something that looked like a bird's-nest made of different coloured wires? Rupert called him a traitor and said he should have his British passport torn up. But Wittingham stuck to it. He was a stubborn old fart and had dug his spindly legs in deep. You had to admire him for it.

If this was a joke, I had to admit, he was playing it all by himself.

He never could explain what had brought on the change. To him, it didn't matter. The change had come and he did not question it.

Wittingham had never been to America, as most people I knew hadn't. But he had read the gangster stories and the money stories and he had seen the pictures. Instead of hating it, the way everybody else seemed to, Wittingham had fallen in love with it.

He said he was going there as soon as he could, and puffed on the end of his pencil. He told me there was nothing for him here in England and least of all at Eton.

'You see, this used to be a place for Empire Builders. People who would go out and conquer the world. But now that's all changed. All it is now is a place for Empire Rulers. Do you see the difference between the Builders and the Rulers? All the Rulers have is arrogance. Some of these old families are resting on prestige and wealth that was won by someone who worked for it and risked their life for it hundreds of years ago. But some of the people who have the wealth and titles now have all grown slack-jawed and lazy. All they know how to do is hold on to what they've got.'

He told me it was different in America. In America, everybody had a chance to make it. You didn't have to live your life based on what your ancestors had done.

I didn't know if it was true or not. That didn't matter to Wittingham. Once when I went to Mr Rosser's study to show him my report card, he looked up and joked that Wittingham had become more American than I was.

It cut me to hear that, the same as when Rupert had said I thought too much. But both of them were right, and I found out that it was only the true things that could cut you and keep returning over the years to cut just as painfully as they did the first time.

The truth was that I had stopped being an American so long ago that I'd forgotten when it was. It was one thing to have other people say that, but another to believe it myself. And now I did believe it.

This crept into the stories I was writing. They were always about a person leaving one place and going to another place and trying to survive. Mr Debenham, my English teacher, had once said that writers usually have one theme that runs like a red thread through all their work. Now I wondered if this was my theme – the search for a homeland, to be worthy of it and to be accepted and to have a homeland at all. I knew that there must be millions of people out there who I had never met and who perhaps didn't even speak the same language as me, but who had the same thread running through their lives. It seemed to me that this was what America was all about – coming to the New World and leaving the old one behind. But you could never leave the Old World completely. It would always be a part of you.

It frightened me a little to think that the theme for my whole life might already have been engraved in my brain, but it also gave me a focus.

There had been no thunder-clap of knowledge or some golden-fuzzy vision appearing at the foot of my bed and telling me what I had to do. Instead, the vision took its time, and more than once I had misunderstood what it meant. I kept very quiet about it, because I doubted if I could have put it into words even if there was someone I wanted to tell.

Twice a week, Rupert and Moriarty and I set out across the playing fields after dark, on our way to Mr Debenham's.

Often we came across two boys named Godfrey and Fletcher, who had built a motorcycle and sidecar from old parts at the School of Mechanics. They always seemed to be rebuilding it and having grand launching ceremonies, which would see the bike about fifty metres down the road and out onto the playing fields before it stalled. Then they'd wheel it back to the School of Mechanics. They were a strange couple, lost in their own world and the world of that old BSA bike. They put so much faith and energy into its dented frame and frayed wires that when one of them heaved his weight up onto the starter, it was as if they meant not merely to fire up its engine but to bring that machine entirely to life.

Mr Debenham was our adviser, as well as my English teacher, and we had to show him our report cards. The time we spent at his house was called Pupil Room. We crammed into his little study and sometimes his wife brought in tea.

He tried to be friendly with us, in a way that he could not have been in class. He tried to make this seem like neutral ground. But that didn't work. We still called him 'sir' and still sat with our backs straight and hands tucked into pockets. He was always the teacher and we were always students. You couldn't switch it on and off like a light bulb.

His house smelled of his baby, who was only a couple of months old. It was a heavy, rancid smell and made our noses twitch, the same way I had seen parents twitch their noses when they came to visit their sons at the Eton houses.

We had to spend an hour at Mr Debenham's. We knew he'd rather be in the kitchen with his wife and kid or at least watching the TV. And we'd sooner have been in our rooms or stealing toast from the prefect Library. But it was the rule that we had to spend an hour there, so Mr Debenham would announce a topic for discussion. Then we'd have to discuss.

Should the Royal family be abolished? (Moriarty calls the Royals fascists and Rupert gets all red-faced. I say something and everyone tells me to shut up because I'm a Yank and this is none of my business. Mr Debenham tries to calm everyone down, but Rupert is mad as hell now and calling us all Bolsheviks. Then Mr Debenham announces that the hour is up. He sits back and dabs at his forehead with a handkerchief.)

Is the National Health system a good thing? (Rupert says he's sick and tired of people who don't work for a living and if they don't work, they shouldn't get free health care. Moriarty laughs in his face and there is almost a fight. I open my mouth and Rupert tells me to shut up. Mr Debenham says that everyone should have a chance to speak but by now I have forgotten what I was going to say.)

If the Eton school motto is going to be changed, what should we have instead of Floreat Etona? (I say – 'We're Only Here For The Beer,' and for the next half-hour we veto every suggestion Mr Debenham makes, with his brave Latin words about Loyalty and Service.)

Should there be Voluntary Euthanasia? (We all say – Yes. If they want to die, let the poor old buggers die. Death means nothing to us. It is too far away. Then there is nothing more to talk about and Mr Debenham lets us go early.)

Mr Debenham was angry with us for not taking his games seriously. As far as he was concerned, he was offering us the change to change our world, even if just in little ways, and all we did was make fun of him.

But what he didn't see was that all we knew of our world was school, and here we were in tail-suits that may have been in fashion 150 years ago, knowing that very little changed at this place and what did change was rarely because of us or any efforts we might make.

That was the way it went with the whole system of being a servant to a senior boy. The Headmaster said he thought it ought to be abolished and asked us all to vote on it. So we voted, and our vote was to keep the system, because I was damned to hell if I was going to serve a senior boy for a year and make his farty old bed and bring him tea which he poured out the window if I had added too much sugar, and then not have the privilege of having someone make my farty old bed for a year when I got to be a senior.

But then the Headmaster went ahead and abolished it anyway. That didn't make me angry. I knew I'd voted for the wrong reason. But it did make me angry to sit there in Mr Debenham's baby-smelling house and pretend that I could change things that I had no power to change. Not yet anyway.

In time, the power would come. That was the way it had been at the Dragon and it was the same here at Eton. You did what you were told and if you did it for long enough, you'd get to turn around someday and tell someone else what to do.

I was angry at Mr Debenham, but angry in a way that could not be put into words without him taking offence. So I kept silent.

Rupert and Moriarty and I walked back to the house across the night-black fields. Some nights, Godfrey and Fletcher would still be out there with their motorcycle. They looked like lost spacemen who had crashed to earth, struggling to leave the planet again and roar back out among the dusty rings of Saturn.

On one of those nights, hearing the cough of their engine turning over, Moriarty sneered at them and said – 'There they go again, trying to jump-start the entire world.'

We turned up the collars of our greatcoats and looked at the sky smudged pink from the lights of Slough, as if the whole city was going up in flames.

When summer came and the Rugby boots, still caked with winter mud, stayed untouched in our lockers, I found myself in the athletics team. I walked out each afternoon to the track and threw the discus or the javelin. I practised until the sun got tangled in the trees and then I wandered home for tea.

The secret of the Eagle House angels was lost now. I won a few badges at the meeting held here or up at the Iffley Road track in Oxford, but I never again saw the spear take off from my hand and rise so far and steadily as I had seen it years before. It didn't matter. I was writing every day now and saved the best of my energy for that. I walked back through the playing fields, seeing cricket teams and hearing the clock of a bat striking a ball, hammering out ideas as I went along.

On Saturdays, when classes ended at 1.15, I'd forget about athletics and head into Windsor with Rupert, overtaken by the sprinting boys trying to make the 1.35 train into London.

Rupert and I wandered down Peascod Street and stared at the tourists. Americans were easy to spot, because they were usually dressed the way they thought the English dressed. They wore their English-style trench coats and English driving caps and the women wore plaid skirts. You could tell the Americans from a long way off.

We bought our usual bread and cheese and fresh coffee. Then in the evenings, we sat in my room, cutting the cheese with an old stiletto knife that had belonged to Rupert's grandfather, who had been a commando in the war. We brewed the coffee and drank it with milk stolen from the Library.

As it grew dark, we'd hear the bands start playing out by the riverside restaurants. If the breeze was blowing right, we'd hear each note of the songs and when they were finished, the sound of people clapping.

One evening, as the clapping died away and I made out the far-away laughter of women and men, I felt my throat tighten up. I was thinking how I had never been to a restaurant by the river and sat listening to the band. I'd never talked to girls. Whole months went by when I hardly even saw girls my age, except to glimpse them on the sunny afternoons in Windsor.

I had never been in love and didn't have a clue what that felt like.

It made me sad to think that my greatest pleasure was to buy cheese and bread and coffee and sit on my window-sill, hearing the distant people laughing in the dark.

I wondered if I'd ever meet a girl and fall in love. I wondered what she'd look like and where she was now and how our paths would cross. If I could just see her, I thought, just catch a glimpse of her and know that someday we'd meet up, then I wouldn't feel as bad as I did then.

I was made a junior prefect. A Member of Debate. The other prefects bust into my room at two in the morning to tell me I was elected. They emptied a can of olive-oil on my head and then followed that with a jar of coffee powder. It took a week of three showers a day for the smell to go away and for my hair to stop shining like glass.

As a Member of Debate, my job was to talk down the hallway each night and check that the New Boys had their lights off. I'd pop open the door and slam it shut again. One boy named Davis rigged up a string to his doorknob so that the light shut off as soon as anyone tried to open the door. I unscrewed all the light bulbs in his room and threw them out into Mr Rosser's garden. The privilege of being a junior prefect was that now we were allowed to have radios. For most of us, all it meant was that now we didn't have to keep our radios hidden under the floorboards. We could also watch an extra half hour of TV each weekend, which brought it up to two hours a week.

If I'd known what was going to happen only a few days later, I would have told them to take back their privileges, to take away my rank and the authority they offered me. I would have done just about anything to have avoided what happened at the end of that same week.

I was patrolling the dorms on a Friday night. I flicked open the door to Davis's room to check that his light was out and that he hadn't rigged up another string on his doorknob. Davis was lying in bed. But standing next to the bed was another boy named Elliot. He was the one who had fallen in love with Wittingham. Elliot wrote him the love letter which somehow fell into Manson's hands. Standing next to Davis, Elliot still wore his tail-coat and waistcoat and shirt, but his trousers were down by his ankles.

At first, nobody said anything.

Then Davis reached under his mattress and pulled out a miniature TV. 'Elliot was trying to buy my TV off me. You have it instead. Keep it. Just keep it.' Davis held out the TV set.

Elliot was shaking. He bent down and pulled up his trousers. Then he went over and stood beside the window.

I didn't say anything. I looked at Davis and then at Elliot and then back at Davis.

Davis held out the TV until it was too heavy. Then he set it down on the bed and took his wallet from his bedside table. He took some money from it and tried to stuff it in my hand. 'Take it,' he kept saying.

Elliot had his face pressed against Davis's window.

'Take the money!' Davis hissed in my face.

I turned and walked out. I walked to Rupert's room and told him what I'd seen. I told him I didn't know what to do. At first Rupert said we should just forget about it. Then he changed his mind suddenly and said we should take it to Rosser.

We went to Rosser's study and told him what had happened.

Rosser sat at his desk, slowly narrowing his eyes and nodding and nodding and nodding. His hands tiptoed back and forth over his blotter, as if he was trying to remember the tune on a piano.

My knees were shaking and I couldn't talk straight.

Rosser smiled at me and said he would talk it over with Rupert for a while and Thank You Very Much.

At first I didn't understand why Rosser had sent me away. But then it dawned on me why Rupert had changed his mind about turning them in. Rupert had his heart set on being House Captain next year. This was a way for Rupert to show Rosser that he knew what was up in the house and would keep Rosser informed. Rosser needed someone who would keep him informed.

I sat in my room and began to realize what kind of a mistake I had made – how it was none of my damned business what Elliot and Davis did behind closed doors. I thought about all the jokes and butt-slapping and doors locked shut with chairs heaved up against them. I'd heard the slippered tread from room to room in the night.

Elliot lived in the room next to mine.

I heard him crying, because he knew I had taken it to Rosser. I heard the gurgle of misery at the back of his throat and listened while he tore his posters off the wall. I dug my fingers into my wrists, as if to punish myself or take some of the pain for him.

Nothing happened. Rosser didn't do a damned thing.

As soon as Rupert realized this, he made sure everyone knew it was me who had turned in Davis and Elliott. He didn't tell about the conference he'd had with Rosser, and no one would listen to what I had to say.

People stopped talking to me. I found myself sitting alone at a table at lunch, while the other tables were crammed with people. My Rugby boots disappeared and I never saw them again. I had a German beer mug that I used for drinking tea. It disappeared as well.

That weekend, I was sitting on my window-sill, eating bread and cheese and watching the sun go down. The door burst open and Wittingham walked in. He didn't say a word. He ransacked the room, looking for cigarettes, alcohol, porn magazines. Anything he could find that would prove I was breaking the rules. He never looked at me while he pulled the books off my shelf and flipped my bed over and pulled out the drawers of my desk.

I didn't try to stop him. I just sat there. As he was leaving, I said – 'I don't blame you.'

Wittingham paused and looked at me, his cheeks flushed red from anger.

'I don't blame you,' I said again. 'It was a terrible mistake and there's nothing I can do to put it right and I won't be forgiving myself.'

Wittingham gave a slight nod. The harshness seemed to leave his face. Then he disappeared.

The bad things stopped after that. People sat with me and talked with me, except we never mentioned Elliot and Davis and what had happened.

I had new steel lugs put on the heels of my shoes. As I walked around checking that people's lights were out, I made so much noise to warn them I was coming, that Rosser complained he could hear me on his side of the house and the Dame said I was ruining the floors.

The whole business made me realize that Rupert and I were only friends up to a point. He had seen his chance to get ahead, weighed it against the cost of our friendship, and the getting ahead had won out. It was a very long while before I forgave Rupert for twisting things the way he did. I'd done a few things and not let myself off the hook, but this was the first time I didn't forgive someone else.

The term ended just in time. I threw some clothes in my rucksack and hopped on a bus to the airport.

I walked into Terminal Three of Heathrow Airport and for a while I just stood still in the chaos of carts trundling past and the boom of the announcer's voice and the muffled thunder of planes taking off overhead.

As I stepped onto the plane, I took a deep breath and slammed the door on England for a while.

But all through the holidays and for weeks and months after that, I woke with a shout from the deepest sleep, calling to the memory of myself as I walked down the short yellow-walled corridor to Rosser's study, with Rupert close behind.

My brother had a job that summer. He worked selling frozen

lemonade for a company called Hippel's. Their sign was a golden palm tree. Everybody knew about Hippel's lemonade, and their antique red and white trucks that you mostly saw broken down on the side of the road with steam puffing out of their overheated radiators.

The owner had a gun, my brother said. Their main office had been robbed a bunch of times, so now the owner packed a .44 Ruger in a shoulder holster. It gave you a funny feeling to walk up to the window and buy fifty-cents-worth of ice and water and lemon peel from a man dressed as if he was going to war.

My brother worked on a commission, but he had to pay for petrol and when his truck broke down, the owner tried to make him pay for repairs, too. Mostly Clive spent his time riding to a beach, selling lemonade for ten minutes and then being moved on by the police. He drank so much lemonade that it made him sick. Then he wouldn't touch it any more. But still he came home sticky and citrus-smelling, with flies landing on his skin and getting glued to it.

I saw Clive once as I was coming back from Newport on the bus. He sat in his Hippel's truck in an empty car-park. The rain was coming down hard. He had his chin resting on his hands and was just staring out at the rain.

Sometimes he met up with Eric and they sat in the truck mixing vodka with the lemonade. Once, as he was riding back to the depot, he turned a corner and his changebox slid out the side window. He said it all seemed to happen in slow motion. The box flew out and then there was an explosion of silver and copper as pennies and nickels and quarters rolled jangling across the road and into the bushes.

He got out of his truck and just started kicking the tyres. He'd never find all the money again, so he kicked the tyres and cussed. People in passing cars waved and beeped their horns and drove over his money.

Clive quit working for Hippel's. After that, we'd cheer every time we saw a Hippel's truck broken down by the side of the road and some poor college boy or girl standing there waiting for a tow.

But we still bought the lemonade, because there was nothing like it in the mad-dog heat of August, when even the ocean wouldn't cool you down.

My brother was American now. It seemed to me that the last trace of his time at school in England had been washed out of him.

He talked differently and dressed differently and he laughed at different jokes. Sometimes it seemed to me that I did not know him any better than Sam or Eric or Allen. And they did not know me, my voice crippled into the voice of a stranger by the English twisting of words.

As the summer moved ahead, I found my old place among them, but each year the place became harder to find and in the end I gave up trying to fit into America, just as I had given up trying to fit into England.

I found myself belonging to a blurred and drifting place somewhere between. There was no mid-Atlantic Watty Dog island, with hard land under foot. I just punished myself by dreaming about that. The place where I seemed to belong was more of a Sargasso, just drifting in the jade-green waves.

There had to be others who drifted back and forth from land to land, but I had never met them. Sometimes in the corral of the British Airways Nannies at Heathrow Airport, I used to look at the other uniformed boys and girls and hunt for some blink of recognition. But these people were usually English, with their parents in the Foreign Office or in some last-ditch stronghold of the Empire. I knew people like them at school, and in their distance from the mother country, they became more English than the English themselves.

So these weren't the people I was looking for. And neither was it the Americans, who when they reached Britain were forced to become like cartoon Americans, ambassadors of TV shows and Thompson-blasting gangsters and cowboys who'd been dead a hundred years.

Sometimes I felt sorry for myself, with this feeling of no solid ground that I could say belonged to me. But other times, I was glad, because I got to see both countries for what they really were. You had to go away from a place to know what it was you took for granted in the land you left behind.

It didn't matter where I was, because a part of me was always floating on the weeds of my Sargasso, spying on two distant shores, not rebelling, but not fitting in either.

There were cliffs at Fort Wetherill and for us they became a kind of sacred ground. The Fort was built around the time of the First World War, to protect the Navy in Newport. Its concrete walls were

173

ten foot thick and the empty gun pits still lay there, green with rain-water and weeds.

On breezy August afternoons, Sam, Allen, Eric and my brother and I would all be out at the edge of the rocks, hearing the waves smack the cliffs and rumble back out to open sea. We'd sit on the sharp rock, avoiding oily poison ivy leaves that bubbled up from the gritty soil. We watched the bright-spinnakered boats sail out towards Block Island. The long hair of the women would trail behind them as the boats reached the mouth of the bay and gath-ered speed, tilting over into the bay. If we had binoculars, we'd spy on the Newport mansions, their endless clean-cut lawns always clogged with party people, men in blue blazers with silk ascots and women in high heels, stumbling on the grass.

Planes flew overhead, trailing streamer messages that announced races at the Taunton Greyhound track or Big Money Prizes at the Newport Hi-Li games.

The Navy had gone from Newport, sometime in the early 1970s. My father had made me watch the huge grey cruisers as they left, knowing they would never come back. He had told me it was the end of an era. I saw the great migration of the steel ships and I wondered if it was like that for the last of the Conanicut Indians, loading up their canoes and paddling out to sea to disappear for-ever among the grey Atlantic waves, with the same strange stillness in the air.

Now all that remained was the Navy War College and the train-ing ships that scudded across the bay. You could hear the orders barked over loudspeakers on their decks. Once I heard a Navy ship blare the 'Ride of the Valkyries' all across the bay, like in the helicopter scene of *Apocalypse Now*.

Sometimes people would park their cars at Fort Wetherill and walk towards the edge of the cliff. Mostly, they never came close. They stood up on their toes and squinted down at the froth of waves that slapped back off the brittle pink and khaki rock, seventy feet below.

Then I would get up and stretch and say – 'Well, boys, she left me and I can't go on any more.'

We had a whole play worked out. The others would say – 'Oh, don't do it. Think of your family. Think of the mess.'

By now the tourists would have noticed. Their eyes narrowed and their nostrils flared as they sniffed around for blood. They grinned, thinking I would only go to the edge, closer than them perhaps, but not over the top.

The thing about jumping off cliffs at Fort Wetherill was that you couldn't allow yourself to pause when you got to the edge. There was a tongue of rock that stuck out a little further than the others. From there you could see all the way down, and once you looked fear would creep up on you and even the shame of having chickened out wouldn't stop you from backing away.

It was almost a relief to step off the edge, the first screams of the tourists already fading from my ears. The air was punched out of my lungs. Blood streamed into my head. I saw the slicks of foam and smelled the salt spray and then it was all around me. The water smacked my feet hard and if I had forgotten to tuck in my hands, the sting would spread along the length of my arm and stay there for days. A sound like thunder whipped past and then the tingle of millions of bubbles shoved down when I hit the water as they carried me back to the surface, but upside down. You always came up feet first. So the first you'd see of Eric if he had jumped in were the suction-cup treads of his Converse Hightops, or Sam's Nike running shoes with their waffle-grid sole. I had my Dunlop Green Flashes, with tread-like bolt after crooked bolt of lightning laid out side by side.

Eric had just had an operation on his hip, and his mother would have ripped him apart like a rag-doll if she had ever known he was jumping off the cliffs. But Eric jumped more than any of us. He jumped from places where it was maybe fifty/fifty that you'd die. He dived and knocked himself stupid on the hard floor of the waves. There was brave and there was foolish and sometimes Eric danced across the line.

Once you were in the water, you had to catch the waves just right, to be carried on to the rocks of the cliff. Otherwise they would spit you up and drag you back down over the barnacles and you'd spend the rest of the day picking crumbs of white barnacle shell from your bloody wrists and palms. As you climbed the rocks, the sun would already be drying your back. There was a path up the steep sides, which brought you out where the tourists couldn't see, so they'd still think you were dead and down below.

Their panic would send them running around in circles like Eric's mad dog Fang. But it wasn't really panic. They were thrilled. They edged a little closer to the cliff, stretching out their rubbery necks, and tried to take a photo as my broken body washed out to sea.

Their nostrils twitched out of control, hunting for the smell of blood. They always screamed for someone to call the police, but they never went themselves. They were too keen on seeing the body. Then their panic would turn to suspicion and they'd scuttle back to their cars, not wanting to be around when the police arrived.

We rode home on the sun-scorched seats of Eric's mother's Delta 88, a car so big it wouldn't even fit on the roads where my aunt and uncle lived in Wales. The car had a hole in its muffler, so the noise of the V8 engine would deafen us.

For a while, nothing could touch you if you'd just jumped off the cliffs. Your heart beat so strong and steady in your chest that you'd think it would never quit. And there was the sun, blinding you and keeping your bare back warm and your shoes still squelching with salt water.

Once, as we tore away up North Main Road, sun shattering off the water, I thought back to a time one winter when I took the bus out to Fort Wetherill. Snow was two foot deep on the ground. I had on seven layers and still the wind blowing down from the North-East chipped its way through each crossed fibre of my clothing. I was alone then. I stumped through the snow to the cliffs and looked down at the ice stuck on the rocks. The sea looked darker, the jade turned unreflecting emerald and muddied with black. It wasn't the same water, anyway. I heard that the ocean in the summer drifted up from the Caribbean. This had come down on the Labrador current, slipping past the pale-blue iceberg mountains off Greenland. You could only last three minutes in that water, I had heard. When trawlers went down this time of year, their crews were almost never saved. They were the only boats that cruised the Newport channel now. The sailboats had all dry-docked for the winter. All that remained of the poison ivy were threads of dead branches. The lawns of the Newport mansions across the bay were clean ivory sheets, and the Newport summer people had crept away back to their cities. I stood there for a long time, feeling my toes go numb, then stumped away home.

I shook the thought from my head and the summer afternoon heat washed back over me. We had all fallen silent. I figured we were all thinking about how it was too good to last. We were growing up now and soon there would be no space in our lives for jumping off the cliffs and no glory in it, even if we had the time. I knew we were all thinking that, but it was never a thing you could say.

CHAPTER 10

AND SUDDENLY, THERE I was again, thirty thousand feet in the air and strapped into my seat. My eyes were dried out and old Rugby wounds cramped under my kneecaps. The stewardesses were handing out little tubs of orange juice which for as long as I could remember had come from the same company – Ardmore Farms in Florida. Sunrise was strips of violent red and pink and yellow across the tundra of clouds. When the clouds broke open, I could see the silhouette of Wales. There was Dinas Head, which you could see from my aunt and uncle's living room, waves rolling in off the Irish Sea and ploughing up the walls of rock. The whole country was the colour of paprika.

I felt the pressure in my ears as the plane began to descend. Reaching above the steady blast of the engines came the scream of babies who didn't know how to yawn and release the pressure from their blocked ears.

I heard the landing gear go down.

The stewardesses folded out their little seats and strapped themselves in. They chatted and looked calm, watched by passengers who were not calm but realized that if anything went wrong, the stewardesses would be the first ones to know. The stewardesses knew they were being watched. They had to – all those dried-out eyes fixed on them and the steady click of hands fidgeting with the ash-tray lids. It was part of their job to look calm. I figured we could have been in a burning tail-spin, coming down from half a mile up in the sky and they would have kept the same smiles bolted to their cheeks.

I usually ran down the echoing corridors to the passport counter. Then I'd stand in line, hearing the clunk-thump of passports being stamped and the mutter of the line controller, telling people which booth to go to next.

My stomach was acid from the orange juice.

I grabbed my suitcase off the conveyor-belt downstairs and ran for the Underground line. More echoing corridors, dabbed with posters advertising Duty-Free shopping (Hello and Good Buy) and one passage with a strange black thread running the whole length of the wall. It traced the outlines of the Taj Mahal, London Bridge, the Statue of Liberty and the Eiffel Tower.

Commuters packed the tube train, which lurched up from its tunnel and sped above ground, dodging through the rain-spattered English morning and the London suburban streets. Men and women read newspapers and stubbed out their cigarettes on the deep-grooved wooden floor. I peered over their shoulders at the headlines and watched the hand-holding springs wobble from the ceiling.

I was glad to be back. At first, the thought surprised me. But I had to admit I'd missed Rupert and Wittingham and Moriarty. I could no longer deny that I took a kind of pleasure in being swallowed up by the school, having nothing but study and sleep and steel-studded Rugby charges down the fields that led towards Slough.

'Slough. This is Sleeeow,' cried the platform announcer's voice.

Sometimes I didn't want to wait for the train into Windsor, so I walked to Eton from there. It was a couple of miles, and by the time I arrived my hands were blistered from carrying the suit-case.

I always got back early. The first deep breath of the house was sour in my lungs. It was all the old boot polish, tea, laundry, boy sweat and chlorine disinfectant cubes in the downstairs urinals. It only lasted a second. Then the smell was familiar again, as if crystals were realigning themselves in my body.

I lay on my bed with the door closed, waiting for the other boys to come shuffling down the corridor and into their rooms.

Now I was impatient for it to begin again. With the great tidal wave of work about to crash down on my head, I knew that time was about to bend out of shape. It would spread itself onto the chart of classes and Rugby games and soon there would be no time to think. And besides, there was something new this year. This year was the year of the Corps.

I was about ready to join the Corps. The Eton College Officer Training Corps. For some it was the most conformist thing a boy could do at Eton but for me it was full-scale rebellion. Even though it was changing one uniform for another, being swathed in camouflage opened up instincts that I had spent most of my time trying to batten down. For too long now I'd been hearing the crash of hob-nailed boots on the parade ground and seeing khaki-suited Corps recruits clatter past in the alleyway outside my window.

Some told me that the two-day field manoeuvres were the most fun they'd had at Eton, and I was ready to believe them. I didn't even go to the speech that the Corps officer gave to draw in new recruits. Instead, I just signed up.

The only hesitation that ticked over in my mind came from something that Sacker had told me just before he left the school. He said that the Corps could bring out a side of you that you might not want to see. It was the side that loved uniforms and being shrieked at by the cold-eyed Welsh Guardsmen who came down from Windsor to train us. It was the side that went out looking for a fight and liked the idea of shooting guns.

That side was there in all of us. There was no way to deny it, and suddenly we were not children any more and playing with sticks by the river-bank. These were Enfield .303s and General Purpose Machine-Guns and Stirling Submachine Guns and Wombat Anti-tank Guns and the Browning Hi-Power Pistol.

We had the instinct for it. At the age of sixteen, I had a better instinct than I would ever have again.

So you had to ask yourself very quietly – Now that you are not a child any more, is this still what you want?

The Corps gave you a chance to decide. It was a trial run, which most of us needed if we wanted to be sure.

If you joined the Corps, you didn't have to give a reason why. If I'd had to give a reason, I probably wouldn't have joined. But nobody asked, so I picked up my kit and for the first time weighed a man-killing gun in my hands.

The first thing I learned in the Corps was that I could not march. I couldn't march now and I would never be able to march, no matter how much the sergeants screamed at me. Sometimes the whole platoon would spin around one way and I would be left facing in the other direction.

It was just one of those things. When the sergeant-major learned that I came from America, he seemed to think that he had found the reason for my bad marching. No Americans could march, he said. He blamed it on the rolling-hipped way that Americans walked, and the fact that American soldiers wore rubber-soled boots whereas the British still had steel on their marching boots. He looked at me with sympathy. Then suddenly his eyes lit up – 'I bet you can shoot, though,' he said. 'There's nothing like a good old Yankee marksman.'

He was right, which made me feel a little better about the fool I had made of myself on the parade-ground. I lay on the hemp-twine mats in the shooting gallery above the gym and fired round after round with an Anschutz target rifle. Then they took me out to a rifle range at Bisley and I fired the Enfields and FNs. I could no more explain why I could shoot well than I could explain why I found it impossible to march. I got used to being deaf after using the Enfields, and I got used to the targets, which were cardboard cut-outs of a man running towards me with a gun.

I found my place in the Corps, in the shooting and the trampled dirt of the assault course and out in the rain on the manoeuvres. My bad marching became a matter of fact. I was even a little proud of it. In time, I did get better, but by then they had made me a platoon commander. Then I was supposed to order others around the parade-ground and I was worse at that than anything else. When an inspecting General came to visit and we marched past him, my platoon did so badly I had to write the General a letter of apology.

Every couple of months, we dressed in the green and khaki and black slashes of British Army camouflage and headed out on manoeuvres. We piled into the backs of Bedford trucks and drove to the training-ground. We each had an old .303 rifle and three blank bullets to fire.

For the next two days, we wandered across the bare hills of Salisbury Plain or slithered through the thick pine-woods of Aldershot, hunting each other down.

After our three blanks were used up, all we could do was say 'Bang!' Or if we were throwing a practice grenade, we shouted 'Big Bang!'

Our rations came in green foil packets, which we emptied out into our mess tins and cooked over hand-size Hexamine stoves. The Hexamine fuel was white tablets that burned with a bitter smoke. It got in our eyes and into our clothes; soon everyone smelled of Hexamine. I kept my pockets stuffed with Callard and Bowser toffees and ate them until the roof of my mouth was raw.

One night on patrol, as I wandered with Rupert to the top of a bare and moonlit field, we saw the huge pillars of Stonehenge on the horizon. For a long time we only stood there watching it, feeling as if we had both somehow been hurled into the distant past.

Then we scrambled down the slope into a deserted village called Imber. When the Army took over the area as a training-ground around the time of the Great War, they made the villagers move out. Now all that remained was the church and the fenced-off graveyard. The other buildings had been knocked down and rebuilt as solid concrete without glass in the windows or wood for the doors. Signs showed which buildings were supposed to be the post office and bank. I was told that this was where soldiers trained for Ireland in the fine art of house-clearing and street warfare.

Rupert and I stood in the shadows. We had come to check out if anyone was in the village. Then we had to report back to camp. We were just about to leave, when Rupert pulled me down and told me to be quiet.

A column of men marched through the main street. We could tell they were regular Army because their weapons were newer than ours and they wore helmets, whereas we only had dark green berets. The soldiers made almost no sound. There was only the shuffle of their boots on the road. They passed by and it was silent again in the village.

Rupert and I kept to the shadows as we dodged away like rabbits back to camp.

The manoeuvres always ended with a big staged attack. Somehow, this always seemed to go wrong and we would end up shooting at our own troops or waiting to ambush people who never showed up. I lost count of the times I lay in ditches, rifle over my chest, chewing toffees and staring up at the sky while our Corps officer swore and rechecked his map coordinates. His name was Oscar and we called him Fuggy. There was not much to say about Fuggy except that if he had been leading us in a real war, we would all have been dead long ago.

Then the trucks pulled up again and we drove back to school. My hands always ached from the cold and from carrying the rifle. Each pore on my face was pinpricked black with dirt and camouflage paint. I spent the rest of the day in the bathtub, big toe wedged against the hot water tap and adding hot water when the bath cooled down.

That evening, Rupert and I would be down in the boot-room getting ready for parade the next day. We melted polish in spoons over a candle and then poured the blue-flaming black liquid over the toe-caps of our boots. When the polish was dry, we'd spit on it and rub the toe-caps with a handkerchief until we could see our faces in the shine.

Rupert left the Corps as soon as he could, but I stayed on a while longer. As part of a machine-gun crew, I was teamed up with a boy named Andrew Thomas. He wore his beret as if he was trying to camouflage himself as a giant mushroom. It frightened him to be out on manoeuvres and many times when we were being attacked and I had the gun set up in a ditch, ready to catch the advancing enemy in a crossfire, Thomas would freeze up and forget to unwrap the belts of machine-gun ammunition from across his shoulders. He would fumble with the bands of brass and steel until I lost my temper and just threw him down. Then I'd pop the belt from around his body and feed it into the gun myself. If we were being overrun, he would be too afraid to leave cover and fight it out, and sometimes I had to drag him back into the woods by the scruff of his neck. It had been different with Rupert around. He was always making pompous comments, even in the middle of the fighting, but he was quick and I trusted him.

After Rupert had left, I would find myself out on manoeuvres and in the middle of some ambush with gunfire and rocket flares all around and Thomas cowering in the brambles, and I would catch myself thinking – I wish Rupert could be here beside me.

Moriarty had decided to rebel that term, although to the rest of us it seemed that he had been rebelling all along. At first he couldn't make up his mind exactly how he wanted to rebel, but then he decided on wearing an ear-ring. They were against the school rules, so he got a little gold stud ear-ring anyway and put a band-aid over his ear-lobe. He told the teachers he had hurt it playing Rugby, but we all knew he had an ear-ring under there. He also wore Doc Marten boots instead of dress shoes, but either because they weren't against the rules for some reason or because none of the teachers had noticed, he got away with it. They were the high-lace-up kind as well, that stretched almost up to his knees.

Rupert took all of this personally. He said you either went to Eton and stuck by it, or you didn't, in which case (he jerked his chin towards the grey industrial buildings of Slough on the horizon) you should just bugger off back into the real world. 'Moriarty's just missing the point,' Rupert shouted to me.

I was only a few feet away, stretched out on his bed and memorizing Goethe for a test. I hardly ever paid attention to Rupert and his little rages. I even played the game of rating his tantrums the way a weatherman gauges the wind. Sometimes it would just be blustery. Other times he would work himself up into a gale and of course there was always the danger of a hurricane if the Labour Party ever came to power. Usually, I just let him get tired out and then dragged him over to Tap for a few pints of Blackthorn Cider, which would always calm him down.

Rupert wasn't finished yet. 'The point is that if he really wanted to leave, he should have left by now.'

'Maybe his parents won't let him.' I gave up on Goethe. My head was stuffed with quotes from iron-chested knights and treacherous brothers. *Weh der Nachkommenheit, die dich verkennt.*

'Rubbish!' Rupert picked up a page of his paper, crumpled it and threw it on the floor. 'He could join the Army, then.'

'I can't see Moriarty in the Army somehow.'

'Rubbish! There's always the Foreign Legion. They take anybody!'

Now I sat up. 'But perhaps he doesn't *want* to join the Army or the Foreign Bloody Legion!'

Rupert sat back red-faced into his chair. 'Rubbish,' he said again. He had run out of steam.

'How about a pint at Tap, Rupert?'

He stood up suddenly. 'Oh, that's a good idea!' He rammed his hands into his pockets, looking for change. Then he poured the coins into his hand and counted them. 'I'm good for a couple of drinks.'

As we walked down to Tap, hands in our pockets and looking at our shoes, I thought about Moriarty and how Rupert said he had missed the point. It seemed to me that no one really missed the point about Eton.

The Point was whatever you made of it. If the Point was to spend the rest of your life saying what crap the whole place was, and how much you had rebelled when you were there, then that could be your Point. Or if you were like Rupert, you might leave the school and think to yourself that since you were an Old Etonian, you had done all the hard work you ought to do in this life. Then you could get fat and loaf around in some quiet town in your dirty corduroys and burst into tears every time you heard the national anthem. To Rupert, that was the Point. I didn't know yet what the Point was for me. Maybe you could never see where you yourself were headed. You could only look at the paths that others had begun to follow.

Whatever the path, this school made people who either loved it or hated it. There was no middle ground. You could not go here and come out not caring one way or the other. You had to stand before your God and commit, but the time for that would not come until you had left the school. Before then, you had no real way of knowing if your time at Eton had helped you or hurt you.

One Sunday afternoon in early spring, when fog had come rolling up the Thames, bringing a smell of the ocean, Wittingham and I were sitting in his room eating bread and pâté that his parents had sent him from Fortnum's.

When the pâté was finished, Wittingham pulled out a film canister and showed me that it was filled with something like ground paper. He told me it was cannabis.

Wittingham said that, coming from America, I had probably tried this stuff before.

I lied and told him yes, but the truth was I had never even seen anything that even looked like it before, except perhaps for one of Nightingale's chewed-up cricket score-sheets.

Wittingham said that there wasn't much marijuana or cannabis at the school because it mostly had to be imported from other countries, which was very difficult. He told me it was easier to get hold of acid, because people made that in labs up in Slough.

I gave some knowing glances and did a lot of nodding because I was a little embarrassed not to know anything about it.

We all knew that nothing could get you kicked out more quickly than drugs. It was the ultimate rebellion, because it wasn't just the law of the school. It was also the law of the land.

After that, I kept my ear out for talk of drugs. I heard some boys were growing marijuana in bell jars in the bio labs and others had planted a crop in a hedge that ran between two playing fields. When I told Wittingham that I didn't believe it, he took me to the spot. Sure enough, it was there, and camouflaged with army netting from the top. They had even stolen a housemaster's pitchfork to grade the earth. His initials were carved on the handle.

I knew a few boys who dropped acid and smoked any drug they could find. They drifted to the fringes of the school and sometimes vanished altogether. They walked around looking lost in a way that reminded me of myself in my first few days at Eton. These boys were like balloons with the air slowly running out of them.

Then one day Wittingham came tearing into my room and slammed the door. He ran to the window and looked out. Two brown cars had pulled up beside a house on the other side of the street. The pot-growers lived there. Wittingham said that the brown cars were driven by plain-clothes policemen and that a group of them had just gone into the house with German shepherd sniffer dogs.

By dinner-time, it was all over the school. Five boys had been Busted and they were already gone from the school. Wittingham said that the sniffer dogs had found pot hanging up to dry inside socks in the drying room. The drying room was where we put our mud-filthy Rugby clothes, allowing the dirt to harden into slabs which we beat from the cloth when the time came for playing again. Another bunch was found stuffed inside a person's half-eaten birthday cake.

It frightened me how quickly the five boys had disappeared. I'd been friends with one of them. Now it was as if he had died, and I knew I would probably never see him again.

I had a hard time making friends and keeping them at Eton, especially since I had seen the limits of my friendship with Rupert.

Partly this was from being an American, however thin-stretched that had become in me. Officially I had dual nationality although this didn't help very much. After so much time in two different countries, I saw exactly how being foreign got in the way of making friends that you could keep. It was hard for me to make friends because I could find no safe harbour among any of the people.

There was more to it, as well. Lately, I had found my moods swinging back and forth so quickly that no one could keep track, and certainly not me. I either seemed to hate things or to love them. I moved from one sweaty-palmed obsession to another and picked up friends and dropped them without knowing why. Or I was dropped by them on the strange see-saw balance of their own moods. We had begun by rebelling against the school in whatever way suited us best, and sometimes with such tiny gestures that they were never noticed. I came to see that in a way Eton expected us to rebel against it. It was a necessary stage of our time at the school. They knew that in the end we would rebel against ourselves and the way the school had made us, and this was also necessary.

I was living in my own kind of black and white. I forgave nothing, not even myself. Small successes made me arrogant. Little mistakes brought me to the edge of suicide.

These were the parts of my growing up that I knew would come rattling out of the dark, years into the future, making me cringe at the harshness I had built around myself.

It wasn't until senior year that we all started to calm down, but by then much of the damage had been done and some of it could not be put right in the time that we had left. I knew I would look back on the middle years of Eton and see how I could have done things better, made more friends and kept them, worked my level-headed way into the ranks of senior prefect Poppers. And if I could have calmed down long enough to see it, maybe I would have done all these things.

But there was no calm. The first threads of stillness came far too late, and for some of my friends, it never came at all. Something always came along to stir up the chaos inside them. Andrew Thomas was one of them. Six months after leaving Eton, he jumped in front of a train. Knowing this sometimes brings tears to my eyes whenever I am standing on a British railway platform at Reading or Cardiff and one of those bullet-nosed yellow 125 trains comes howling past without stopping.

Leaving Eton was a shock to every boy, who constructed in his mind an idea of how he thought the world outside might be. Perhaps Thomas did not enjoy his time at Eton and perhaps he had built in himself a happy vision of the outside that would save him from being miserable if he could just last out until it was time to graduate. I guess that he was wrong, and the last barricade against his misery collapsed. The world he found was not worth living in, so he leap-frogged life and jumped off to his death.

Another one who died was Jim Godfrey, the motorcycle man, who pushed his bike more than he ever rode it. He did make it into Pop and seemed to have reached steady ground. But within a year of leaving, he put a loaded shot-gun in his mouth and pulled the trigger. I heard he fell deeply in love with a German girl, but she did not love him. Before he killed himself, he sent her all his possessions. I couldn't help wondering then if he had sent her that damn motorbike of his. I spent a long time wondering about why it had happened. To me at Eton, the idea of true love seemed very far away. Maybe it was far away for Jim Godfrey, too, and suddenly to feel the full force of it so soon after he left Eton, raking each fragile nerve like claws across piano wire, perhaps it was too much to bear.

I heard a rumour of another boy who died, by jumping out of a window. His name was Julian Renfield. But the rumour was wrong. A long time later, after I'd left Eton, I was sitting in a train that had stopped at Temple Meads Station in Bristol. I saw Renfield hobbling across the platform. His legs were in braces and he had to walk with a cane like an old man. It gave me such a shock to see him that the train had moved on by the time I thought to get up and say hello. But then I was glad that I didn't because in my mind I had already buried him and said prayers for him and stuffed his grey body into a cemetery in my head.

CHAPTER 11

WITTINGHAM LOOKED UP from his Sunday paper one foggy morning in May and said that the way to really hurt an Etonian's feelings was to call him a queer when he arrived and then to call him straight just as he was leaving the school.

Now that we had reached this final stage, with only months to go, I saw that he was not altogether wrong.

Wittingham had been a Pretty Boy when he arrived. It was true he looked more like a girl than a boy. He had a girl's complexion and a body so frail that he would have been killed on the Rugby field, if Villiers, who was Captain of Games, had wanted to send him out there.

Instead, Villiers wanted Wittingham to come and sit in his room and he wanted to run his fingers through Wittingham's hair. But now Wittingham had grown hair on his chest and ought to have been shaving twice a day. He was a thug on the Rugby field. Being tackled by him could knock out your lights for while.

Now Wittingham had his eye on a boy called Hewlett, who lived in another house across the school. He had fallen in love with Hewlett and could no longer deny it. He didn't talk to Hewlett. That would have been too obvious. Wittingham just liked to watch him from a distance. It was as if Wittingham had fallen in love with the reflection of himself three years before.

I knew half a dozen people who were in love with Hewlett, and if anything had happened to the boy, I don't know what they would have done. They cared for him like guardian angels, and never laid a hand on him. Most knew that when they left Eton they would go out and find girlfriends and eventually find wives. But I doubted if they would ever love their wives the way they loved Hewlett. It was a harsh thing to say and never to be said out loud, but for some of them, it was the truth.

Rupert had a question to ask, but he didn't know exactly how to ask it. He walked into my room and shut the door. Then he just stood there with his hands in his pockets and a fierce expression on his face.

'Yes?' I set the gold cap carefully back onto my Parker 51 and rested it on my desk.

He still had nothing to say. He strode over to the window and opened it. 'Stuffy in here. How can you work in a place so stuffy?'

'Well, I don't know, Rupe. I'm sure it's a miracle I've survived as long as I have. Was there something else?'

He held his watch to his ear, then slowly moved it away. 'I think I'm going deaf.'

'Is that what you came here to tell me?'

Rupert sighed and pinched the bridge of his nose. 'I've been thinking about what Wittingham said the other day and I tell you, Paul, the truth is I'm at the end of my bloody rope.'

'Which rope is that?'

'I suppose we could call it the Sex Rope, if we have to give it a name.'

'The Sex Rope?'

'Yes.'

'Well, for God's sake, Rupe. You're not suggesting you and I . . . we . . .' I couldn't even finish what I was going to say.

'Oh, Christ almighty! No!' Then he asked me if I wanted to go up to London with him and go brothel-creeping. 'I'm fed up with looking at magazines,' he told me. 'If this keeps up, we'll all end up as slobbering dirty old men like Wittingham.'

'Wittingham's not old.'

'Well, he's slobbering.'

'So you've finally decided to do something rebellious, Rupe. I always knew you'd be the last one to go.'

'Well, I joined the Corps, didn't I? That was pretty rebellious. You said so yourself.'

'Yes, but it was only rebellious for me. You joined because you had some idea that they would make you an officer in your first week, and when they didn't you quit as soon as you could.'

'Well,' He frowned and swallowed his lips, 'I suppose there's some truth in that.'

'I think it seems a little dirty to be going brothel-creeping.' As soon as I had said this, I wished I had kept quiet.

Anger was stamped on Rupert's face. 'You still think too much. I've always said so.'

We went up on a rainy day, knocking back Strongbow Cider at the orange-walled bar of the 125 train from Slough to Paddington. We had told Rosser we were going to look at an exhibit at the National Gallery. He sounded so enthusiastic that we thought for a minute he was going to ask if he could come with us.

We got out of the underground at Leicester Square and weaved through squads of Italians, down the backstreets of Chinatown. In Chinese restaurant windows, I saw ducks that looked as if they had been painted with creosote and then run over with a truck. Then more backstreets, and suddenly all around us were lights flickering in the dingy air and washed-out colour pictures of women in bikinis. Men in tuxedos handed out flyers in front of peep-shows and porno cinemas. They said to come in, so we did.

Rupert ducked inside so fast that at first I didn't know where he'd gone.

It was pitch-black with disco music played through crappy speakers. Someone shoved me into a booth and told me to put 50p in the slot if I wanted to see the show. I dropped 50p into the slot and a panel slid back in front of me. Behind the panel, on a little stage, was a big black woman and she was dancing. She didn't look sexy or even very happy and she moved as if she had been dancing for a long time already. It was damned dark in there and I couldn't really tell what was going on. She sat down on a chair and kicked her legs as if she was swimming and then the panel slid back. I didn't have another 50p and I wouldn't have spent it if I had.

I stood outside for about ten minutes, looking at my watch because I was embarrassed to look up. Every time I raised my head, I was staring at some tuxedoed man telling me to come into his porno shop or else some faded colour picture of a mostly naked woman. It was a street where people walked by quickly. You never caught anyone's eye. The dozens of disco songs all piled together in the air and rose up into the sky. I just stood there and looked at my watch, until Rupert ducked out into the street, squinting in the light because the peep-show place had been so dark.

'Well, that wasn't worth five quid,' he said as we walked on down the road.

'Five pounds? You watched that thing ten times over?'

'I kept waiting for something to happen.'

'And did it?'

'Well, she fell off the stage once, but it wasn't very erotic.'

We walked down an alley that was only a hundred foot long. It opened out into a vegetable market which boomed with Cockney voices. In the alley was a theatre. A woman in the doorway took hold of my arm and told me to come in. She said there was a live sex show and it only cost six pounds.

I shrugged her off and kept walking.

Then she called after us, almost in a whisper, 'Well, maybe perhaps you're looking for the real thing.'

Rupert stopped and so did I.

She said it cost forty quid.

Rupert took out his wallet and slapped the money into her hand.

'Right.' The money disappeared somewhere under the folds of her dress. 'Here's what you got to do. You go up to Oxford Circus and wait there for a girl named Angela.'

'How will she know what we look like?'

'We? Well the forty quid is only for one of you.' She looked at me. 'Where's your money, love?'

I just shook my head. The rest of me was shaking, too.

'What does she look like?' The blood had drained out of Rupert's face.

'Tall and blonde with a big chest. Go on now, or you'll miss her.'

Rupert took off running so quickly that I lost him in a crowd of Germans. I had to ask a policeman where Oxford Circus was.

Rupert was still there when I arrived. He looked disappointed to see me. 'Oh, it's you, Paul.'

'Well, I can go away again if you like.'

'No, stay.' He rested his hand on my arm. 'At least until she arrives.'

Hundreds of blonde women walked past us. I thought this place had to be one of the busiest spots in London.

We waited half an hour and then forty minutes. It had been dawning on us slowly, but when Rupert looked at his watch and saw that we had been there forty-five minutes, the knowledge reached us as a kind of choking feeling, as if someone had thrown dust in our faces.

'We have to go back and get your money.' I started walking, but Rupert didn't follow. 'Well, come on!'

Rupert shook his head. He flagged down a taxi and we drove back to Paddington station.

'You know, Rupe,' I said on the train home, 'maybe it's better if you wait. You know,' I held up my hands and said again, 'you know, until you get married and all.'

'Oh, fuck off, Watty. I was this close.' He pinched the air in front of him. 'This fucking close!'

'It would have been shabby, Rupe. Just damn shabby is all.'

'It's always shabby the first time.'

'And bloody expensive, too.'

We laughed then and could forget about the shame. The train gathered speed out from under the glass roof of Paddington. We slid by concrete walls that separated the railyard from some concrete houses on the other side. On one of the walls, someone had painted – I AM A PASSIONATE SOUL CRYING OUT IN THIS TORTUROUS MEDIOCRITY.

We roared past the platform at Ealing Broadway, people standing back from the tracks with their hands covering their ears.

The train pulled into Slough and again we heard the woman train announcer on the tinny speaker system. 'Sleeeow. This is Sleeeow.'

Rupert and I took the train back to Windsor. There was evening chapel and we knew we would be late. That meant hiding out until the service was over and hoping that our empty seats had not been noticed. The carriages swung along a viaduct that ran above the fields outside Eton. Looking down into the tall grass, we could see some boys hidden away, still in their tail-suits, red-labelled bottles of Woodpecker Cider set out beside them and feathers of Silk Cut tobacco-smoke rising up around their faces. They were dodging chapel, too. We'd all probably be caught, but for once I didn't care. We would be leaving this school soon, and its rules were losing their grip on us.

Being late to chapel got you the same punishment as being late for class. Otherwise, I would probably have dodged it every week. There were often antique fairs in Windsor on Sunday mornings and I would have spent my time there, if it had been allowed. Looking at the old things gave me ideas for stories, especially things that carried the marks of long use – an old pair of boots or a worn-down inscription on a cigarette case.

We were always giving thanks to God and singing to him and getting down on our knees in chapel. I sang the same hymns so many times that often I didn't need to read the hymn book. Sometimes in the holidays, when there was no church and no mention of church, I would catch myself singing hymns and being surprised that I knew all the words. What surprised me more was that I had never once thought of what the hymns were about.

The Eton chapel was designed to be much bigger, set out in the shape of a huge crucifix that would have stretched half way across school. But King Henry VI who commissioned it ran out of money, so his church just looked like the head part of the cross.

Being in the chapel did not make me think of God. Instead it made me think of how many hundreds of boys had come here before me. Because so much had stayed the same, I felt as if I could have met an Eton boy from a hundred years before and started up the same talk with him that I could with Rupert sitting next to me now and mumbling his French subjunctives as he prepared for a test. I thought of the boys who had gone out and what had become of them.

For so many boys, their lives had ended as soon as they left, and their names were plastered by the hundreds across war memorials from Waterloo to the Falklands. Most died in the Great War. The reason for it, a teacher explained to me, was quite simple. The majority of boys joined the Army and became second lieutenants. Then they were sent to the trenches. Whenever a trench raid was launched, and the soldiers went over the top with fixed bayonets, it was the second lieutenant who climbed up first. And if the enemy had staked out the position or was expecting the raid, the Eton boy would go down in the first volley and maybe they would call off the raid but probably not. And rank after rank of boys would climb up and get punted back dead by the hammer of the Spandau guns.

I thought back to the white marble busts of Old Etonians who had become Rulers of the Empire, the ones I had seen on my first day at Eton in the hall above the main entrance gates. I remembered that voice I had heard, or thought I heard, that told me of the two extremes of memory – the ones who died too soon and the ones who lived long and worked hard and made their names immortal.

Now in my last weeks, that voice came back to me. It warned me how short my life was, even if I lived it out and grew old.

There seemed to be so many things to cheat you along the way, the way my father had been cheated. I knew how hard he worked, even at a time when work meant nothing to me. It was as if he knew his time was almost up. I remembered when my brother asked him to explain about dying and he said it was like a cake. He told me and my brother that we had only eaten a little piece of our cakes, whereas he and my mother had eaten a little more, and our grandparents had eaten most of theirs. I thought about that at his funeral; what he would have done if he had known that by then his cake was already eaten and he was just dabbing at the crumbs.

I looked around the chapel, the preacher's voice a constant beehive hum at the back of my mind. I stood when the others stood and sung the hymns without opening the book, but all the time my eyes moved back and forth across the faces of masters and boys, and the cartoon ecstasy of saints painted on the walls.

I felt as if we were all in a race to leave our mark, and the day we left Eton, which was only a few months away, would be like the firing of the starter's gun. Some of us would only be cheated. It was inevitable. Others would drop out by themselves. And still others would discover what they wanted to do with their lives. Then they had to move quickly because there was no time to lose. They could never grow tired and never give up, or time would overtake them.

This became like a religion to me. It was not clear at first, so I chiselled away at the idea until it made better sense. I was impatient to be good at something, in case there lay sleeping in me the same cancer that had brought my father down like some trophy animal shot by a hunter.

I couldn't bring myself to think of the chapel as any kind of Holy Ground. My heart did not beat quickly when I walked under the arch of the titanic organ, with its pipes racked up like leg-thick javelins above us and little Bewley beating on the keys as if he was insane. It gave me no inspiration to stare up at the stained-glass window, which was newer than anything else in the chapel because the old one got blown out by a bomb dropped from a German plane as it went down in flames over Slough.

When I imagined Holy Ground, I found myself thinking of the end of Narragansett beach, where the Narrow River meets the sea. Whenever I reached home, I'd walk out there as soon as I could, past the beach clubs and the dunes, to the fast-running river and the rock beyond the surf that tricked you into thinking it was the humpback of a whale, even if you knew it was just a rock. When I reached the place, I said to myself that I was officially home. And when I voyaged back at night from my fold-up bed at Eton, it was this beach where I arrived and from this place that I left again.

All of us had Holy Ground, although we called it different names. Sometimes a boy would bring it up, and the rest of us would pretend we didn't understand, because the sacred fields or roads or woods or back alleys would have lost their sacredness if we spelled them out and shared them. So we kept it to ourselves, and it was about the only thing we never shared.

I signed up for the Career Aptitude Test. Mr Rosser said it might help us leavers figure out what to do with our lives.

It was like an exam. There were lists of questions, asking which jobs you would prefer and then it gave you the options –

1   Banker
2   Soldier
3   Farmer
4   False Teeth Maker

I put down that I would rather be a farmer. I didn't want to be one, but it was a better choice than any of the others. There were dozens of these questions and they were all very similar, except in each one, a new job would be put in. They kept asking if I would want to be a False Teeth Maker.

After I had sat through the test, I wandered home and lay on my bed. I stared at the ceiling and wondered why they hadn't asked me if I wanted to be a writer. As soon as that thought straggled through my mind, I realized that I already knew what I wanted to be, and I was just hoping that the Career Aptitude Test would spell it out for me in black and white.

But it was too late by then. I'd already taken the test and now I had to wait for the Career Aptitude Representative to come by and tell me what he thought I should do with my life.

It was Mr Bixby, my old physics teacher. He leaned very awkwardly against my window-sill, thumbing through his notes but not saying anything.

I wanted to say I was sorry about busting his Ripple Tank. He never did get around to charging me for it.

I had tidied up my room and was sitting in my green chair for the first time in about two years. Usually it was covered with books and clothes. It was a comfortable chair, and I made up my mind to sit in it more often, instead of on the floor with my back to the radiator, the way I usually did.

Mr Bixby said he got the impression that I would like to be a farmer. Then he glanced up at me nervously, as if maybe I would lunge at his throat.

My face stayed blank while I pictured myself wearing dungarees and a straw hat and shovelling hay with a pitchfork.

Mr Bixby saw my blank expression and it must have looked to him like I was having a revelation. That all my life I had wanted to be a farmer but never knew it until now. 'Yes,' he told me, 'I definitely think you would like to be a farmer. But you must decide whether it will be an arable farm or a livestock farm.' He shook his finger, no longer nervous and fidgeting. 'That's a difficult decision to make.'

He went on a bit longer, balancing arable against livestock farms and saying how the Common Market was a risky proposition for British farmers.

I sat numb through all this, thinking – Well, I'll be damned. I'd always imagined myself riding around on a Harley. Now all I'm going to ride is a combine harvester.

When he had gone, I went back to my place on the floor by the radiator, took out my notepaper and started writing again. I needed to prove Bixby wrong, and there was never, never any time to waste.

I did not know about the career of a writer, how books were edited or published or about contracts and negotiations. And I was past the point of worrying whether my mother would approve my decision. For now, I could think no further than the fact that I wanted to write more than anything else.

I remembered back at the Dragon when Cuddly told me about the old men in Portugal, where he lived. All he ever saw them do was sit around and talk about whether or not they were constipated.

Sometimes, while our time at Eton came to its close, straining every tendon of our patience, Rupert and I sat around like a couple of old Portuguese men.

Whole afternoons and evenings would tiptoe past, when we sat in the same room together but hardly spoke a word. I knew everything about him and he knew everything about me. We knew everything that was going on in the school and even though the veins of the grapevine were wide open, nothing travelled through them.

It wasn't that we were cut off from the rest of the world. Rupert had his paper delivered every day, and I read Moriarty's racing news before he shambled downstairs in the morning to claim it.

Things that happened outside the gates of the school seemed blurred and unreal. Floods and coups d'états and Royal visits to African kingdoms came and went. Rupert and I read all about them, but with the glazed-over expressions of having half our minds on homework or the forthcoming Rugby game against another house in which we knew we would be slaughtered.

The safest thing to do was not to care about what happened outside Eton. If you worried too much about it, as I did sometimes, you began to feel trapped in your ancient uniform and boxed in by the crumbly brick of the houses. The closer you came to leaving, the more trapped you felt. You'd walk onto the playing fields and see people using all the strength they had to smack a Rugby ball one way, run after it, then turn around and chase it in the other direction. You saw the whole pointlessness of it. The rest of the world thundered into the future while you hung in the past like a bug trapped in a spider-web. It was painful to think of it like that.

More than once I walked across the fields to the motorway bridge and climbed up the grass bank to the road. I stood watching the cars scream past me towards London and wished to hell I was in one of them. Then I'd stump back to my room and stare at my homework and the hundred-year-old grafitti on my desk.

So you had to push that aside. You had to fool yourself in taking pleasure in the muddy body-slamming charges down the Rugby field. You had to use your strength almost suicidally, even if there was no hope of winning. It took time, but eventually the pleasure would become real. I dived at the legs of boys running with the ball, knowing that if I misjudged the dive, I'd take their steel-studded boots in my face, and I enjoyed it.

I enjoyed my classes and the novels that we trudged our way through in French. On our twentieth class of discussing Balzac's *Eugénie Grandet*, even Monsieur Dubois' eyes would start to roll back into his head, but I enjoyed it without completely knowing why.

In English, I had to stop myself from grinning as we haggled over one line of *King Lear* until the class was ready to start a brawl, and the teacher's fist was red from pounding on the desk as he shouted for us to be quiet.

The outside world seemed a cold and distant place. The travelling and parties and epic love-affairs that we allowed ourselves to dream about were never meant to find a place in what was real. We all knew the truth, that the outside world wasn't distant at all. But still we couldn't reach it, except for brief moments on the weekends. We had to wait with the patience of statues for the time when we could bust out and wallow in the things we had imagined.

*

One day I looked up from shaving, and peered across to Rupert, who stood a couple of sinks down, scraping away at his stubble with a silver-handled razor from Woods of Windsor. 'Rupert?'

'What?'

'I'm never going to be a Popper, am I?'

'Well, you might. I mean, you *might*.' He squinted over at me.

It wasn't a thing you were supposed to talk about. If you had to ask someone, then it was already a sure thing that you weren't on the list. 'But I won't, will I?'

'I'd be a bit surprised.'

Every boy wanted to be a Popper, because being a senior prefect was the highest honour, and one that was chosen by the boys instead of the teachers, so it counted for even more. There were people who said the whole organization ought to be abolished, and who said that if they were elected, they would turn down the offer. But I never heard anybody say that and actually believed them. Sometimes I cared and other times, it seemed like nothing to me. That morning I did care. I looked at my fold-down collar, not the stick-up kind with a bow-tie which meant that you were a Captain of House or Captain of Games or had some other privilege. I'd won prizes for writing and for shooting and for Orienteering and for Discus and Javelin. I got a cup for being Cadet of the Year, although after the job I did of marching in front of their inspecting General, I think the Corps people wished they'd chosen someone else. But none of those things added up to much.

No, I was not going to be in Pop. On the day when the Pop elections were taking place, I went walking in the fields, when hopefuls like Rupert stayed in their rooms, down on their knees and praying that the door would be kicked open and a crowd of Poppers would storm in and tear up their clothes. They'd throw the person's books out of the window and all his underclothes. They'd cover him in shaving foam and then dump a tub of coffee powder on his head. And from then on, he'd wear the black-and-white houndstooth trousers, silk brocaded tail-coat and the funky waist-coat of a Popper.

I had to laugh when I got home and found Rupert still in his room, head down on his desk and tired out just from the waiting. He looked up at me when I walked by.

I said I was sorry he didn't have any luck.

'Luck with what?' His face was turning red again.

'You know damn well with what.'

'I don't know what you're talking about.'

I leaned in his doorway and grinned. 'No, Rupe. I don't suppose you do.' The truth was he cared so much about being a Popper that he couldn't bear to admit he'd even considered it.

Nobody in our house was elected into Pop. I felt glad about that. We all got to be social cripples and for the first time since our first month at Eton, we banded together like brothers.

With only a short time to go before the end of my final term, I began to think not just about leaving, but about what I would do after I left. The idea sent me into a kind of shock. Between lessons, when the empty streets and alleys suddenly ran in a black-and-white river of Etonians, I slung my books under my arm and waded through the new boys with their squeaky voices and rosy cheeks and too-big uniforms, grunted hello to the people I knew and jabbed my index-finger skyward in the motion of Capping, whenever a teacher walked by.

I memorized *Die Judenbuche* by Annette von Droste-Hülshoff for my German 'A' level exams. I knew *King Lear* by heart for English and had forced myself to learn *Eugénie Grandet* for French. My head became an Enigma Machine of nonsense-words which I could unravel into dozens of quotes and themes and background information. I wrote exams in my dreams and barked out the answers to questions fired at me by Mr Callendar, my German teacher. In every lull of silence, all I could hear was a chorus of other people's words and for the first time in years, I had no time to do any writing of my own.

Everybody I knew who stood a chance of getting into Oxford or Cambridge was going to try and get in. The few who knew they wouldn't make it had already decided on other universities. I'd heard it used to be that an Etonian had an almost guaranteed place at Cambridge, just because of being an Etonian. Not any more. Not even close. Rupert went for his interview and the first thing the interviewer said to him was 'I have a very low opinion of Etonians.' The way Rupert explained it, it only got worse after that.

When he arrived back to school, he locked himself in his room and smoked himself silly on his Roth Handle cigarettes.

Moriarty would get in wherever he wanted. The same was true for Wittingham.

Others were heading for the Army, the way Villiers had done.

The ones I knew chose the Welsh or Coldstream Guards, with a few in the 17/21st Hussars or The Greenjackets.

Some already had posts waiting for them in the Inner City banks.

I decided to attend Yale University in America, because I had come to know what it meant here not so much to be an Etonian, but to be an Old Etonian. I knew what people thought of you, whether they admitted it or not, and I knew what they expected of you, both the good and the hideously bad. Moriarty would be spending the rest of his life trying to hide the fact that he went here, and Rupert would tell people at every chance he got until he keeled over dead in his worn-out corduroys, his lungs a smelly bog of old Roth Handle smoke.

It seemed to me that my horizon was getting narrower instead of broader.

I knew that in America, being an Old Etonian was more of a novelty. It had the same effect on people as saying you stormed ashore on the Normandy beaches in the Second World War or that you used to be an astronaut. They treated it as an experience that they could not expect to understand completely and they usually left it at that.

It gave you space to breathe.

As soon as I decided, and had actually chosen a place where I would go, it was as if I had already left. The smells of the rooms and the gym and the classrooms became suddenly unfamiliar and sour in my lungs. I felt as if I had already said goodbye to Rupert, Moriarty, Wittingham and Manson, and I realized that we really were friends after all.

We might find ourselves isolated from many of the people we'd meet over the rest of our lives, but we would also be banded together; we who had gone through it from the start. And because the place changed so little from decade to decade, it also banded us to the ones who had gone before. With them we could bridge the crevasse of years and find communion that perhaps could not be found in any other way.

My last few days at Eton were not sad. There was no Grand Finale, no big party or diploma-giving speech, no last-minute slackening of the rules. You said goodbye and you left, and I preferred it that way. I was busy with selling the beat-to-hell furniture that I had dragged with me from room to room over the years. In a box, I packed my Harris Tweed jacket, which was hopelessly ruined but which I could not bring myself to throw away. Then I crammed in all my stories and mailed it home surface mail to the States. The box would take months to arrive.

I threw away my uniform, which by now was mostly held together with safety-pins. As soon as it had gone, I wished I'd kept it. I knew other boys who felt the same, who had slashed their uniforms to shreds with knives and cackled like witches as the cloth turned to ribbons, but who then fell silent when they saw what they had done.

I took leave of Mr Rosser at a time when it looked as if his house was going to cave in around his head. Rupert had got into an argument with Moriarty and Moriarty had turned him in to Mr Rosser for his years of smoking and the fact that he let junior boys smoke in the room, too. I just shook Rosser's hand and said goodbye. The last I saw of him, he was sitting at his desk and staring at the blotter. Rupert was once his Golden Boy and he had been badly deceived.

But Rupert was the only one of us who could have been House Captain. Moriarty would have tried too hard to change things. Wittingham was too far out of touch and lived in the more reliable world of his gadgets. Nobody trusted Manson and never had. And I had drifted away, too. After that time of walking in on Elliot and Davis, and how terrible I felt after I'd turned them in, I could never have Busted people or ordered them around. Rupert was the only choice, but that might have been the most unkind thing that anybody ever said about him.

I dreaded saying goodbye to Rupert and Moriarty and Wittingham. Each time I saw them in the dining-hall or the corridor, I did not know if it would be the last time. In the end, I didn't say goodbye, convincing myself that I would see them again soon enough. But the truth was that I could find no words to finish all this time we'd spent together, and at a time like that, no words were better than ones that did not fit.

I said goodbye to the Head Man. It was all very formal. You had your name on a list and a time when you were supposed to appear. You wrote down on a piece of paper all the things you'd done at the school and what your grades had been in the 'O' and 'A' level exams.

I barely knew Mr Anderson and had almost never spoken to him before. And he did not know me. But somehow he knew more than I had written on my list of grades and prizes. He recalled shaking my hand one rainy Saturday in June when I had won the school discus award out at the track. He knew that I had won a short story prize and even remembered the content of the story. It was only a handful of unimportant details but this caught me off guard.

I sat in his dark study and looked out across the College field, over the bronze statue of Perseus holding up the chopped Medusa's head, and I realized that this was the last goodbye.

There were still two days of school left to go. They were meant for packing and settling accounts at the school stores. But I had already packed or thrown away or sold all that I owned and I had no bills to pay.

I left as quietly as I could, carrying my last few things in an old canvas rucksack.

I did not look back as I walked down the High Street towards Windsor train station and the castle snubbing an early summer sky. I kept wanting to turn around and take one last look at the place, but I did not allow myself to do it.

This was the break and it had to be clean. I doubted if I would ever return and it would not be the same if I did.

It has been ten years since then, and what I see now is that we are always looking back. It is as if there are questions that we ourselves don't even know how to ask, but whose answer lies buried somewhere in the chalk-dusty classrooms, in the stamp of marching boots and in the slamming of our bodies onto the muddy Rugby fields.

So we may never return, but far into the future we will still look back, until we understand the questions and have put them into words.

Then we will stay silent, because this knowledge was not meant to be shared. We will keep it hidden like a pearl, in the oyster of our grey and ageing hands.